Joyce and Martin

with best wishes for

Christmas 1997 from

Robert and Susan

Erskine.

"A book of verses and causes, to confront glitches in British public life, by don, Robert Erskine".

First Published by Robert Erskine, 1997

Department of Management,
Glasgow Caledonian University,
City Site,
Cowcaddens Road,
Glasgow G4 OBU

Telephone 0141 331 3000
Fax 0141 331 3269
E-mail: r.erskine@gcal.ac.uk

Contact : Robert Erskine.
British Library Cataloguing in Publication Data
Erskine, Robert

ISBN - 0 9531886 0 4

Dedication

This book is dedicated to my precious wife Susan, who tolerated with indulgence the role of 'book widow', while it was written, and without whose support and inspiration it would never have been written.

Preface.

This is a book in two parts. The first is a collection of 25 verses. The second is a selection of 20 memorable newsletters and papers from a pool of 200 written initially as family newsletters between 1994 and 1997.

This book is an unconventional autobiography. Instead of being written chronologically it is a selection of interest directed themes. The material was originally written to inform and amuse family friends and relations but inevitatably as a reforming don many academic research themes also had their first airing in these newsletters. The verses initially were written as 'party pieces' for family or charity promotion events, but also some were used as an extra dimension of communication in the teaching of business management.

The reader is advised to read the preface, and the index and then proceed in an interest directed fashion throughout the items.

Table of contents.

List of illustrations

35. Buckingham Palace response to the Erskine newsletter in tribute to HM's state visit to South Africa . P205

36. HM Treasury response to the Robert Erskine intervention to save £3 billion / year in Britain . P206

Acknowledgements

1. To Major Philip Erskine, author's brother, for permission to use his material in the Biography of General Erskine, and for the text of the account of HM Queen's visit to South Africa.

2. To Lady Edmonstone, author's sister-in-law, for permission to use her photograph of Duntreath Castle.

3. To Sophy Bristol, niece, for her permission to use a copy of her painting of Sonya Madam.

4. To Iona Andrews, daughter, for her photographs of 'Maxwell Court' scenes.

5. To Margaret and David Moore, Coll neighbours, for permission to include verses 'Shrimps for supper'.

6. To Sandy, Hamish, Erskine, sons, for permission to include the 'Anniversary Song'.

7. To 400 friends and relations, who were the readership of the newsletters and academic papers and who frequently responded to me with comments and windeups.

8. To Kip Poulson, Coll artist, for permission to use his cartoon of the 'Wuffler'.

9. To Mairi Hedderwick, Coll author, for permission to use her cover sketch, 'Robert and Susan and the Yorkies'.

10. To Sir John Starkey, 2nd cousin, for material informing my academic work on the Church of England Commissioners.

11. To Professor Ambriola of Pisa University for his many e-mail contributions relating with the intervention to Tony Blair.

12. To Professor Helga Drummond, for so much of the material on the 'blow by blow' account of the Taurus case study.

13. To Rev Denis Robertson, for his flow of relevant press cuttings on the property dealings of the Church of England Commissioners.

14. To Diana de la Rue, author's aunt, for permission to use the picture of Sir Evelyn de la Rue and his Rolls Royce.

Chapter 1. Family events and fund raising promotions

In the first theme it is the birthdays, anniversaries, weddings that are the objects of the poem, and they are all optimistic, appreciative of the central character, and the portrayal is heroic, promotional. The author is a grandad, and he loves getting involved, to the extent of being exploited as cheap labour. But the exploitation is really 'tongue in cheek' as his labour is love, unconditional love. Everyone wants to be wanted even grandad in Ireland. Robert Junior, grandchild is dedicated in Liverpool, a child threatened in his 20th week of pregnancy with a doctor's recommendation to terminate the pregnancy. His recovery seemed to be a miracle. In this chapter too there is the joy of travel to new countries and exposure to new cultures. The verses on charity promotions profile the sheer fun of running the event and getting the buyers into a buying frenzy. The episode at Duntreath Castle, Susan's old home, is also a chauvinist male's view of what women do when they go en masse on a shopping spree, but this seems all right as the money goes to the disabled and extravagance is excusable. The temptation is there to buy those piles and piles, miles and miles of stunning hats. Niece, Sophy gets this promotional treatment too when she runs her 6th exhibition of pictures in fashionable Dover Street and uncle gets the red stickers up. The momentum continues when author's wife, Susan, promotes her Sue Ryder charity at a luncheon; that summer the family run a charity tea party for the whole Isle of Coll to raise money to send Jessica overseas for a year to Zimbabwe. Jessica becomes the Coll champion and the islanders are legendary in the hospitality as they pour £624 into funds from a Saturday tea party, with the entertainment a selection from these verses! The final verse is a sad lament for the late Diana, Princess of Wales.

1.1. Susan's birthday verse. January 1997

*

We come as guests this happy day,
To celebrate and make the hay,
To raise a toast to precious Susan,
And ensure some love profusion.

*

Here we have a son and grandson,
To ensure that we have some fun.
Carina too has made the trip,
To see some love that will not slip.

*

Granny is a tireless knitter.
Fingers move to make her fitter.
Granny does so love her Carl,
To her he is a real true pal.

*

She was a mother great and true,
And children took to her like glue.
They never wanted to go to bed,
Until their dad was nearly dead.

*

Her doggies loved her all the way.
Every weekday was like a birthday.
Chocolates sweets and runs galore,
They barked their way in total uproar.

*

The brave Life Boat men adored her too.
The funds she raised would see them thru.
The gales and seas and rescues wild,
Till they returned to homestead mild.
*
Her banner making is not lost.
Christmas, Harvest, Easter, Penticost,
With colours now they decorate,
And give much joy to every mate
*
Her cooking done for precious Hubby
Gives him joy and makes him tubby.
Homemaking is her pride and thrill.
Her wit and fun are all a drill.
They make all days like golden days.
The sun can send no warmer rays.
*
The birds know she is good news.
She feeds them for their winter doos,
With fat and nuts and all things nice,
They know they are in paradise.
*
Fund raising is her natural skill.
She does it as a soldier's drill.
Sue Ryder Homes are Susan's pet.
She strives for them in dry and wet.
*
She braves the dogs that bar the doors,
And psyches them till they give her paws.
She comes away with nothing under,
A £5 note or bigger plunder.
*
Susan is a champion true,
Everyone will say they knew.
So let's give her a birthday toast
That will resound from coast to coast.
*
Happy birthday Susan dear.
And many more, hear hear.
Happy birthday Susan dear.
A super star you have become.
Our love for you exceeds a ton.
*End

A portrait of Susan

1.2. The Erskine Grandparents go to work at Christmas

*

'Oh we want you, so we do,
To join this team and see us thru.
This Christmas tide when all are busy,
And we are all just in a frizzy.

*

The 'flu has struck and laid us low.
The drains are blocked as you well know.
The boat needs scraping,
And then painting.
The garden weeds are no illusion,
The work is here in much profusion.

*

The wains are wanting more attention,
No good sitting back on that great pension,
Come at once for Christmas cheer,
We will give at least a beer.

*

And a panto to delight your wits,
And keep you all the time in fits.
Morna wants to sing and clap,
And not let that Grandpa have a nap.

*

The invitation is accepted,
And a plan is soon erected.
A passage booked to the Emerald Isle,
And travel done in super style.
To engage in all that hoch,
And sweat and sweat around the clock .

*

The Christmas spirit is all alight,
And plenty of work is there all right.
Tommy must be fed at once.
Grandpa cannot start his lunch.

*

Two spoons for the hapless boy will do,
And Grandpa takes another two.
Efficient feeding all will see,
Shrieks and shrieks of happy glee.

*

Then comes the indigestion, bang!
And wheatabix and milk go wang.
One spoon is more efficient than four,
If the youngster decides on more.

*

Daddy isn't that amused.
'You will have that child confused.
Granny you go on the feeding.
Grandpa you must start the weeding'

*

'Here's a spade, and there's the garden.
All day's work will earn a pardon.
Granny go get Morna dressed,
And we will all be so impressed'.

*

Grandpa feels he is a mug.
As a bed for artichokes is dug.
For punishment he is a glutton ,
There's never time to eat the mutton.

*

Whatever next will he have to do?
Just run and catch the turkey too?
But no it's to the roof he's sent;
The guterings have all been spent.

*

The new ones need a lick of paint,
And Grandpa is the local saint.
Up the ladder 20 feet,
A fall would be a rotten leap.

*

But oh, the lovely view from there,

Takes away all his dispair.

Granny, meanwhile, has finished the feeding,

She stuck her nose up at the thought of weeding.

*

She must start the darning now.

Or else there will be such a row.

A jolly lot of shirts are pending.

A 100 tears are there for mending .

And the missing buttons too,

Need some fixing all the noo.

*

The panto breaks the hard work schedule,

With lots of jokes and fun and ridicule.

Mother Goose rides on a goosemobile,

But grandpa thinks about a meal.

*

And sometimes has a little snooze,

But Granny will not let him loose.

She nudges him with lots of relish.

'That snoring is a wee bit hellish'.

*

The Yorkshire terriers are in great heart.

No poos at all, not even a fart.

They steal the slippers of boss Johnny,

And they think it is so funny.

*

Another day we go and hasten,

To see the precious Edmonstone bason.

Still in use in an Antrim Glen,

A really right true Christening gem,

A silver piece of great delight

It is antique, a gorgeous sight.

*

When Friday comes the tears are there,

The Andrews family are so dear.

They may carry on as best they may

But it is a wrench to come away,

When all that work was all that fun,

It glittered like the rays of sun.

*End

The Edmonstone Christening Bason

Morna Andrews on the staircase at Maxwell Court

1.3. Dedication of Robert Benjamin Miracle, 1997

*

Thank God for your gentle touch,
To give us babe we love so much,
He is so precious to us all,
As we wait to see him crawl.

*

Young Robert comes and gives us joy,
He is a gorgeous little boy.
To mum and dad he is delight.
He turns their life and makes it bright.

*

To brother Carl he is a mate,
And so much more than birthday cake.
Robert, Benjamin, Miracle is our toast today.
In unison we cry hurray hurray hurry.

*

The Lord dedicates these names three,
With an overpowering sense of glee.
Young Robert will be a Christian knight,
To join Christ's army in the fight.

*

He will know what's right and wrong,
He will sing a happy song.
The Lord will guard him all his life.
From womb and, childhood, manhood and all strife.

*

He will want to praise the Lord,
And give him songs of one accord.
He will want to join his church.
And go in glory on his perch.

Growing up will be such fun.
Following Jesus Christ, the son.
With the joy of God in every stride,
And games with Carl in every ride.

*

Granny Sweden and Granny Scotland do adore him,
And will run to his every whim;
And the grandpas do agree,
To stimulate the repartee.

*

Granny loves to knit all day,
And teach wee Robert how to pray.
Dedication day is treasure;
All are here to share the pleasure.
*End

Robert Junior with grandparents

1.4. Verses to celebrate Carina's 30th birthday June 7th 1997.

*

Carina is a wonder mum,
And all around enjoy her fun.
It is today we celebrate,
And put us in a joyous state

*

Her birthday is a great event;
Good wishes say one thing is meant.
We love you very very much,
We love your very gentle touch.

*

Carl has a mum he just adores,
His kisses better than guffawws.
Young Robert too adores his mum,
Without her he would be so glum.

*

Sandy loves his birthday bride,
Warm and welcome at his side.
She is the toast of all her patients;
They do so love her sympatique,
To her charms they want to leap.

*

Her Mum and Dad adore her too.
She is the gem that sees them through.
Her friends enjoy her Christian spirit,
Her friendship manifest and with it.

*

Sweden's lass is Scotland's joy,
And yet she is so very coy.
She sings and dances with decore,
Amidst the cries of all encore.

*

She is the youngest of some six,
A gorgeous baby full of tricks .
Her wonder smile will make you melt,
And joy oh joy was all you felt.

*

Let us toast this lovely girl,
Who always puts us in a whirl.
Many happy returns for you,
With joy and love and coo and coo.

*

Carina, Carina happy birthday.

*End

1.5. Poem of Hamish, Sandy and Carina - The Anniversary Song to parents, 1996.

*

Robert, Robert, ask me the question do.
I'm half crazy all for the love of you.
What would you think of marriage?
I can cook your cabbage.
I'll be sweet, I'll cook your meat,
And I'll do your housework too

*

Susan, Susan, give me your answer do.
I'm half crazy all for the love of you.
It <u>will</u> be a stylish marriage,
If <u>you</u> provide the carriage.
And we can float,
On a ferry boat,
To a honeymoon on Coll.

*

Mummy, Daddy, tell us the secret, do.
You've been married, thirty years and two.
How did you ever manage,
To have such a good marriage.
You still look sweet, upon the,
Seat of a Fiat Panda made for two.

*End

1.6. Shrimps for supper - From David and Sadie Moore of Coll, 1996, a contribuition to anniversary celebrations.

*

One day as I was walking on the lovely Cornaig shore,

I chanced upon a scene that I'd never seen before.

A silver-headed gentleman at the edge of the deep blue sea,

With his shirt and tie still on his back,

And his trousers up to his knees.

*

I watched quite fascinated as he paddled up and down,

With a really strange contraption that was orange, white and brown.

A net of some description was clasped between his hands,

And he was marching up and down trawling in the sand.

*

I ventured over closer to inspect the trawling patch,

And to witness at first hand,

What this poor man was trying to catch.

Then Robert caught my gaze and he,

Exclaimed "Come here and see -

I've caught a multitude of shrimps, and I'll have them for my tea".

*

"Would you like to join me - Susan won't object.

She'll put them on sandwiches for supper, I suspect".

So off I went to share this meal - I was assured a treat.

But sandwiches with crunchy shrimps I found too hard to eat.

*

I won't forget that day - indeed the memory's ingrained,

Of eating crunchy shrimps for which my palate was not trained.

But still this man of 60 years and wed for 32,

Goes paddling for his supper and perhaps his breakfast too.

*

So here's to you, wha's like you - you really are sublime,

To Robert and to Susan - a legend in your time.

Happy birthday to you Robert - happy anniversary too;

Long life and lots of happiness from us to both of you.

*End

1.7. The no courting culture of Yemen, 1996

*

Courting is banned in Yemen.

There, you have to wait till you get to heaven.

In school, boys are taught in the morning.

No girls are there adorning.

And this is all in primary,

So the boys can't see their finery!

*

The girls go in the afternoon,

With no chance of a swoon.

At home the boys are upstairs,

And the girls live downstairs.

*

When visitors come they are segregated,

Or they might get too animated.

And marriage comes from a deal.

That is life and it's so real.

*

The contract is based on dollars.

That is rather hard on all those fellahs.

Six year's savings will win a bride;

It is a rather expensive ride.

*

The money's hers as a life long pledge;

And it is a massive wedge.

He must please her for all he's worth,

And give her all his heart and mirth.

*

If she absconds with all those dollars,

Then he has to cope with bothers

Another six year's savings are required,

Before he can get once more fired.

*

Hamish one day stops at Immam's Palace fair,

To see the goods and relics there.

For a guide there, is one of his friends.

Abdul comes and chats and greetings sends.

*

Oh dear, oh dear Abdul, is so upset,

There's a dreadful story about his pet.

A party of Japanese came to Taiz,

To see the treasures and the flies.

*

This party was mixed oh dear.

And Abdul saw this lady there,

And Hamish said, "there will be romance in this".

And Abdul said," it was just bliss."

*

He took her round and showed the town.

His face was happy as a clown,

He did so want to marry Pearl,

Just the perfect Eastern girl.

*

The hotel manager noticed all,

That courting comes before a fall,

Only men may Abdul take.

The law was written for his sake.

*

In a jiffy he's in the cells;

No, no, there'll be no wedding bells.

And down the dungeon he must stay,

Till darling Pearl has flown away.

*

So Hamish says, "Abdul, friend,

That Eastern girl would send you round the bend".

Why not take a Yemen bride?

Then no need to run and hide".

*

Abdul turns and says with passion,

"That lovely bird and all her fashion,

Did not require the dollar duty,

She really was a cut price beauty".

*

Hamish, wise bird that he seems,

Cautions Abdul on his dreams.

"Ladies from the West and East

Have expectations for a feast

It is lifelong and far in excess

Of the dowry and your distress."

*End

1.8. Snipe shooting in County Down, Boxing day 1996

*

Two grandpas, a dad and an uncle, and Black Bess, the Lab,

All armed with guns and hats, so they looked fab,

Trudged to the bogs of Comber,

All intent on shots of thunder.

Their quarry was the little snipe

So slickit, fast and wavering in flight.

*

These four worthies were determined on good sport,

In the bogs in which they fought.

But oh dear the bogs were owned by others,

So they had to chat up all the Mothers,

'Happy Christmas to you, from our merry band.

Please give us the sport of your boggy land.

We've nothing to give but the smiles of our faces

If on the bog we can put our paces'

*

'Of course you can, you gallant men,

But mind not shoot the pheasant hen,

Or the cock that came this spring,

With his intent to have a fling'.

*

With permission now to have a go,

The gallant four were in the know.

One sniffed the air for tactics sake,

Into the wind the snipe will take.

*

Three guns are carefully placed around the bog,

And grandpa and Bess the dog,

Plunge in the bog and make to seek,

The snipe rise with a cleek,

Bang, bang, these birds give super sport;

The best in the world and few are caught.

*

The gallant four become the gallant three.

There is another tugging, see.

For grandpa one has another quarry,

And he has to make a rapid foray.

*

The three are left to enjoy the snipe,

And find the bogs till nearly night.

They win the sweet talk on the owners all the time.

Greetings are exchanged some ten times more and all is fine.

*

Picnic lunch is some event at Paisley's bog.

Grandpa, dad and uncle, the gallant three are munching,

And Cupid comes to join all this lunching.

Uncle has his mobile, sweet voice says, 'you're a hog.

You should be with me, not stuck in that bog'.

But uncle had his sweet talk too.

'I'll be with you after shooting, right the noo'.

*

The Paisley bog is more than an ordinary spell.

The snipe are there galore, and some teal as well.

Bang, bang and the quarry is down with a big sound,

Behind the six foot drains a long walk round.

Bess, the lab, and uncle with Cupid inspiration,

Trudge and trudge with desperation.

Till they pick the birds with a real hard jog,

And return triumphant from the bog.

*End

1.9 Wedding speech for Niece Lucy 1995 in Stellenbosch.

*

When Lucy got engaged it was her lovely wish,
To get that Uncle Robert right inside her niche,
And make the bridal speech.
He knew she was a peach.

*

Cape Town was his destination,
To make the speech with inspiration.
It was a long weekend half way round the world
But his joy was there just to be unfurled.

*

Lucy got engaged to Patrick on a moonlit beach at night.
Her spirits were much higher than a kite.
When she accepted his advance,
He wanted much to do a dance.
Patrick was a pilot of a jumbo jet.
The courting miles were millions till he had won his pet.

*

Then when he got back to duty,
He thought this would be fruity,
He got in to the simulator and did a loop the loop.
To win his darling Lucy was a mega wonder coup.

*

This speech must serenade Lucy lovely bride.
She is already uncle's pride.
Just gorgeous as a flower,
Love groweth by the hour.
She was brought up in Ida's Valley,
Under that wonder artist, who is her daddy.

*

At 19 she went to Florence to learn Italian art.
In no time as pupil she played her part.
Signora Simmi no chicken at 93 put her through the mill;
Drawing was to her a regimental drill.

*

In the mornings nudes were drawn;
Sometimes the models were forlorn.
In the afternoons it was portraits,
Of models in gorgeous corsets.
In the evenings it was still lives,
No time at all for any drives.

*

Then to Chelsea School of art Lucy came,
Just another step to get her fame.
In 1987 she became young master,
She could not get attention any faster.

*

Then the take off really came,
With exhibitions in sun and rain.
She broke down the door of the Royal Academy.
Her pictures were hung with smug hilarity.

*

Burlington House was the natural gallery,
For to win and earn her salary.
Her pictures were the gems of sight.
That brought extravagant delight.

*

She travelled half the world and more,
To study art we could adore,
And paint the places of the globe,
As in triumph there she rode.
She is a super star we know;
Her reputation does just glow.

*

Lucy has a real compassion.
This is more than just a fashion.
Dachshund Otto gives her licks and kisses,
As he adores his human misses.
*
10 minutes of this standing ovation,
Is the style of Otto's motion.
How the politicians would envy her.
The way she gets her friends to purr.
*
But now his doggy nose is out of joint.
You'll be the first to see the point.
For Lucy was all his own,
And now he will be left alone.
*
For Patrick now has place of honour,
And poor Otto feels a gonner.
And Lucy has some other loves,
She skis down slopes as fast as doves,
She rides her horses with some skill,
And never never has a spill.
*
Dancing reels is also a must.
Giddy are her partners just,
And as she swirls in the eightsome reel,
All can see she has appeal.
*
But Patrick is so hard to get,
And that we'll not forget.
He is so used to flee at 2 mack speed,
The other ladies who him heed.
*
Now Patrick and Lucy are a couple,
Let us have a toast that's subtle.
We wish them life of happiness,
And grace and joy and togetherness.
*
Lucy and Patrick.

Lucy's Royal Academy 'Iona Cathedral'

Lucy and Patrick on wedding day

1.10. Dedication of Jessica's year with Project in Zimbabwe, 1997

*

We are gathered here today,
To send Jessica on her way.
Zim must look out,
For this girl with such clout.

*

She's going to be a rover,
Sure she is no pushover,
When her anger is inspired,
And you nearly get devoured.

*

Coll's envoy is her role.
God bless this happy soul.
She's going to the bush.
It's dry and wild and not very lush.

*

There is a canny thrill in going on a jumbo jet;
But oh so sad Jessica cannot take her pet.
Her pony will have to stay,
By the Manse and have a bray.

*

'I will wait at least a year,
And more if you prefer.
I will think of you in Zim,
And the pupils you will win.'

*

To a school Jessica is going,
To help them with the knowing.
She will teach them all some English,
Till their tongues are wagging fiendish.

*

Her charms are there in tons,
Forgive my fickle puns.
To children she's delight,
They won't let her out of sight.

*

No trouble keeping order,
They cannot afford her,
Going to some other place,
Where they will have her face.

*

Zim will be such a pleasure,
There will be time for leisure.
The swimming pools are warm,
For one with elflike form.

*

But she will need a checking,
There is no hippo lurking.
She'll take a pole to probe,
And touch the hippo's lobe.

*

And if she tries the rivers,
She could so get the dithers.
There are crocs to hold her down,
That would make her Mother frown.

*

But it's well known as she goes hence,
That Jessica has some sense.
So Mother can relax,
Jessica will return intact.

*

We must applaud this super girl,
Who sends us in a whirl,
To give a year of toil,
In a country where you boil.

*

She goes with our goodwill.
So we want to pay her bill.
We need to rush like lemmings,
To maximise the givings.

*

Your fingers must go numb.
You mustn't think it dumb,
To write those cheques so fast,
The pain will hardly last.

*
Good luck our Island lass;
We want to make a fuss;
We know you will come back,
Or Lavinia will get the sack.
*
God bless her mission there,
May joy shine every day, my dear.
And like the rays of sunlight,
Bring grace and awesome might.
*End

1.11. Coll Easter Revue 1997

*
Coll is an Island with magical beauty.
The people there are equally fruity.
The drama talent is there so deep,
In tragedy they will have you weep.
*
But the Easter revue is full of fun;
The humour there is by the ton.
The event is out to raise the money;
Coll's champion Jessica is out to claim the honey.
*
Look out Zim, Jessica's coming.
The pupils of the school will come running.
But £3,000 this champion needs.
To that challenge the community heeds.
*

The Coll band starts with violin, drums, piano, guitar, fiddle, flute and clarinet.
Two encores are the outcome as you would expect.
Then 1960 songs are sung;
John Porrelli had begun.
*
Little Amy only nine,
Gave three spots fine,
The keyboard banged with great accord,
And cries were up encore, encore.
*
Her sound and smiles were captivating;
The howls and yells were excruciating.
This is a star we've seen for sure;
She will ne'er be shown the door.
*
Little sister, Jessica's supporter,
Amy is Lee's younger daughter.
Lee the Mum should have gone on the stage;
Her drama antics in Coll cover many a page.
*
Her concert reppertoir,
Is so full of satire.
Her tummy dancing has your smiles a-flash;
Later tonight she plays Miss Whiplash.
*
Pete Smalley is the compere;
As usual he plays only in top gear.
A comic he is so very game.
He is superb as a pantomime dame.
*
You will laugh with every pressure,
As you follow every gesture.
And the ad libs leave you weak,
As Pete takes you to his peak.
*
Tonight he's compere,
He' s that bril my dear.
He pretends to forget his lines,
To trick our clever minds.
*

He goes behind the curtain,

A subtle rouse for certain,

Then he ad libs some more,

That's funny to the core.

*

Then Lee and Moira come and dance,

Clad in tartan bonnets and sashes they prance.

Fran and Anna, Scottish comics, they impersonate.

They put the pulse in double rate.

They sing roaming in the gloaming,

As their audience starts foaming.

And stop your tickling jock,

And the audience is in their pot.

*

Lorna Barr brings on the Island choir.

These youngsters bring a special primary fire;

And a solo act with recorder is Helena's contribution;

So accomplished is her tuition.

*

Ali gives a recitation of proud MacSporran.

What did this Scotsman wear underneath the sporran?

The ladies shut their eyes,

They didn't want to be wise.

*

The spread is so refreshing in mid evening.

All the platters are left gleaming.

Then the second half is there for fun.

This will leave your truly done.

*

Pete gives the recitation of his life;

No, it's not about his wife.

It's Albert and the lion, poor Mum gets vexed,

As morsel Albert gets perplexed.

*

Moira and Brian are given 'This is your life',

A tale indeed of awesome strife.

The midwife starts with nurses outfit.

The birth was there and don't you doubt it.

*

Then Nanny came with strict regime.

Poor Brian was given a painful clean.

Grandparent Pete could not find the babe.

He duly went into a rave.

*

And Mairi was the tough school teacher.

Brian's hand got the strap, poor creature.

Then up he grew and went to the city,

And indulged in a few things flighty.

*

The foreign frauline did him embrace,

Then other girls came a pace.

And there was Miss Whiplash,

To enfold him in her sash.

*

From this wild city life,

Brian fled to somewhere nice,

It had to be a farm on Coll.

From whence he could not have a fall.

*

The standard of the concert was so very high.

That was no sudden flippant cry.

The talent was in tons.

And raised £614 to put Jessica in funds.

*

A Royal Command performance would never out play,

The staunch island spirit, I say, I say, I say.

*end

Portrait of Pete Smalley, Convenor Coll Show, Island Pantomime Dame

1.12 The Coll Show and dance 1997

The Coll spirit is alight;
It really does burn bright.
First Friday in August the joy overflows,
As whole families compete to the standard of the pros.
*

There are classes for sheep;
It doesn't matter if they leap.
The vegetables are in classes;
On the tables they stand like mountain passes.
*

Seaweed mixed with muck makes the soil alluvial;
The carrots are so big they are unreal.
The potatoes are so good they are judged the best of best.
And that was said without a wince of jest.
*

The floral decorations fill front stage.
Two hundred and more entries, they really are the rage.
These wild flowers have such a pungent scent,
They catch the nostrils of every island gent.
*

Another 200 items are on the baking table packed,
Bread and scones galore, cakes and pancakes stacked.
The smell is just delicious,
Aromatic not fictitious.
*

And the centre table is dedicated to knitters.
The Coll knitting Beeb just puts you into jitters.
These Coll ladies work throughout the night.
The standard achieved is higher than a kite.
*

We must not forget the children's classes too.
They attract attention right the noo.
Shell gardens are a form of art,
That pulls and tugs the heart.
*

And pieces on the shore,
Give interest to the core.
There was a dutchman's clog.
It would be perfect in a bog.
And neptune's candle stood,
A light to eat the pud.
*

Spectacular was the metal weathervane,
The painting and welding all so very game
Adult's art and children's art,
Were another pleasing part.
*

The exhibits were an eyeful.
Yes, they were much more than cool.
Outside the children danced the Highland Fling,
And 'best kept pet' competed in the ring.
*

The winner was the collie;
Which was so very jolly.
Pony came nowhere,
Despite washing and brushing and other loving care.
*

The cross country event got a lot of attention.
The ladies cup went a-missing, what a mention.
Charlie won the mens,
To applaud of all his friends.
Alison won the ladies, the fastest in the Isle,
The cheers she got were quite a pile.
*

Pete Smalley was convenor;
No, he was not a dreamer.
He commanded the show together
A sergeant - major could not do better.
But the humour was in tons,
As he ad libbed with all his puns.
*

Heroes he made the cup winners.
They knew they weren't beginners.
Some had baked the night right through.
To grace the judges' chew.
*

Some had slaved the year and more,
To make their gardens give galore.
Some had knitted till their fingers got a cramp,
In the small hours by a lamp.
*

Some had fed their sheep on oats,
And had carefully brushed their coats.
The children had practised their dancing.
When they could have been out prancing.
*

The cup winners were the super Collachs,
Won, I would say with some super frollicks.
Catriona Brodie was the tops, the cups she won were legion.
She was the champion of this region.
*

The show is a huge endeavour,
Which the Coll folk will never sever,
They celebrated that night,
When the lights were shining bright.
*

They danced the evening thru,
And the Mallin band was true.
And the raffle they did draw,
And the goodies were galore.
*
A tv set for starters,
And a lawyer's will for afters,
Coll show day was a treasure,
With lots and lots of pleasure.
*End

Best Kept pet being judged at Coll Show

1.13. Duntreath Castle Christmas Fare

*
Stall holders of the world unite.
Give to charity with all your might.
The poor disabled want your money;
This is earnest and not funny.
*
The place for all this enterprise,
Is Duntreath, Castle of surprise.
The pheasants strut across the lawns.
A large marquee the tower adorns.
*
40 up market exhibitors come.
The 'County' ladies must be won.
This is the hen party of the year.
2000 are shopping, do you hear?
*
They have come to buy their Christmas presents,
Far more dear than Duntreath pheasants.
For these stalls are so up market,
Only the best is there to target.
*
This might just be a fashion show,
As those hats and dresses glow.
There are handcrafted wonders there,
Made with lots of loving care.
*
The jewels they sparkle on the stands,
All set to attract the fans.
Fountain pens are bargains too,
Five or six at least will do.
For Christmas pressies must be bought,
And price can hardly be a thought.
*
Multi-coloured cushions stare.
The buyers love this super fare.
And scarves galore all haut coutour,
And bonnets sure,
Combine to take them all by storm,
As this army works in form.
How they love this spending spree,
With all those gifts and all that glee.
*
Only to Duntreath and Glamis we go;
The class is there we have you know.
Duntreath and Arundel is another pair,
For pressie displays and lots of flair.
*

But the Arundel stall is full of woes.

The cash, it keeps them on their toes.

They are struggling with the Scottish money,

And they don't think it's funny,

Their £ twenties and £ fivers get all mixed,

So their prices are unfixed;

Their cut price gems are bargains true,

As those ladies make their coup.

*

Oh how these ladies love their shopping spree;

As they sign the cheques in glee.

Their minds are crazed,

Their eyes are glazed.

*

How they love those gorgeous hats.

They will outshine society rats.

And multi-coloured ties and boxer shorts,

That make men glam on tennis courts.

*

And children's ware is there as well.

The dresses cute would make them swell.

And toys and games would send them dizzy.

The mothers now are in a frizzy.

All this choice and no men about.

To guide the mums and check their clout.

*

These ladies shop and shop with zeal,

For everything looks like a deal.

The stall owners too exude panache.

They're not thinking spending's rash.

*

You need to know your Debrett as well,

To recognise the rich and swell.

A duchess there is doing trade,

So county ladies be not afraid.

To show your brass,

And let all see this spending pass.

*

And when they tire of this shopping thing,

They ascend the Tower for another fling.

Delicious eats are there hurrah.

There's smoked salmon and pots of caviar.

And champers champers by the gallon,

Flowing freely from the flaggon.

*

This hen party is quite unique,

With 2,000 ladies at the peak.

Their happy chatter is quite a noise,

As they buy for all their boys.

Their taste is good, their mission sure,

Their riches there to pour and pour.

*

The route is long thru marquee and castle,

When they trudge with one huge parcel.

40 stalls of Harrods quality

Bought to ease disabled poverty.

*

Every room contains some stalls.

Four poster beds are a wow for shawls;

And hats in piles and piles and piles,

You would have thought they stretched for miles.

*

The dining - room is decked with dresses.

Oh, they are the best of pressies.

Evening gowns and super swimwear

Tempt the buyer in her lair.

*

In the kitchen are doggy coats.

No, no it's not a silly hoax.

The pets must have a part to play,

On this Christmas fare today.

*

Clever Julie is the organiser of this ware.

She has raised a standard for Christmas fare.

Like Crufts it is the best of best,

Nowhere, nowhere are the rest.

*

Hen party of the year is her inspiration.

And the men will pay with perspiration,

And pressies make a Christmas mountain,

As no loot is left for counting.

*end

Duntreath Castle, Susan's old home

1.14. Verses for commemoration of Sophy Bristol's painting exhibition June 10th 1997 from Uncle, Robert Erskine

*

The socialites of London descend on Dover Street.

They are going for a very special treat.

Sophy's pictures are hanging in an exhibition;

This is a mega event and no part of tradition.

*

Did you ever have a taste for very modern art?

For this is how Sophy has made her instant mark.

Groups galore in very gaudy colours,

Are there to entice the rich and famous Mothers.

*

The pop stars have their places,

Which glamorise their faces.

Sophy's subjects are from imagination.

She can paint flirtation.

*

Her eyes are on the Royal Academy of Arts.

Her pieces portray swinging London parts.

Her pictures will be put to the hanging committee.

No worry there, they are so pretty.

*

A whole room will be apart,

With Sophy Bristol art.

In only just a jiffy she will be proud RA,

This is a very special day.

*

The rich and famous come.
Other artists can't help run.
She's the one that sets the style,
Leading, leading by the mile.
*
They come from every part.
They think this is a lark.
Uncle jets in from Scotland.
He should have brought a band.
*
Their hands are on their chequebooks.
Sophy has them all on hooks
It simply is a race to get red stickers up.
Before they go for sup.
*
Investment prospects glow,
As the viewers pass their doe.
Their fingers get quite numb,
Their spouses go quite dumb,
They write the cheques so fast,
How long will this craze last?
*
Uncle is quite captivated,
And his chequebook is gyrated.
'Relaxed' is the purchased piece,
From his ever joyous niece.
*
She is always walking tall,
But when she's had a ball,
She is 20 feet above the buyer;
It's not good to be any higher.
*end

'Sonya Madan' by Sophie Bristol

Sophy Bristol

1.15. Verse for fund raising money at Sue Ryder Charity Lunch 1997

*

Welcome welcome to the steadings.
You have come here like the lemmings;
For it is the chance to give and give,
So that others may live and live.

*

Sue Ryder in her wisdom great,
Did so want to have a date,
To get donations flowing through,
Enough to put you on the brew.

*

Her cause is just so wonderful;
It speaks a thousand words of pull,
To give the sick some care and love,
And comfort as a cooing dove.

*

Binny House needs more space;
To offer more the gems of grace,
And bring some smiles to treat the sick,
And give them life that has a kick.

*

Love glows for the cheerful giver,
As long it's done without a dither.
Let your riches go where they cannot rust.
Lest Sue Ryder should go bust.

*

Give and give till it hurts today.
Sue Ryder will say hurray hurray.
And joy there is in bringing comfort,
And it makes you feel triumphant.

*

The cause is good;
It's like rich pud.
Your pocket's deep;
This is no time to go to sleep.

*

Reach down and sign your cheques away.
There is no fear is what I say.
Sue Ryder will love you a lot.
Don't be worried by this plot.
*end

1.16 Lament for Princess Diana 31st August

It was a Sunday full of tears,
It bode the worst of all our fears,
Diana icon for us all,
She did so have a tragic fall.
*
We heard that morn at six o'clock
That her car had hit a rock,
And turned around at dreadful speed,
As Dodi had her homebound fleed.
The paperazi bikes were giving reckless chase.
We never will know what was their tragic pace.
*
From these tigers she had fled,
But now this heart throb of the world was dead.
We all were truly stunned to see this light go out.
Her love and compassion still lingered around about.
*
As our minds went completely numb,
We reached out to let her memory come.
This fairy like girl had had a sad childhood,
At six her parents split, no mother there to give her pud.
*
But at 19 she met her Prince Charming.
In no time she was the nation's darling.
The bride of St Paul's admired in every land
And feted everywhere with the fanfares of a band.
*
She touched the hearts of millions
Till she went to America, then it was the hearts of trillions.
She loved the young and frail and sick, the old and vulnerable
She brought such a kinda touch they simply could not stumble.
Her charms were there in tons.
She was such a hit with mums.
*
This was the people's princess.
No wonder her death would make such distress.
She had her causes too,
And made some politicians boohoo.
*
The land mines wrought such horrors,
To children they brought such sorrows.
Her campaign was so simple;
To abolish land mines all in a twinkle.
*
The power of her charisma
Stretched from London to Tunisia.
She would tackle AIDS head on,
And make sufferers think it had gone.
*
The lepers felt her hand,
They didn't think her grand.
She cuddled them in pity,
They laughed and called her witty.
*
Her presence gave a sparkle,
Her glance was such an article,
Her smile would have you melt,
With warmth and pleasure felt.
*
Her own life was full of sorrow,
As her wife role got so narrow.
Divorce was very painful,
But her life could still be gainful.
*

In life she lacked for love at home,
In death the flowers formed a dome,
London florists were cleaned out,
As mourners showed their clout.
*
For charities she was a winner,
£1,000 to join her for the dinner,
In one day alone she raised half a million dollars,
To help young distressed fellahs,
To keep them off the drugs,
And free them from the thugs.
*
She found her role at last,
She was the queen of hearts.
The world has lost today,
The heart throb of the world, I say.
*End

Chapter 2 - Sattire, causes and politics.

The poems on causes bring out emotions of anger and despair and desire to reform and prevent future waste and abuse of power and incompetence at the highest level. They are full of invective and satire. The sling is loaded and the villains are so very villainous. The archbishop is chided for sleeping through 8 years of accounts till the church is nearly bankrupt and the First Estates Commissioner goes on an unstoppable spree of gambling with commercial property! The under performance of the Church exceeds a gob stopping £5 billion. In the house move, however, it is authority in the form of the policeman who is the butt. And he has his leg pulled unmercifully.

The three principals of the University of Oz abuse their positions of power in an awesome way and the final principal, Dr. Mopkin finally gets felled by united staff action on the university e-mail system. The poem is written to draw attention to the authorities to revise the instruments of university governance and prevent more re-occurances of such abuse. The resonance of this poem is to bring a reform of democracy to the QUANGOS of Britain. The most promising instrument of reform is to adapt and adopt the 'Cadbury' rules of governance to restore credible accountability in the public sector.

The verses on the London Ambulance Service highlight the horrors of badly managed computerised systems, which deliver chaos instead of improved response time. London glitches while Avon comes to terms with the help of robots. The crucial difference between success and failure in use of high tech solutions is dependent on the adoption of 'best practice' in design and implementation. The failures in Britain in the Public Sector exceed half a billion pounds / annum, a sure target for satire.

The verses on Taurus explain how £400 million went down the plughole owing to a major glitch between provider and client, in which the chief executive found himself powerless to abort an unviable project for 4 years. A provider tried to impose a Canadian solution to a London Stock Exchange where stakeholder interests were very different. Solutions to the computer glitches are offered in chapter 7.

The poem on the Hustings gives support to nephew Jamie in the General Election of 1997. It portrays the fun of battle in getting votes but also rouses anger about waste and extravagance manifested in a £64,000 binge programme laid on by the Stornaway Council.

2.1.When the Fire rescued the Law.

Happy was the day Robert moved into his Farm

Two police officers came next day to still the calm.

The law was there to break the fun.

Their mission was to check his gun.

*

One officer, a wee man, stood thin as a nail,

A tasty morsel for a killer whale,

The other, experienced with 20 years on the beat

Substantial with large bottom and size 12 feet.

*

Robert led them to the loft and set the ladder straight
The fat officer climbed in confident state.
After panting and puffing he squeezed thru the hatch,
To see the gun and check the serial match.
*
The wee one waited on the net,
There might be a call from the Met.
But no it was from Falkirk that the panic came.
'Come immediately; there are robbers here to claim'.
*
The fat one in the loft said 'damn this alarm,
There's no time to dither in this farm.'
The big bottom and size 12 boots of this old buck,
Lunged to the hatch and got stuck.
*
He was stuck fast as a cork in a bottle.
*
There were pulls and tugs and ouching and ripping,
But no sign of the officer slipping.
His legs did kick and muscles strain,
His gestures frantic as he took the pain.
*

He was stuck fast as a cork in a bottle.
*
The thin one saw his superior's middle,
And became speechless trying to suppress a giggle.
There were pulls and tugs and ouching and ripping,
But no sign of the officer slipping.
*
He was stuck fast as a cork in a bottle.
*
He showed his long-jons as his trousers rent,
There was a clatter and bang as the hand cuffs went,
Next his hat to the bottom of the cupboard fell,
This officer knew he was going through hell.
*
Long-jons, long-jons, have you ever seen a finer uniform?
*
His truncheon next was to make the clatter.
His whistle last to make the batter.
His face was red; the sweat was on his brow;
Oh dear, oh dear, he did so want his freedom now.
*
He was stuck fast as a cork in a bottle.
Stuck fast as a cork in a bottle.
*

The frog had left the thin one at last.
Composed he called the fire brigade to come fast.
They came with saws and a great long rope,
The harbingers of the constable's hope.
*
Two fire officers applied their tools and cut the hatch.
They hosed him down to prepare a snatch.
They pulled and tugged for all they were worth.
This was no matter for joyful mirth!

*

Long-jons, long-jons, have you ever seen a finer uniform?

*

Then bang at last his bottom fell,

He knew that now he was free from hell.

Debagged, disarmed, exhausted, what a fate,

While all that crime was still in spate.

*

He was revived with tea downstairs.

It soothed his mind and calmed his fears.

The Yorkie barked behind the door,

Then Susan gasped at what she saw.

What's this, a constable in debagged state?

'Get back to duty to seal the Falkirk robber's fate.'

*

'Carry on policeman'!

*End

2.2. Gambling by the Commissioners of the Church of England by Robert Erskine

*

Margaret Thatcher has a day of glee,

As Sir Douglas Lovelock comes on bended knee.

First Estates Commissioner is the job he gets.

Bishops and clergy will become his pets.

*

By Jove, he will improve their lot,

Don't say he might yet start the rot.

Pensions, stipends and cars galore,

All are there if he can get rapport,

With all magnates of the City,

And make his patron's plan look pretty.

*

What a job is this says he.

No-one, no-one, but the Queen can sack me!

I'll drive a wedge through the high and mighty,

That'll make the bishops flighty.

*

With the billions I'll go,

Into property like Metro Centre Co.

I'll make the Church a cut-price bank,

To entice the knights of rank.

*

Sir John Hall, partner, made some booty,

Oh that success was really fruity,

Newcastle United earned his love,

As £ millions descended from above,

From 3rd to 1st division hike,

They got there faster than by bike.

*

Sir Douglas will lend galore,

The hard won givings of the poor.

In rough times the losers run,

The Church as bank is left with none.

The debt is sadly written off.

Sir Douglas merely has a cough.

*

Oh what risks Sir Douglas made.

For Ashford £80 million he paid;

A mini town he was to build,

But then, oh dear, it was all killed.

*

The planners rejected all the plans,
And out the window went his fans.
And the value left, a poor ten grand,
Not enough to pay the band.
*
He had to keep the clergy sweet,
And make them want to lick his feet,
And he paid them far more money,
As the capital went runny.
*
The dividends, he stripped them bare,
No longer under tender care,
Sold ex dividend the income roared,
And expectations further soared.
*
The capital flowed into the breech,
But losses were kept out of reach,
They hid behind an elegant screen,
In which the truth was short and lean,
*
Mr Plender blew his whistle.
The news he gave was an epistle.
The Financial Times gave all a jolt.
For some it was a near revolt.
*
For a full 8 years the archbishops slept,
But when they knew the truth they wept,
£800 millions in one year had gone a-walk,
And not a trace could now be sought.
*
But that's not all I'll have to say,
To load you up with more dismay,
The under performance when he did the rounds,
Exceeded more than Five billion pounds.
Eight years was a long time for the archbishops to sleep
And lose and lose an enormous heap.
*
Their provinces, pay, pensions and palace,
Had gone with Alice,
Through the looking glass,
This was a mega farce.
*
Archbishop Carey, new in his Sea,
Twitched as he were bitten by a flea,
Roused in anger and dismay,
He nearly threw his crook away.
*
Then His Grace took hold,
And he played bold.
And poised and calm he sent for Baring,
And a Lambeth group for hearing.
How the money had been lost,
And what did all this gambling cost.
*
The Lambeth group responded fast,
And nailed Sir Douglas to the mast.
Field MP set up a pension's hearing,
Not impressed with Peter Baring,
With his bank about to fall,
When Leeson made that fatal call.
In charge of both the front and back,
He was destined to get the sack.
*
And the House of Commons sat,
And put Sir Douglas on the mat.
When he made a proposition,
He brooked no opposition.
*
He was in charge of 16 groups,
And made the most of all his troops.
The message coming from his lips,
Was that his property chums were drips.
They were like beasts who prowled the land
No worries if they were underhand.

*

Advisers tried to restrain his style,

But all attempts were tossed a mile.

A lone protester did his best,

But he got no more joy than all the rest

*

He resigned in anger in the end,

But Sir Douglas would not bend.

The pensions man near had a stroke.

When he discovered they were broke.

*

The audit staff of NAO did blush,

Their recommendations had a hush,

For 8 long years they were ignored,

No wonder that the reports were flawed.

*

The annual report had a circulation wide,

PM, Home Secretary, the House of Commons, the Archbishops the Synod, on every side,

Yet none did see the flaws were there,

And none did so much as turn a hair!

*

The Lambeth group did stop the rot,

And put new players on the spot,

With retrenchment as the theme of day,

And wise men only had a say.

*

Their Graces next to Turnbull put to write,

New rules, new structures, an archbishop's council with bite,

To recover leadership and zest,

And rid the Commissioners of their pest.

*

And radical was this reform ,

The Commissioners a meek 15 from 95, they are reborn,

As the family stockbroker assumes its residuary role,

And power returns to the Archbishop's soul.

*

No more, no more, will gambling be done,

And magnates allowed to boss and be won.

The archbishops at last will lead us in Grace

And spend for the cure of souls in every place.

*End

2.3 Three Principals of the University of Oz

*

In the 1970s this institution was born.

Its three principals became ever so forlorn.

Dr Pipkin was the first;

One must not say he was the worst.

*

An engineer he built the structure.

Needless to say there was no rupture.

But his pals were hard to find,

When they found that he was on the grind.

*

He had a hate against the rates,

And all the local authority mates.

He plotted for Central Government control,

But alas there was around a mole.

His deputy Dr Popkin had ambition.

Perhaps he could generate some friction.

Pipkin glitched in the industrial court,

Sex discrimination, unfair dismissal were the causes fought,

And lost amidst a harsh critique.

The judge did not like Pipkin's pique.

'Unreliable are you' said he,

'A principal you are not fit to be'.

*

Another glitch was soon to come.

The CNAA came down like a ton.

'Your style is not mature enough,

With people you are far too rough'.

*

Popkin saw a bigger prize.

He was astute and worldly wise.

He burgled Pipkin's secret files.

Treason was there for miles and miles.

*

And now as mole to the council he went.

'Your hold on Oz will soon be spent,

HMG will take Oz on.

Your wonder flagship will ere be gone'.

*

The council were so very angry.

' Pipkin, Sir, we don't like this hanky panky.

This treason cannot be forgot;

We cannot have you make this plot.

*

The CNAA have had their lot;

The judges could not believe your word;

We are giving you the bird.'

*

Popkin rubbed his hands in glee;

Now he would get a better fee.

Acting Principal was his next role;

Soon it was Principal for this happy soul.

*

Power was glorious to wield;

It could enhance his every deed.

For technology he had a passion,

To get the robots into fashion.

Tubes and tubes in great profusion,

But they were to cause confusion.

*

The committee men were a bunch of experts;

And they had no time for perverts.

They clashed with Popkin on many grounds.

On contracts he was out of bounds.

*

He made the experts rubber stamps.

All their work got no thanks.

And they were miffed as you would expect,

When they saw all their counsels wrecked.

*

The suppliers had a better deal,

And Popkin got the odd free meal.

He bought from them some tons of junk,

While all the experts' hearts were sunk.

*

Mopkin, Vice Principal, was appointed;

By Popkin he was anointed.

But the friendship didn't last,

Mopkin thought he was so fast

*

He told the local papers that,

Oz would be no longer flat.

The new broom would be sweeping clean,

And Oz would be a super dream.

*

Popkin, a flop, was made to look.
'This upstart must be brought to book'.
He threatened Mopkin with discipline,
The shouted charges made a din.
*

No quarter must be given now.
To Popkin's will he must bow.
Mopkin knew that he must win,
And get once more his natural grin.
*

He saw all the junk in piles and piles,
And went and burgled the suppliers' files.
Irregularity was there in heaps;
So much was there it gave him creeps.
*

To the governors he sped along.
'You must give Popkin the gong,
This irregularity must be stopped.
T'is time that he were chopped'.
*

The governors listened quite aghast.
Indeed this day was Popkin's last.
He left without an ounce of grace.
The departure was at a shocking pace.
*

There was no time for a goodbye party.
For Mopkin it was all hilarity.
No more public humiliation,
He set to build his own reputation.
*

From deputy he became the boss.
His broom was there to sweep the floss.
An entrepreneur was he just,
For power he had a hungry lust.
*

For eight long years he stayed in power,
As it gathered hour by hour.
At first he had a honeymoon,
And he created quite a boom.
*

He binned all Popkin's tons of junk;
All this waste was just sunk.
He made the institution hot,
Till university status was its lot.
*

It grew and grew as years went by;
And all the while he was on the sly.
The power he had went to his head;
He did so much he ne'er went to bed.
*

Deans and HODS were anointed too,
But they were put on a leash the noo.
Three year contracts and bonus schemes,
Tied them totally to his dreams.
*

He recommended nominations for most of the governors too;
So they would not tell him what to do.
The Munich spirit wafted through the campus,
Yesmen everywhere would make no rumpus.
*

Bolder, bolder, he became.
He tried to make the staff insane.
Kangeroo courts went into action,
At the first sign of reaction.
*

Intimidation was the order of the day,
For the hapless ones to stand in his way.
And at spending sprees he was no novice;
A million pounds was spent on his new office,
While all universities were retrenching,
Mopkin geed on all this spending.
*
The luxuries there would make King Farouk blush.
When the cleaners saw it there was a hush,
Then 'hang', they said, 'what waste is this?
He must be trying to take the piss'.
*
How did the governors approve the extravagance?
But they enjoyed all this flamboyance.
They paid Mopkin twice the going rate.
One wonders how they did debate.
*

He had them on the leash its true,
Never never would they say boo.
And what about those men of senate?
They just said they did not ken it.
A whisper seen as an epistle,
Would have earned instant dismissal.
*

When power's abused it knows no bounds.
Decisions are made on very dicey grounds.
Academic mayhem was the order of the day.
Delayering was the instrument, I say
*

But the staff were very angry,
When they found this hanky panky.
The HODs would be no more;
They would all be shown the door.
*
This Mopkin's grand notion,
Was planned to be done in vacation.
The talk of consultation was just a little farce,
When all the staff were out to grass.
*
But when they returned from holiday,
Revolt is in the air, I say.
The auditors were sought.
They were the only group not bought.
*

No confidence votes were passed.
Mopkin merely laughed.
'The lunatic fringe are wingeing',
But the e-mail was soon spinning.
*

Intimidation stories were wafted on the net,
Then the majority could have their little bet.
How long could Mopkin last,
Amidst the fury of this blast?
*
The local press were in the door;
They had a field day, cor!
The staff confronted Mopkin with financial irregularity.
The auditors picked this up with much hilarity.
*
The governors were embarrassed.
They really did look harassed,
As their champion was laid low,
Principal Mopkin went below.
*

There was not enough grace for a goodbye event.

We wonder what all this meant.

Three principals were out for abuse of power.

They really were an awful shower.

*

Why could not Oz learn from its errors?

And rid itself from all those terrors.

But a university is the last to learn,

Even when it is about to burn.

*End

2.4. On the Hustings May 1997 in the Western Isles.

*

The uncle must give the nephew support,

And help him with political rapport.

The Constituency is the Western Isles.

The work is there in piles and piles.

*

No Tory fighter has been seen for years.

Now Jamie wants to get the cheers.

Uncle Robert flies the Friday plane,

And with Lord McKay he has a refrain.

*

The Minister will be there just;

Him and Jamie will be a must.

The tv cameras they think are waiting,

But their absence is a baiting.

*

Candidate, minister and yours truly,

Think this was a nasty gouley.

Anyway the Minister's visit must go on,

And VIP events are done.

*

The town walkabout is quite a thing.

The minister enjoys his fling.

Then to the County Hotel we go,

To have some soup and eat some doe.

*

And meet the local Tory Committee,

Oh they are so very pretty.

Their hats are at least a metre wide,

With flowers fragrant oosing pride.

*

But then the rival party come,

Lorn Gillis and the SNPs to spoil the fun.

The minister's briefing,

Is soon ceasing.

*

Then there is more VIP speeches,

At Ardesir he is in the breeches.

This is a yard with 400 men,

And they must know that Jamie's a gem.

*

Uncle Robert goes on his own,

To canvass in the streets alone,

He knows by heart the manifesto,

And his message goes hey presto.

*

Willie Whitelaw gives some tips.

They are essential for canvassing lips.

'If the voter is sore committed,

Don't just stand there half witted.

"Jolly good show," and give a handshake warm.

You mustn't leave support forlorn.

*

If the voter's a committed anti,

Don't let him get so very panty.

"Well that's it isn't it" and move on just as fast.

It's to the floating voter your words must last'.

*

Next site to catch the voter's eyes,

Is outside the Coop as they emerge with goods and pies.

When they see that huge rosette in blue,

They charge their batteries anew.

They state their politics in grace.

And encounter canvasser face to face.

*

Next day in expectation the Tory Party goes,

To Isle of Scalpay, the Tory Party rose.

This is an amazing Isle,

The toffs there are quite a pile.

*

With a population of 400 in just a mile of Isle,

The fisherfolk have a very special style.

When herrings were there in profusion,

There were millionaires in some confusion.

*

But now with the more modest prawn,

Some of that wealth is shorn.

And there is some irritation when the boats from Isle of Man,

Don't heed the Sabbath ban;

And fish the place right out.

Poor Scalpays are down the spout.

*

But there is still goodwill in Scalpay for the Tory cause.

And canvassers can still get some applause.

The Queen Bee Tory Colonel of the Nursing Arm lives there.

For Politics she has abundant flair.

*

The canvassers this day got cakes and buns galore.

The food would have fed 1,000 hungry poor.

The breakfasts were for winning,

When the Tory tale was dinning.

*

The Scalpay's Highland hospitality,

Does outplay any charity.

At last the canvass's done,

Oh dear that Lorn Gillis comes to spoil the fun.

*

The SNP loudspeakers make a dreadful din.

How could those millionaires want to see their thing.

On the ferry going back,

The two parties exchange some flak.

*

Next day is the Sabbath, at last a day of truce,

And a trip to the Free Kirk, ever so tidy and spruce.

300 ladies are there with hats in modest colours,

For it wouldn't do to get a wink from awful lively fellas.

*

There is a little time,

To read of local crime.

The councillors have hogged the scene.

This one will make you keen.

*

They have approved a wonder binge,

That will make you want to winge.

£64,000 must be spent on 80 Eurocrats.

They will occupy the many island flats.

*

They will the lovely seashore adorn,

But it might be a little forlorn,

After imbibing £3,000 of spirit,

Their minds will hardly be with it.

*

The Tories must get in to stop this spending glitch;

To wash away extravagance must be their vital pitch.

It's worth it on the hustings just to have this subtle cause.

It's time the spending spree had a long long pause.

*

After all this Tory hype,

They were all sent on a bike.

They held their vote in Stornaway

But no seats in Scotland I say.

*End

2.5. When the London Ambulance Service glitched, 1993

*

London is not the place to have heart failing,

As the 999 men may keep you a-waiting.

In October 1993 the robots were installed.

And you will be quite appalled.

They glitched the service thin,

And Bottomley made the din.

*

There was a call unanswered for a very long 10 hours;

Time enough indeed for many autumn showers.

And when the ambulance came at last,

They found they weren't as fast,

As the Coop undertaker,

Already there to lift poor soul to his maker.

*

This was a little rough,

And Ginny kicked the robot to the touch.

'There must be a reason why,

This poor man had to die.

I will set up an enquiry to be a natural focus,

To get to the bottom of all this hocus pocus.'

*

The LAS director had been put on the spot,

To improve response time or it was his lot.

Two attempts had failed to get the robots there.

£5 million down the drain, oh dear, oh dear, oh dear.

There was one more attempt to go,

With another £2 million or so.

*

But the project was so fraught,

No lessons had been taught.

They only knew about glitching,

And that had Ginny bitching.

*

LAS called on a provider,

He proved to be a glider;

To get programs to the robots and intelligence therein,

And hopefully some added value win.

The tender had to be,

The cheapest one you see.

*

At the time of this development there was labour unrest.

Crews and operators thought the provider was a pest.

The design they wouldn't validate

So provider just did abdicate.

*

There were technical hitches all the time,

And weak testing was a crime.

The providers knew quite well that bugs were truly seated,

And that they were untreated.

*

And that training for the crews was a farce.

The new system simply couldn't last.

They used to hear a voice of a human controller, sure,

Now it was a robot which was such a bore.

*

When the 999 call came in,

The robot had to win.

It sent the nearest crew,

Which seemed to be the most sensible thing to do.

*

But the crews often forgot to tell the robot where they were,

So chaos did occur.

The crews were also miffed,

As their place of work did drift,

And when they wanted home,

Across half London they did roam.

*

Three days of this did last,

Then total breakdown came so fast.

All memory had been filled with incidents galore;

Nothing left for the robots to chew on any more.

*

But don't just think that robots can never work.

In Avon they are really quite a perk.

They help the controller to verify conditions,

And track the crew's positions.

*

They are a model service there,

And deliver lots of loving care,

They are user friendy to the crews,

And never make the news.

*End

2.6. Taurus - losing nearly half a £ billion

Its kinda bullish to want to lose the millions.

You have to be kinda bril to lose the billions.

To lose anything on computers most would think it kinda daft.

But the losses on Taurus will make you quite aghast.

*

Four years till abandonment and £400 million down the plughole,

That's just enough to tittivate the soul.

You must wonder why the high and mighty glitched in such style,

To lose that money in such a pile.

*

The Stock Exchange wanted to introduce paperless settlement,

While relationships with clients were most inclement.

The stakeholders never agreed the business solution,

But the providers pushed ahead with determined resolution.

*

Canada had a system for rolling settlement.

They thought they could adapt it for betterment,

Of London and make it world centre of finance.

That really was an idea of romance.

*

Watson was their champion with discretion,

And a clause of non interference to keep him in direction.

Rawlins was chief executive and warned to leave Taurus alone.

Or there would be such an awful moan.

*

Stock Exchange Council were determined as the day.

To get this project going without any more delay.

They never thought that HMG would make demands to protect,

The small investor against those who might defect.

*

The Canadian solution already patched galore,

Was then like Humpty Dumpty after his great fall.

Rawlins wasn't convinced but didn't know how,

To get the board to abort,

This mega project for which they had fought.

*

Watson kept saying he could pull it off,

With a little time and money for this computer toff.

But he never had the grace,

To come to his stakeholders face to face,

And accommodate their needs,

Instead of giving weeds.

*

After 4 long years and precious little progression,

Watson's programmers predicted a day of commission.

It was that glorious date infinity.

It was a date bereft of any dignity.

*

So Rawlins pulled the plug.

'No budget for infinity', he said it with a shrug.

But all the same resigned;

All his credibility impugned.

*

The City firms were so frustrated.

It was Rawlins they castigated.

Who had led them for 4 years with a 'no hoper'.

And had absorbed their funds as a soaker.

*

And the cause was so very simple.

Understandable to a baby with a dimple.

The client should never let the provider take over.

As he then becomes a helpless pushover.

*

He should monitor the contract with 'best practice' embedded.

An arms length relationship is better than being wedded.

He should respect the stakeholders too,

Or he should abort the project the noo.

*

There isn't any point in imposing robots clever,

From a system in Canada which never had a dither.

When your clients are in London,

And requirements for a very different run down.

*end

Chapter 3 - Impact of technology

The changes in technology were originally written for the Coll magazine and were full of romantic memorabilia about old farming methods, but gradually the author realised that this embraced a more serious theme about social change and could be used in university to explain the impact of modern technology and the impact it could make for new winners and losers. This section is developed with some satire aimed at robots. They stuff poor granny into a dustcard; they ensnare a business man at Waverly Station, but are so unfriendly they succeed in losing their owners £2 million / year in carpark revenue. They trap brother Philip in his high tech Land Rover so he has to be 'talked' down by mobile telephone. The Coll theme occurs again in the verses about the Coll ritual - the Coll show and dance. The theme of this is the profusion of the Island talent in gardening, baking, knitting, and the sheer capacity to enjoy themselves.

3.1. Farming memories on the Isle of Coll from Robert Erskine

*

Those were the days of 1963,

When Coll was the nicest place to be.

Gathering sheep was an ordeal.

For some it had a great appeal.

*

The evening started in a boat.

We hoped it would keep afloat.

The destination was Eilan Mor.

For the party of the gallant four.

*

The island sheep were wild as goats.

The seaweed fired them more than oats.

They didn't like losing their fleeces,

As the gatherers went to pieces.

*

They jumped the cliffs,

And took the biffs,

So one or two did get away,

All ready for another day.

*

By dark the party left the isle.

Their bags of fleece were quite a pile.

The seals were honking all the way;

Mission accomplished should we say?

*

Next week at Sorisdale the task was making hay,

With uncles, aunts, cousins, friends and no pay.

The old men supervised the scything.

The volunteers did all the turning.

*

The technology was oh so quaint,

You never saw a lick of paint.

The centre piece was a wooden rake.

The teeth were mainly there for good time's sake.

*

The stacks were really works of art,

With nets and stones to charm the heart.

The old folks much indulged their craft,

As the others did the graft.

*

The weather could cause awful pique.

Haymaking could last a month or a week.

That's a lot of time for the friends to stay.

All that time with no pay.

*

The corncrakes creek and creek so much,

And all the more when they have a clutch,

The courting males will creek for all they are worth,

For mating makes for so much mirth,

And cornfields are the perfect place,

To indulge in mating's chase.

*

At Cornaigbeg they decide on innovation.

Some might see this as commotion.

Sileage will be a better bet,

And can be made in dry and wet.

*

A high tech operation starts

With Wuffler banger and a 1,000 parts,

A banger tractor, and young crew,

The grass is cut and rolled by two.

*

Banger vehicles have abundant care.

Punctures are so all that rare.

This banger Wuffler had a burst;

And all around they cursed and cursed.

*

They ran around the byre in haste,

And found an old wheel encased.

Thy laughed and laughed at this great find.

They knew this Wuffler would not mind.

A large wheel one side and a small one the other,

There was no thought of future bother.

*

The Wuffler went again to work.

It seemed as solid as the kirk.

But no it really was unstable,

The vibration was worse than any fable.

The ground did shake,

The walls did brake;

The farmhouse roof lost some tiles,

Then they fell in piles and piles.

*

The cockeril crowed in great dismay.

Nothing would his fear allay.

And then the sides of the Wuffler shook,

Poor Susan dare not have a look.

*

The vibration had reached commotion;

The sides had got a violent motion,

And crashed with bangs upon the ground;

And then was silence all around.

*

So sileage making that day was done,

But next day sure there was more fun.

There's a kind neighbour up the isle,

And he will loan his Wuffler for a while,

Till grass is cut and sileage is in the pit,

And all the friends and helpers quit.

*

And 10 years on the Wufflers are no-where,

No more that loving tender care.

For the bangers of the isle are gone,

Just a memory in island song.

*

Technology has changed alas!
No more pits to roll and fill with grass.
It's contract men that come in force,
High tech methods they will endorse,
With cutters, bailers, wrappers, huge black bags are there,
In just a jiffy the sileage is made, my dear.
*
In just two days the island sileage is done.
But where have all the corncrakes run?
No more creeks and creeks and mating moves,
And displays enough to light a fuse,
No more helpers with the hay,
And cracks and jokes for many a day.
*
And the crofters are no better off.
They cannot swagger like a toff.
All that labour
Was just a favour
But the contractors are so dear,
They have the crofters in such fear.
*
Oh, for the days of scythe and rake,
For old time's sake,
When haymaking was really fun,
And friends and cousins gave for none,
And corncrakes made their mating calls
For the blessing of men's souls.
*End

Picture of Cornaig Lodge

The wuffler collapsing

(By kind permission of Kip Poulson)

3.2. The robot dustcart, 1997

*

In Scotland robots are moving in apace.

Everywhere they confront you face to face.

Outside the Gyle they are in the petrol pump;

The plastic card just makes it jump.

*

No operator is there to leap;

Robot petrol is so cheap.

Noone's there to take your money;

That plastic card is just so canny.

*

The robots move to shops as well;

The people there stock and sell.

You scan the goods into the trolley,

Then the plastic card goes to the robot dolly.

*

There is no queueing any more,

You are very quickly out the door.

And now the robots go to other fields,

To dustcarts and things on wheels.

*

Stirling county is the pilot for this game.

Dustcart collection now will never be the same.

In good old times three did the job;

The driver there he was called Rob.

*

Two tippers followed up behind,

As down the street he did wind.

They turned the baskets to the cart;

Not much rubbish came apart.

*

But now the men behind are gone.

A robot arm comes right along.

The rubbish bins are hoisted high,

And turned around without a sigh.

*

Rob in the cab feels oh so great,

Alas he's there without a mate.

The pedestrians must watch with care,

This huge cart can give them quite a scare.

*

The arms are like a whalebone jaw,

They could so snatch you at the door.

And lift you high and turn you round with such a flourish,

And dump you in with all that rubbish.

*

What a bit of luck that Rob is there.

He controls the robot from his chair.

A tv in the cab keeps him on the straight.

He is in charge of all men's fate.

*

One day there was he had a snooze,

And even worse a wholesome booze.

Then Granny's fate was quite ghastly,

As she got grabbed with all that parsley.

*

The police did not know what to do.

As granny disappeared without a clue.

The safety men came on the scene with all their files,

Indeed they stretched for miles and miles.

*

There were county regs for just a start.

Then Scottish regs in another part,

And Brussels regs to take on board,

More regs than anyone could afford.

*

But nothing on the robot cart,
For this was more than state of art.
Then Rob awoke from inebriation,
And quickly turned to consternation.
*
He switched the robot in reverse.
No, it was not too perverse.
Granny reappeared in one,
And said 'My goodness I am done'
*
Why can't men collect the bins,
And let poor granny have her dins?
We would rather pay a higher rate,
And send that robot to its fate.
*

3.3. The Robot at Waverley

*
We may admire what the clever robot does,
Indeed it can give us more than a buzz.
In faraway Mars we can see the rocks.
In dangerous places they take the knocks.
*
In business they sometimes come in to play.
Their owners want to make a fortune a day,
But don't forget they can be stupid,
And gather results that are quite putrid.
*
In the car park at Waverly Station,
They will not get a great oration.
They are there to control it all,
But pride is there before a fall.
*
The robot assumes the role of picket,
And issues the business man a ticket,
When he returns a few days hence,
It's smart and can compute the pence.
But no, its pounds, that are the bill,
Rather more a juicy kill.
*
Ticket stamped Rob's got to pay.
£28 it was one day,
When off the nightsleeper he did sally,
But money bags he did not carry.
*
The note reader was out of action,
And very angry was his reaction.
'Damn this robot has made me a prisoner
Across the park I could have driven her.
*
No plastic money would she take,
Although there was no risk of a fake.'
In high dudgeon Rob stormed through the station.
He really was in great commotion.
*
Eventually he found the man behind this fiendish thing.
'Your wretched robot has got me by the chin.
Take my money and let me run.
Or I will surely have you done.'
*
'Sir, this robot is a wonder mate.
I used to be on that gate.
I slaved in hail and snow and rain,
And now in comfort I can live again.
*

Quite often clients lose their temper,
And it's not only in the winter,
When like you they find that they're trapped
But it is quite simple, Sir.
This is what I do aver.
*
They never want to come back again,
And give me any more refrain.
Unfriendly robots clear the park,
And this is where you'll have your lark.
*
We lose £1.5 million every year,
Rather more than a glass of beer.
Men who carry money bags are so very rare,
For fear of thieves who would have them for a dare.'
*
Rob draws a breath and has a cogitate.
'I never knew a robot could so irritate.
To lose the car park millions,
In time it may be trillions,
All for the want of a plastic reader;
It cannot be a leader'.
*End

3.4. When the robot went to sleep

*
The robots are so clever;
Don't say they are no bother.
They can catch you by the short and curlies.
They have no respect for worthies.
*
Brother Philip gets his dream come true,
But that robot makes a wretched poo.
The dream that becomes a wreck,
Is a Range Rover, very high tech.
*
Four wheel drive, immobilizer, central locking,
There is yet more to get your brain a-rocking;
Aerodynamic trim for cruising,
No energy for losing.
The windows move on the touch.
You could drive the car with a crutch.
*
The dashboard has a panel;
This is not a little flannel.
The dials you would expect,
Would outshine those on a jumbo jet.
*
The commissioning is soon begun.
Brother Philip wants his fun.
The family all go out,
They will soon be down the spout.
*
The clouds lift around them.
The blue sky is a gem.
They want to get some breeze,
No, there really are no fleas.
*
But dear, oh dear, oh dear,
This is worse than you could fear.
The robot's gone to sleep,
And we cannot get a peep.
*
The windows are right jammed,
And the hot sun rays are fanned,
The air conditioning stops,
As all the family flops.
*

They stop at the next shade.
It is a leafy glade.
The dogs want out to have a wee,
But there is no luck you see.
*

The robot's gone to sleeps.
It could be for keeps.
The family are locked in,
And now they make a din.
*

'We could stay in here for years,
While no one sees our tears.
How will we ever get out,
And make that robot nought?
*

The future of the family may really be in doubt.
But the mobile phone is there and it has a little clout.
Contact at last is a barrage,
With supplier in his garage.
*

'What can we do to awaken,
The robot that's mistaken?'
'The immobiliser has been triggered.
The robot must have figured.
That you were a rotten thief.
It never thought it might have caught the chief.
*

You will have to wait an hour.
Don't let it make you dour.
Then we can re-initialise
The robot you despise'.
*

'This robot's far too clever.
It gives me so much blether.
I would rather be in charge,
Than have this awful thing at large'
*

Brother Robert says in jest,
'When the robots know best,
They make a glass cockpit syndrome,
And take the pilot's kingdom.
*

This is a common thing.
We should stop the robot's fling.
You never know what mischief they can make,
Till we have a proper robot brake.'
*end

Imprisoned by the car robot, Major Philip Erskine, author's brother, Cape Artist.

Part 2 - Notable newsletters and correspondence.

Chapter 4 - Newsletters mainly about travels.

The theme of these newsletters are the joys of travel, particularly in the Western Highlands of Scotland, and to members of the family abroad, and meeting places for academic conferences. The newsletters offer a vivid first hand view of the culture and events. Most of the material was written within a few days of the visit, and the tone is always cheerful and optimistic.

4.1. Walkabout in Venice

Diary for weeks beginning 28/4/1997

Gathering my academic colleagues with e-mail invitation

All week is a bit of a rush in university. My room becomes like a doctor's waiting room with line after line of the students coming for advice before they put in their dissertations. I am also rather keen to get local criticism of my Italian presentation, so send an electronic mail invitation to over a 100 colleagues inviting them to a pre-presentation dry run on Thursday, just the day before I fly off to Italy. But sadly we just do not have enough research culture and there are only 2 who turn up. Perhaps it was a no hoper to expect a good turnout on election day! But anyway my class of 30 managers in the afternoon gave a rousing reception to the presentation, so I went home with lots of 'feel good' in my make-up, the fun slides popular, the timing within 15 minutes, and such a bullish message to the providers of the computer industry to pull their socks up and get rid of £ billions of waste by following a simple pathway of good practice.

Jetting to Italy

Friday is brilliant sunshine and the first leg of the flight is to Amsterdam over the centre of Britain. In May it is a mass of brilliant yellow. The oil seed rape has become ever so popular a crop. My pocket computer is doing me proud and I can use it at the airport and at 25,000 feet to write newsletter copy and assessment reports about student presentations. Wonderful to be able to be so productive on the hoof.

Holland from the air

I am fascinated at the view of Holland from the air. The fields are in pristine condition but there are no fences like on a British landscape. All the land is marked out by water dikes, miles and miles of them, all so very symmetrical and straight; the fields are large units, economical. The succession laws in Holland must be like the British, eldest son takes all. Then as you get to Amsterdam the waterways are so broad, like super motorways, and very busy with shipping. Amsterdam Airport, Schipol, is a nightmare as the incoming Glasgow flight is 15 minutes late despite a tail wind, and I have to run round the airport to get my connecting flight to Venice. I am wondering what has happened to my luggage. Perhaps I will have to collect it tomorrow. Oh dear, what if it is delayed beyond Sunday, and all my precious presentation slides are missing. The presentation will have to come from the heart!

The Alps and Venice from the air

We are soon in the air again for an hour and a half and we get a spectacular view of the Alps. The mountains are white and the valleys deep sunken gorges. Then just as suddenly we come to the plains of Northern Italy, and they are all small fields. There must be different succession laws in Italy and they will like the Common Agricultural Policy which keeps uneconomic farmers in business. We are soon over water and the City of Venice comes into view. From the air it glows a rich red, the colour of bricks. One's immediate question from the air is 'Where are all the skyscrapers and the city smog cloud?' Venice is an ancient city dominated by towers and domes and basilica and palaces, no concrete carbuncles in sight. There are also hardly any cars in the city as all transport is by boat taxi. Anyway I need not have panicked about my suitcase. It was almost the first to be put on the conveyor.

Around the Grand Canal

I then got a taxi into the city at rather an expensive fare. I suppose airport taxi drivers the world over know how to rip off the tourist and I was dropped off near the Railway Station at the boat taxi rank. (Later one of my computer conference pals said that he got maps of Venice down loaded on to his computer in Nottingham and even bus and train timetables, so knew exactly where to go). After queuing a while I went on a boat 'bus' and as it was rush hour it was strangely like being on a London Tube everyone standing and holding on to handles; I knew that if I slipped I would be in the drink in no time. Fortunately, I was out at the first stop and the hotel was within sight. After unpacking I did a mini walk along the Grand Canal taking photographs all the time. I was walking along the canals and over the delightful canal bridges. It rather reminded me of walking down the Backs of Cambridge but on an infinitely larger scale. The beauty of this lovely City is that it is a huge pedestrian walkway of about 45 square kilometres, (Isle of Coll in Scotland would be approx 101 square kilometres), and along the streets are countless cafes and tables and excited tourist chatter and shops ablaze with gorgeous Venetian glass. The canal was packed with tourists in richly decorated gondolas, mostly Japanese and accompanied by an Italian singing songs from the Great Caruso. I found a cafe with spaghetti bolonaise on the menu for a modest price, and a cheerful tourist companion from Vancover, who said he was a 24 year old burnt out stockbroker, so we had a little 'City' talk and swapped disaster experiences. I was soon tempted in the shops buying a cut price 1997 calender richly illustrated with the Italian Master, Botttichelli, and lots of good quality postcards just in case my own photographs glitched, and of course a video of Venice, just so that I can share with Susan some of the magic of this trip.

6 hour walkabout / boatabout in Venice

Saturday is a delicious day, no rush , no hassle, an early awakening with the bells of the adjacent bassilica, a breakfast of rolls and Italian honey, then just miles and miles of walkabout with no awful motor sounds, and honking, not even really crowded with people. Last night I woke up at 2.00 am and read the history (!) some of it, of Venice, and the abiding impression

I got was that Venice has almost stood still for at least 200 years in terms of its architecture and culture. Today my first stop was the huge bookshop by the station and my attention riveted on a book about Canelleto and there on a plate for a modest sum were the 38 masters he had completed in the mid 1700s, (the originals are in the Queen's collection at Windsor), and a quick appreciation of these and it must be game set match; today's Venice is not that different from Canallello's, except that now there is an invasion of Japanese tourists, whereas in his time it was the aristocrats from the rest of the world doing their 'grand tours' and then stuffing their English gardens and stately homes with Venice style culture in art and architecture. Yesterday, everyone kept talking to me in Italian, French, Dutch, but never English, so today I had a cunning plan, to get English first time and avoid all the rigmarole of what touristie I was. The answer was so very simple. Go in the streets wearing the Scottish glengarry. Philip calls it rudely my 'Harry Lauder' hat, then Scotsosia is the only possible response. My first contact is with a Buckinghamshire man who helps me find the post office. "I love Scotland", he says, "where do you live?" In no time we are having an animated conversation and I am getting him to mark the places on my map that are top priorities for a two day stay, and he marks the key art galleries, and basilica. "When I went to Basilica Rocco and saw the rendition of the crucified Christ I wept for 30 minutes. You will have to be strong not to be overcome by the religious art in its home environment". "And what brought you to Venice?" 'I worked here for 6 months and got so well looked after by the family they invited me back for this week's wedding feast, and it was a ball". Anyway with map marked for the first destination, Basilica Rocco, was easy to find, a modest entrance fee, and handkerchief at the ready, and I was fully prepared for an eyeful. This is a 14th century Gothic masterpiece on a vast scale and with walls steeped in Italian masters up to 80 metres. I have never seen such a concentration of masterpiece art placed in harmony with the architecture and sculpture work. It is wonderful to see great pieces of art in a museum or gallery, but a new and far richer emotional experience to see it harmonised with the other forms of art and in its home environment. My friend from Buckingham was quite right, one did need considerable strength not to be overcome by the sheer pressure of these fantastic Bellinis and bible scenes, old testament and new, and the wonderful carvings of the pews. I must have been at least an hour and a half absorbing the treasures of this place in such spectacular concentration. There is a huge distance in seeing the masters on the Christmas cards of the world and then in their original setting, generally without frames and the harmony is breath taking.

Shank's pony to The Art Gallery

My next destination is the premier Gallery of Venice, and according to the map is just 40 minutes walk, but of course that would assume that you were a Venetian who knew the way. My map did not have street names, so I was for ever getting into a maze then endless cu de sac. Never mind, these little alleyways are absolutely enchanting. The walls are often rich with Russian Ivy, or wisteria in full blossom, and as you look up there are generally three stories and each has a balcony and window boxes of luxuriant geraniums, a splash of red colour. Occasionally you come to a bridge over a mini canal and there are photographic opportunities in every direction. Sometimes in the narrow streets you get a whiff of pong. Oh dear the tide is not strong enough to carry away the smells. I noticed about 2 feet only of tide in the Adriatic, and that is the spring tides. If you are there in the neapes there is only a foot of difference. So if you want to avoid the pongs go to Venice two days after a full moon or a new moon, otherwise grin and bear it! Then one comes out onto a square and a flood of sunshine, and cafes with tables outside and gaudy coloured sun canopies. You can indulge in rolls and fruit, and Italian beer, and this walkabout seems to last for ever. To my amazement a lot of the passing visitors pause and I find myself caught in the eye of a Japanese or Dutch video camcorder, the latest tourist attraction of Venice, but of course when you are 60+ eccentricity is indulged! Clearly a Scottish glengarry is touristie box office appeal, and there is no shortage of eating companions. My walkabout mile is about 3 normal miles, so I am quite weary on getting at last to the Art Gallery.

The Picture orphanage of Italy

I should have been prepared here too for the handkerchief, as once more there was a huge concentration of the key religious works of art of the world, but here they were carefully hung together for harmony and impact There were 20 rooms of these masters and after following the guide notes one soon realised that this gallery is the picture orphanage of Italy. As soon as a church has a glitch and cannot continue its planned existence then the treasures are absorbed into the Gallery of Venice, so the pictures are hung among friends, which is the next best thing to being in the original place of commission. The hanging rooms are huge, and the works of art equally large, 6 metres by 30 being the largest companion piece. The compositions are so very vivid. Cain and Abel breathes a passionate hatred as the dagger is poised for its final thrust. Adam takes the apple so enthusiastically from Eve, and there are such sensuous vibrations from that picture. All the biblical stories are set into brilliant Italian landscape, and the clothes are the finest of Venetian design, rich in blues and reds and yellows. Each room in the gallery has sitting space down the centre so you can relax and then follow the guide notes through one side of the room, swivel around and then repeat viewing from the other side. My son-in-law, Johnny, loves icons (!); one room here hangs a modest 200 alone. He would have had such a ball here. After 20 gallery rooms I am emotionally numb, cannot absorb any more of the world's treasures, already on the second handkerchief.

Tracing the steps of Canaletto

Outside the Gallery I am the immediate target of a young lady in brilliant 17th century costume and long white wig in trestles almost to her ankles. She is selling tickets for that night's performance in the Scoula Grande Giovanni Evangelista, a concert, with soloist, dance, ballet, unavoidable, and as a senior citizen (!), I qualify for the best seats at third class price. This is a bargain I cannot resist, and I find the Scoula Grande is just 10 minutes walk from the hotel, so even now exhausted, in 3 hours I will be re-charged. I cannot face another 3 hours walking through the Venice maze, so return to the hotel via boatbus a mile and an a half down the Grand Canal. Luckily I find the last seat at the back of the boat which is open and in 20 minutes my camera operates like a machine gun and I am capturing many of the 38 Canaletto prints. I really will be able to test whether there has been any changes since 1740. Later on I read that Napoleon captured Venice and made his influence felt and even built his own palace. The editor of the Canaletto book reveals that some of the pictures were painted from a very high vantage point, but without helicopters how did he do it? The suggestion was that he made lots of mini sketches on the ground and then in the comfort of his studio re-configured them from a simulated high point, so it was Canaletto who inspired what the computer buffs now call cyberspace! Anyway the book on Canaletto reveals a lot of the mini histories of the palaces and families who lived in them. I could not help smiling at the aristocratic family that was so very nearly wiped out by the plague in the 12th century. In desperation they got the Pope to release the last male heir from his monastic vows, and got him married off to the Doge's daughter, who promptly produced 9 sons in 10 years. Having decided that he was rather exhausted at fathering so many children he returned once more to the monastery.

Concerto

After a welcome snooze for an hour my batteries are re-charged and I am out in the town getting a huge helping of spaghetti bolonaise and half a kilo of the most succulent strawberries you have ever seen. Well fortified I make the 10 minutes walk to Scola Grande and wait till the doors are open. This is another architectural masterpiece. After climbing a long wide staircase one enters the main aisle of this church. It is an elongated cube, 1x1x6, but the proportions are immediately satisfying. The front altar has a brilliant sculpture of Christ and on either side are marble pillars, and at each corner there are three oval masterpieces. Each side of this church are huge biblical paintings and on the ceiling there are friezes and paintings of the Ascension of Christ. Somehow the artist has delivered a sense of levitation which is awe inspiring. I could not help wondering if Scottish architect, Adam, had not been inspired by the Venetians. The hall is packed and on come the artistes all in wigs and 17 century costumes, and the programme begins with pieces from Vivaldi, Martini, and Haendel. The violin soloist is international star Ana Trentin, the soprano is another international star, Nazareno Balduin, and the final superstar is ballerina Veneziano. This is the superb environment for this concert; there is a synergy of sound, architecture, sculpture, religion, art. Once more one's emotions are under attack from the intensity of this mega cultural pressure. I loved the first dance of the programme. A set of 6 dancers came down the centre of the aisle and gave us a rendition so like the Scottish 'strip the willow', then they went to the front by the high altar and gave us a shortened version of 'Hamilton House'. I could not help wondering whether the Stuarts in exile in Italy may have brought these Venice traditional pieces back to Scotland with the Jacobite cause? So Scottish Country dancing is really an extension of Venice traditionals. The soprano is out of this world as she generates mega decibels of sound and feeling. Then the dancers come on once more. The male, (a devil I suppose), wears a terrifying mask and he cart-wheels a whole 30 metres down the aisle persuing 3 terrified virgins. The effect is spectacular. The concert lasts just 1.5 hours, and is so very popular the artistes respond to 3 encores. So ends my second day in Venice of a heaven on earth experience.

Sunday sightseeing in Venice.

I am up early on Sunday and on the waterbus by 9.15 right down the Grand Canal to the Doge's Palace in St. Mark's Square. The first sightseeing stop is the Great Basilica, but tourists are shut out while a mass is in progress, so I decide to visit instead an exhibition of Van Gough in a mini gallery by St. Mark's. I get a few postcards and a Van Gough Book. The assistant goes to great trouble to reveal to me the secrets of his works on display, where he conceals in his landscapes other pictures of children, cats and even portraits of other artists, Leonard Da Vinchi, Reubens, Goya. He is so very clever at this hidden art.

Correr Museum St. Mark's Square.

My next stop is the big Museum. It is the old Palace of Napoleon and as such reflects gaudy and luxurious furnishing and paintings of the early 19th century. Most of the display rooms are beautifully proportioned, cubes or double cubes, and ceilings elaborately painted on. The third room is a 'Cupid' room devoted to lovers and with paintings and sculpture and a set of mirrors so you can see both sides of the figures at once. These Italians are so very clever in doubling the impact of their work. But the theme here is less religiously evocative. Venice is portrayed as the dominant seafaring nation of the Mediterranean, so there are brilliant paintings of naval victories, and Venetian men of war, and huge globes of the world to indicate that Venetians were the powerful discoverers. There is a room of gorgeous ceramics, but the guide told me that there is no longer an active ceramics industry in Venice, but a lot of Venetian glass, too vulnerable for air trips. There are rooms showing off the gambling of the time and the first roulette wheels and then packs of cards. I looked out for mention of de la Rue cards as I knew that the family had set up a card making facility in the early 1830s, but these cards were older than that and of poor printing quality. Then there are rooms showing off weapons both naval and military. The other theme is the stability of the Republic and portraits of the Doges and other aristocrats. I never really mastered the political system of Venice, but bought books and videos which hopefully will reveal all. Of course there are also religious compositions. I found the most striking one was the last supper, and all the disciples had mini halos except Judas. He was kneeling the opposite side of the table to the others. All their knives were pointing towards him and he was looking up and he had just dropped his golden purse with the 12 coins. A rival picture for sheer horror was the 'Dance of Salome with the Head of John the Baptist'. A brilliant composition was of the wedding in Canaan and the virgins were filling their vessels. They were such beautiful young ladies, clad in the most luxurious and aristocratic finery, yet surely at that time women were heavily veiled?

St. Mark's Tower

It would not be possible to visit Venice and not go 300 feet up to see the whole Archipelago of 100 islands. Needless to say the views were spectacular and another reel of photographs was taken in a few moments from every one of the four sides of this tower. Lunch was a delicious rest from sightseeing with prawn sandwiches and beer in St. Mark's Square by the band playing lunch time waltzes. The Square was busy with Sunday trippers and families out for the afternoon and feeding the pigeons, which are all so fat and overfed they can hardly walk and mate! There is a thriving trade selling nuts for the birds and they are so tame one feels the rush of air round the back of the neck as they mob one. But be careful. Italian beer is so sweet you can forget how strong it is. I bought an ice-cream, tripped slightly, and plop the delicious strawberry was on St. Mark's Square.

The Doge's Palace

One could not leave Venice without a tour round the Doge's Palace. Susan has a picture in our dining room of this scene. It was a present from her Mother for her 21st birthday so I felt this was somehow home territory, but what treasures would the interior reveal? The guide notices warned that it would take 1.5 hours to see around, and by this time I was rather wilting as a tourist. I could not be exhausted before delivering the Conference paper in Udine. Anyway I made the tour through the Palace as fast as I could cope with. This glorified both the religious life of Venice and its political life and its pride in its democracy. The main rooms of interest to me were the huge public rooms of the Council of State, the Collegio, the Senate, the Maggior Consiglio. 300 elected members could be accommodated at once, presided over by the Doge and his Council of 10. Once more there were striking pictures of memorable events in the history of Venice. The rooms were all elaborately decorated with pictures, and freezes, and brilliant ceilings. Italians certainly expect citizens to walk tall and look up. The guide book refers to the splendid interior decoration, both majestic and scenographic, is the work of the major masters, Titian, Tntoretto, Veronese. If I had had more time I could happily have spent 2.5 hours and taken in much more and really digested the guide material. Instead I had to compromise by buying postcards and a video.

Off to Academic Udine

This is my first experience of an Italian train. Will they run on time? My only annoyance was that most of the stations did not have names on them, so after 1 hour I had to ask a passenger, Udine?? And they kept coming back with giggles. I should have invested in a map of Italy while I was in Venice. I could not help notice that several carriages were covered with graffiti. What a relief after all the world class art which had to be appreciated! Anyway I was much taken by the landscape of Northern Italy. We travelled through a lot of wine country and also tree plantations. No, they were not Scots pines, but beautiful elegant eucalyptus. We also sped across many dry river beds with sparkling white pebbles and just a trickle of water. Then I noticed the landscape which was the background to the crucifiction picture by Bellini from the Correr Museum. When eventually I arrived in Udine I was struck by the wide streets lined with chestnuts in full blossom, the white candles ever such a pleasing sight. The Hotel 'Fruili' is modern, smart, bright and I have an ample double room with tv and plenty of space to put my clothes and papers, and a huge collection of touristie trophies from 2.5 days in Venice. In no time my newly acquired Tintorettos, Canalettos, Van Goughs, and Bellinis are up on the hotel walls and I am enjoying my recent booty. I had never realised it could be such hard work being a tourist! I have a light meal of spaghetti and muscles cooked in butter, served in their shells, delicious, world class spaghetti. I expected to see lots of conference delegates at the hotel bar or in the dining room but alas just a glimpse of a gentleman from Oman. Where have all the academics gone? You never know quite what to expect at these international conferences. Sometimes it is a bunch of world experts, sometimes it is a bunch of out of work professors looking for chances to get off the dole! One should just expect the unexpected. A week later I drafted a conference report concerning the papers presented. To give you the flavour of the conference I enclose just a few of the paragraphs, which I hope do not blind you with science.

Conference Report, Software Quality Engineering University of Udine 4th - 7th May 1997 from Robert Erskine, participant, Department of Management, Glasgow Caledonian University.

Partners

This conference was set up jointly by the University of Udine in Italy, and Wessex Institute of Technology, (a division of the University of Southampton).

Publication

The proceedings are published hardback under editors Tasso, O, Adley, R.A., Pighin,M. 'Software Quality Engineering', CMP 199, ISBN: 1-85312-406-6,

Participant profile

There were 48 participants from 24 countries. Organisations represented were leading software providers, university departments of computer science, management, public administration, informatics; telecommunication companies, research organisations. This represented a fair mix of the Information Technology provider community, with the IT user community, and academics and advisers of government.

Hosting and Ambience

The hosts of Italy were the University of Udine, who had offered the hospitality and facilities of the Udine 'Il Palazzo Antonini-Mangilli-Del Torso'. This is the local palace and the main conference room was the historic place of 1867 when Garibaldi came to Udine to declare the new Italian State and persuade the local people to accept Rome as capital. This conference room was a cube room, with beautifully decorated walls and ceiling and a huge original chandelier.

Overall Comments on SQE'97, participant point of view from Britain.

SQE'97 was a very rewarding conference. Leading edge operators were reporting progress in many fields and sharing their successes and concerns. There was no complacency anywhere. Most interesting of all to the British were the reports of the Italian contingent of professors of Public Administration and Informatics. ("Italy is run by academics. The mayors of the major cities are nearly all academics. They realise that governments must be monitored to reduce waste. The professors of informatics worked with the professors of public administration and articulated a change in the law so that all large public contracts are now monitored by an independent Authority. Informatics is the instrument to generate the pressure to squeeze the review process and prevent large scale waste.") The conference participants responded to Erskine's call to set up a world database on the internet to report on Information Technology glitches and the prevention strategies. The Italian Professors of Public Administration and Informatics were positive to the suggestion that they come to Britain and offer their Informatics based solution to the new government of Blair. This is an opportunity which cannot be lost!

Social dimension with the leading edge fraternity

The 3 days in Venice convinced me of the advantages of playing the 'Scottish' card in Italy - at least people would speak to you in English first time. On conference opening morning I am just wearing a tartan tie. In the evening there is a reception in the Palazzio in a gorgeous cube room with beautiful furniture and ornate decoration, and I wear the tartan jacket, which I might add is much admired. "Robert, we want to see the kilt too". "No, no impossible". However, on Tuesday night there is the Conference dinner held in a restaurant in the old part of the town just beneath the castle, and the leading edge fraternity of the computer world are granted their treat, yours truly, Harry Lauder style complete, glengarry, tartan jacket, kilt, belt, beaver sporran. I am about the last to arrive at the reception having lost my way on the walk from the hotel in the rain, protected only by my tartan umbrella. Anyway, on arrival there is a great cheer, and in seconds there is a forest of flashing bulbs from the cameras! The dinner is a very jolly affair. On my left is a Hong Kong / Canadian, ("I remember the Star ferry well in Hong Kong"), on my right is a Greek, opposite is a Polish professor, ("How do you find your new freedom in Poland"? "It used to be red rule in communist era; now it is black rule, the rule of the priests, and not much more freedom"!); one further down is an Australian, ("A long way to come to Italy for a conference"? "From Australia everywhere is a long way, and I like every year to visit my relations in Ireland so Italy is half way".) Later we move round the table and there is a Virginian with a grandfather from the Isle of Barra in the Hebridees. We are soon talking about Hebridean life and the snob corncrakes, and they tell me about their Virginian cats. "We have two cats back home, Mary and Molly, and they both gave birth to litters of 10 in the same week. We put them in the same room with a basket at each end. They both loved their litters, but Mary would always wait till Molly was out of the room and then steal all Molly's litter and feed 20 kittens. When Molly came back she would retrieve her own ten and be quite content. This behaviour went on for 3 weeks. We never understood why Mary wanted to be mother and auntie at the same time." On Thursday we make the train from Udine to Marco Polo Airport, and travel in one of these marvellous 'double decker' trains. "Come on Robert, we want some Scottish entertainment". Anyway never to be non-plussed and with my poems on my pocket computer, they are given the recitation of the policeman who got stuck, so we are all a merry band of friends by now after 3 days of conference and partying. Then oh dear, I find my hotel room keys are in my pocket. They must be posted back before I leave Italy. After a little hassle and a lot of sweet talk I get an Easter Egg box from the duty free confectionery shop, wrap up the key and take it to the post office. To my huge surprise the assistant takes out a ruler and says, "Your parcel is too small. We cannot accept it". They don't sell envelopes, so I have another hassle. Eventually the manager in the Bureaux de Change takes pity on me and gives me a huge envelope, easily big enough for the Easter egg box. Triumphantly, I return to the post office, but oh dear now there is a 'close' notice hanging on the front door. Anyway, I knock frantically and wave and catch the manager's eye once more, and he takes pity on me. The ruler comes out again on this enormous envelope, and he says, "Fine, that will be 15,000 liera", about £4, which is a huge ripoff. I was accompanied by my pal from Northampton, "Robert", he says, "Does this happen to you every day? Is your life just one long bananaskin"?

*End

Author in Venice

4.2. Trip to Yemen

Newsletter from Sunday 14/7/96 - Trip to Yemen

The convenient Olympics

On Wednesday morning I am up at the crack of dawn. Kind niece, Lucy would not let me escape without a cup of tea from her home in Clapham Common, and I have a cut price cab with gets me to Heathrow in 40 minutes; all the road is clear. The taxi driver is doing a 'master's course for being a professional actuary', and is very interested in the courses on offer at Glasgow Caledonian. At Heathrow Raymond, (son's father-in-law), arrived to meet me at the Royal Jordanian Desk with the parcels. At check-in the cases hit the scale at 62 kilos, and my heart started beating that little bit faster. The Joranian check-in operator looked me straight in the eye, and I immediately said, "I wonder how many gold medals will Jordan pick up in the Olympic games?" "Oh, gosh", she said, "We have an eye and a book on the Karati Team". For a couple of minutes I kept up this banter and in no time the cases disappeared with a forwarding ticket to Sanaa, and I received my boarding card - miraculously, no questions about the 40 kilos of overweight, with a paddling pool, a small wendy house kit, and a library of computer books for Hamish and his computer buff friends who are waiting on getting connected to internet.

More sweet talk

Our flight to Amman had a stop over in Berlin to take on more passengers. About an hour before landing at Berlin I talked to an air hostess about the chances Jordan had in the karati team, and then told her about jumbo jet nephew Patrick and his 747's and how I had longed to see the flight deck of an Airbus, and whoopwee, in 5 minutes time I was in the cockpit looking down on the Hague. Pilot and co-pilot were in cracking form also betting on the karati team, but conversation was a bit limited as there was a lot of buzz on the radio with the air traffic controllers, but there were a few lovely one-liners. To the co-pilot, "What do you have to do to become a captain?" "Oh nothing, just grow a few white hairs or get a wig". To the captain, "Do you ever have to retire as captain"? "No, work to 60 and pass all the 6 month medicals. I have been captain 15 years now and Royal Jordanian has increased its fleet to 18 aircraft". We were flying at 33,000 feet, temperature - 50 degrees C, autopilot in control and soon to begin the descent through the weather. With throttle then automatically back and a hand touch of the altimeter target meter and we were soon at 15,000 feet and then a wink and a nod and I was back out of heaven and the flightdeck of the Airbus and those masses of flashing dials and into my seat, and on to chapter 2 of the Leeson Story of Barings, bought an hour earlier at Heathrow. Kind Raymond had also provided me with a book giving a blow by blow account of the air disaster at Kegworth, and the health service disaster recovery procedures that were the aftermath, but for me one book a day was enough, and I would look at Kegworth on dry land!

The Leeson Story read in transit.

By the evening we were once more landing and that was Amman. The airport shops were closed, but I had 5 more hours to kill before getting my connection to Taiz in Yemen. By this time Leeson had had most of his drama. He was sinking deeper and deeper into the mire. The profit dealings were being reported to London and winding up to £30 million enough to fuel his own personal bonus of £450,000, and Peter Baring's of a cool £1 million. Meanwhile his losses accumulated into the secret 88888 account were peaking to £100 million. He tried a desperate throw into foreign exchange expecting to make a profit and clear the losing account, but no, he clocked up a 78 billion yen loss, which was even more difficult to explain away. But with a little ingenuity he forged a couple of faxes, which made it look as though Citibank had done a deal and lost, and for the next 8 weeks amazingly no-one from Barings asked Citibank for the 78 billion yen, nor anyone ask how Leeson could have dived off into unauthorised dealing in foreign currency. Then in December the top brass of Barings flew off to America for a mega conference and Barings world wide were told that Leeson was a role model for them bringing in millions of commission every day, and they all ought to be talking to him to absorb the magic touch! Leeson found all this so sickening he quit the dinner dedicated to all this unearned glory. He had to face that sooner or later the bubble would burst, but not before he was lent on for another £2 million profit to seal all the annual bonuses. Later in London he was shut in to Barings building to trade all night for three nights to make the extra £2 million. He was very tempted to stay in London and quit, but he could not tell his wife, so back he went to Singapour, and every day doubled up to clear the mounting losses. They were soon escalated to £150 million and then the earthquake in Japan sent the index into free fall on his trades - his losses were at the £200 million mark. Every day he was getting London money to pay margin calls into the SIMEX exchange, "London is the cash cow. In Singapour, that is where we are making the £ millions in commission". No hint that London were really feeding a black hole of ever more extravagant trading. The bosses came out, a little worried about where the Baring reserves were being poured; (the Bank of England was miffed that they were exceeding their 'position' by more than 25% of their capital), but Leeson sweet-talked them with football stories and sent them off to play tennis at the Singapour polo club. His local bosses didn't like London interference, so they set every kind of decoy into play to put off any heavy weight external auditors, (he sweet-talked Coopers and Lybrand) to sign the audit, but when the losses got to £300 million and a further set of internal auditors were scheduled to see him, he realised the game was up, turned off all his telephones and went on holiday, faxed through a letter of resignation and went white water rafting for three days, and then realised that he was the most wanted man in the Far East. When the bubble burst and the market knew where Barings were both long and short the market makers reacted and within three days the £300 million lost had escalated to £600 million; this was the coup de gras to put Barings into the knackers yard. So much for rather racy airport reading material.

Sanaa Yemen 4.00 am Thursday, The ancient Realm of the Queen of Sheba

Another 3 hours flight time and we were in Sanaa. Hamish had sweet-talked a tourist policeman, who greeted me at passport control and rushed me through to customs as though I were a VIP. They opened everything and could not make head or tail of the paddling pool. I think that they thought it was military equipment, but with a little reassurance about the two little boys of 1 and 2, and in no time my 62 kg cases had white chalk marks and I was free for Hamish. He was really cock-a-hoop. That very afternoon he had taken and passed his Yemeni driving test. The sweet talk on the taxi driver was so effective that he was permitted to take the test using the taxi, and as the taxi driver and tester were old friends, he sailed through everything in an hour. On average it takes 2 days to get through the test driver rigmarole and all the medical tests that go with it, but sweet-talk can work a dream. So Hamish was meeting me and driving a friend's car through the city to his friend's house. I was a little nervous when we were stopped at a road block and two armed soldiers beckoned us to stop. Hamish greeted them in English and they waved him on. If he had been a Yemeni, he would probably have been expected to pay a 'stopping tax', but today we were lucky. Our onward lift to Taiz was to leave at 8.00 am, so there were a few hours for a sleep, and at 6.00 am the cock started crowing outside my window, and for 30 minutes it out crowed every other cock in Sanaa. I was in a Yemeni style house in the old City with gorgeous coloured carpets and a view onto the very distinctive Yemeni architecture. It is beautiful beyond words, but the streets even of the capital are full of pot holes and uncollected rubbish and baying wild dogs who snarl at the tyres of the car.

5 hours across the highlands - an adventure, getting stranded

The ride to Taiz is with a friend, Denis, substantial 6'6" and broad as well. Sanaa is about 7,000 feet and on a plateau. We are soon driving down a pass in the mountains on to a lower plateau. The view is out of this world. There are masses of small terraces and very luxuriant crops, from maize to potatoes, to qat, which is the local drug taking up to 30% of the national income. It is so widely chewed that the Yemeni men grow up stunted, rarely more than 5' tall. Even 'little chap' me is a giant in this country. The terraces have such rich cultivation, like Uganda, 4 crops a year, no bother. Vineyards would do wonderfully well here, but Islam doesn't like wine so that is a 'no hoper' now. Apparently before 1948 there was a substantial Jewish community in Yemen and they grew their own wine, but Yemen was shut off to the rest of the world, so there was no wine trade ever developed. These terraces are so small they are ploughed by donkeys, not a tractor in sight till we get to the big fields of the plains and then they are there mixed with oxen doing the ploughing. We are soon going through villages and masses of fruit on sale, pumpkins galore, sometimes stacked in huge walls by the roadside, or along the entire roofs of the houses, water melon, bananas, potatoes, tomatoes, cacti fruit. This is peeled and then delicious, but with hard seeds; you could break your teeth on them easily. Then there is a nasty ping, a smell and Denis, the friend's Toyota, loses power and we glide to a stop just off the main road. Despite the presence of three engineers after still an hour of probing we decide to flag down a car - one stays with the car, the rest of us use the hospitality of our rescuer to go to the next town and call for electrical help, meanwhile the rest of us negotiate a passage for the further 100 miles to Taiz in a Peugeot taxi. These have 10 places. I count as two people because of tubbiness, and the 62 kg luggage for another person, but the whole bill is still only £5. Money goes a long way in Yemen. The countryside is still stunning, but not so visible from the back of a Peugeot. The green of the mountains is very lush. The mountains bring a good rainfall, and this country, home of the Queen of Sheba, is the green pearl of the Arabian peninsular. After an hour we stop for food in a minor town, and we get a delicious meal of Salta and bread, the bon surprise dish of Yemen. Suddenly outside there is a burst of gunfire. Violence, oh no, just a wedding procession, and the 'best man' sending off a few rounds in celebration! Coming out of the cafe I remarked about three lovely calfs tied up. "They are there waiting to be made into tomorrow's main meat dish"; oh dear they did look so calm and innocent, and not very fat. The houses in this typical Yemeni town are all built with pillars of reinforced concrete and the top storey invariably is left with metal spikes for another storey when there is more money available. When the Gulf war was fought Yemenis were sent packing home from Saudi and Kuwait, where big money was being earned and now the harvest of that is a nation of houses with a storey yet to be built! The rest of our passengers soon returned with large plastic bags of qat, and chewed with glee for the rest of the journey. By the end they all looked as though they had been to the dentist with large bulging balls in the left of their mouths. That is the qat stalk which is eventually spited out. The passengers tried to share their goodies with Hamish and me but our excuse was that we were used to Whisky, not qat. Anyway we got them buzzing getting them to guess my age! They thought I was 80, not 60, but if the drug did them no more harm than that it must have been pretty innocent! In this country old age is respected, so as an 80 year old giant I felt to be quite a swell in Yemen!

Progressive consumption taxes

We ended up in a taxi rank in the middle of Taiz on the main street by the famous gate where Paul Bristol used to reminisce about the heads of traitors being impaled on sticks. Mercifully, we were spared that horror; there is now a much more liberal regime in power. I was positively discouraged from looking for the prison where Paul was held a captive for a few weeks in the 1950s. I was told that if I took a photograph of it I would be scooped up inside myself! We transferred to another taxi and went about a mile and a half up hill alongside the bank of the main wadi which descends from the hills above at 10,000 feet to Taiz at a modest 5,000 feet. Hamish's house is 'above the old electricity centre', no street name, no number, no address, but also no mail; that has to be collected from a PO box number in the city. I could not understand how taxes could be collected by the authorities if there were no addresses. Apparently each house has both an electric meter and a water meter, and a telephone meter, for the few, and twice a month a collector comes and reads these and demands payment. The cost is a progressive tariff. For the first few units you just pay £1 a month, then if your consumption is over that minimum then you pay £5 a month, and if you have a smart house with air conditioning then you will have to pay £200 a month. In Britain we expect a discount for volume, but in Yemen volume gives a savage penalty. The politics of this are to make the rich subsidise the poor without having a complicated income tax or benefit system to administer. This approach comes from the North Yemen tradition of a benevolent dictator, or now republic.

Hamish and Nicola's home - an engineer's dreamhouse

This is a high second floor flat on a high penthouse style site overlooking the bank of the central Taiz wadi. There are two lovely reception room decorated with traditional Yemeni carpets and low cushions, a dining-room / guest room, a room for the two children, a main double room for Hamish and Nicola, a kitchen with gas cooker, and a wash-room / shower and loo, which must not be flushed too often as the main water supply only comes on once every 18 days. But Hamish is an engineer by nature. He has put plugs into every room; he has fitted fans for cool breeze, he has a most elaborate water pumping system from a main tank to a roof tank controlled by an enclosed gravity switch; he has imported these ideas from Coll; he has plumbed in the shower and 'tuned' it for temperature; he has fitted a small electrical heater insulated so there is constant hot water for £1 / month, beat that if you can. Shower water is also collected for flushing the loo. There is so much 'added value' in his ingenuity and re-cycling going on, no waste anywhere. Outside he has his own protected balcony for the children to play on. This has a stunning view up the wadi to the really grand houses on the mountainside, across the wadi to a huge tower with microphone which is connected to the nearest mosque, and down the wadi to the main street, the suk and the mountains in the far distance. In Taiz one is acutely aware of the rhythm of the five daily calls to prayer. The one at 4.00 am usually sets off the dogs howling in the wadi for at least two miles and 20 minutes. Below

Hamish's flat on one side there is a typical flat roof house and several times we saw a chameleon, a small lizard in bright colours scampering across the roof. On another side there is a large drop and a small garden where a Yemeni family have sheep. The little children were in fits of laughter when I made my sheep sounds and got the ram really worked up. On the other side of the house were eycalyptus trees and the delight of the dawn was to see the branches loaded with bright green parrots. Later in the day one would see lots of kites soaring in circles making use of the thermals. From the back window one would see large bats hanging on the electricty wires upside down. In the evenings there were hundreds flying about under the balcony.

Two little boys - Jonathan and Timothy

When we are home the 62 kg luggage has to be unpacked. The two mega important items are the paddling pool and the wendy house in plastic. In no time these are erected from the instruction leaflets and are positioned on the balcony. Bonus, today the water is on so with a hose the paddling pool absorbs a foot of water, and a little chlorine to keep it bug free, and my goodness how those children love it, and such fun splashing Mum and Dad and Grandpa. In July it is too hot to go to the Red Sea, so we brought the sea home instead! Jonathan had a water pistol, and you may imagine that target practice was 80 year-old Grandpa. The chuckles of glee were fantastic. Jonathan (two and a half), still has those incredibly long eyelashes, that send every Mum into a tizzy; Timothy has a broad smile and has been walking for two weeks now; still a bit wobbly and with feet slightly out-turned, typical Erskine style, but he goes wizz. How they do love the pool and the wendy house from Sandy and Carina, and both in a completely safe environment. There is cover over part of this fantastic balcony, so from 3.00 pm there is plenty of shade. The two little boys are so very lively. Jonathan has a trike, and loves bedtime stories, 3, 4 or even 5 of those little books with pop-ups have to be read from the 'animal tales pop-up book series'. Nicola is in fine form and delighted that the 62 kg got through, and is amazed at all the sweet-talk.

The Sabbath

This is Friday and after a wonderful morning of splash and counter splash on the balcony we see the 'muezzin' on the very high tower opposite adjusting the microphone. His mosque is 100 feet below us just the other side of the wadi. We see all the faithful troop in and then the call is extended through the microphone. Most of the service is a one hour sermon. The voice is very emotional and excited; I am already vibrated into a religious frenzy and I can vividly imagine the muezzin gesticulating with extravagant arm movements as he works his congregation into an even greater frenzy. I ask Hamish why he has to broadcast his sermon to the whole district. Well, that is to get at the naughty ones, who have missed out on mosque and the women who generally don't go. They stay at home to prepare the mid-day meal.

Walkabout Taiz

In the afternoon we go walkabout in the town of Taiz, 5p a head for a taxi to the City Centre and we go through the suk. At the entrance is a huge crater, the site of dreadful flooding 2 months ago when the wadi was in spate and broke its banks and then cascaded through the suk. This disaster had been partially anticipated and a diversion channel had been constructed but not quite completed when the big rains came. It is quiet being a Friday, but trade is still on. I cannot resist getting a golden coloured belt from a shop selling djambias and holsters. The djambia is a deadly curved knife awarded to a male at about the age of 10, a horrific knife in ornamental sheath, a symbol of manhood and authority. The golden belt will do on my kilt, now the black belt and buckle is too short for comfort, and the gold colouring will go so well with Erskine tartan. It is the longest one in the shop and after a little bargaining we get the trader to stitch on a special extension strap to make it comfortable. We are next in the market for a colourful cotton embroidered blouse for Susan and after lots of lively discussion find one with golden butterflies, and hope that she is pleased. We then walk through the town taking pictures of the sites, the magnificent 1,000 year old mosques in dazzling white, so bright my eyes get sore in the equatorial sun, and I deliberately have to look at some green cactus growing in the street nearby. At the back off this magnificent mosque there is an exit into the town's rubbish dump, filthy and flies everywhere. Such a contrast this culture with magnificent and ornate architecture and yet very poor hygiene and rubbish collection. The Swedes could teach them a lesson or two, with the spotlessly clean streets of Stockholm. We then find 'The park', the children's favourite outside cafe, for cool drinks. The park covers a large area in a maze of box hedges and chairs and tables, not a public park, but so like one, with luxuriant trees everywhere. How the two little boys love this outing place and the man at the entrance who sells toffee chocolate from a wheelbarrow. What a clever contrivance of trade. You find the best pitch in the day and move whenever you want! The restaurant sports a magnificant sign with Rothman's logo. Any trader supporting a Rothman's logo gets a free board. Players used to do that in Britain in the 1960's.

Saturday 2nd trip to Taiz - the wild taxis

This afternoon we attempted to get to the Museum, the old Immam's Palace in the centre of Taiz till the 1962 revolution, but they had closed at 1.00 pm. I am amazed at the traffic in Taiz. The cars all seem to be dated about 1971, and the motorbikes from the 60s. They are a very important form of cheap taxi, and the driver rides round with two, sometimes 3 passengers, behind him, sometimes they ride normally astride, sometimes they ride sidesaddle, no helmets, but wizzing about the streets. And the old taxis - the driver can be as young as 12. Officially you need to be 18 to get a licence, but with a little bit of influence and you can get one much younger. Hamish had a lovely tale of one of his rich Yemeni friends, who got given a Mercedes and a wife at 13. At 14 he was a daddy. At 34 he had a 20 year old son. When the two of them went to Egypt on holiday the immigration wouldn't believe that they were father and son!

Visit to Hamish's school

We then changed plan and went to Hamish's school and I saw around all his classrooms and met some of his teacher friends. I was the great hero for bringing in the computer book for his Indian friend and they were in stitches about the 62 kg airline luggage and about my other stories about the girl on Valentine's day who sent the luncheon invitation by mistake to all members of the Caledonian University. Computer glitches were just up his street! But lots of more news on the school home front. A new principal has been appointed, Sultana, the head of primary, a lady with 20 years experience, but a lady principal in Yemen is unprecedented. Recently the school has had a representative in London and hired 10 new teachers of English, which is quite a handful.

Sunday - a trip up the mountain with a load of chickens

Hamish and I were out in the morning visiting one of his NZ / American couples, just about 10 minutes from his house up the hill. They had a spacious house, beautifully decorated, nice garden with fig tree and guarva tree and figs that tasted like honey, wife called Susan from Chicago, two delightful children. When we got home our shadows had disappeared completely, sun vertical. It was rather hot to go out in early afternoon but out we went at about 3.30 bound for a taxi trip for half an hour up the mountain. Top cars in Taiz are 1994 and after Toyota Land Cruisers with 4by4 drive and sturdy roof rack, much more fashionable than Mercedes, which hardly exist in Taiz. However we had 8 in our 1971 'Land Cruiser' 4by4 taxi, 2 more on the roof, plus two cases of chickens, two cases of eggs, and a large basket of cacti fruit. A full but typical taxi cargo; at least we were not on the back of a motorcycle! After five minutes we left the tarmac road and were on the mountain road, hairpin bends, gradient from 10% - 20%, often there were huge overhanging boulders by the roadside; it would be so dangerous in a heavy rainstorm if there were a landslide. Amazingly the mountain was a mass of terraces, a lot less than 5 yards in width, fully cultivated and fortified by stone dykes from mountain quarried stone. Frequently we came to a mini plateau which supported a mini village, As we got out the roof passengers followed and the chickens squarked no end on being landed. The village was full of goats, chickens, the occasional cows and masses of brightly coloured children, all so very curious to see a foreigner. They all wanted their photograph taken and then of course a little tip, but how can you divide a modest note among 20? It reminded me a little of feeding the geese at Linlithgow Loch. We were at 8,000 feet looking down on Taiz far below. You never would have thought that steep mountain was a mass of hidden villages. Hamish and Nicola had been to that spot before, by a primary school, and befriended the local taylor, so we made out way down a rocky path past a lot of cacti plants and flame trees to his house and he was ever so welcoming. Hamish and I went into one room with Jonathan; Nicola and Timmie into another room with the wife. There is no mixing of the sexes in this culture. Our host was surprisingly well informed about Britain; he asked about Ireland and Dunblane, and Mandella. Most Yeminis have tv and get the world news. He had 5 daughters and 3 sons, an average family! Jonathan and Timothy were very popular with the Yemeni children. They had never seen such fair ones before. Our host told us that he spent the morning making clothes on a Japanese electric sewing machine; in the afternoons he worked on his terraced farm with his brother. He did his best to persuade us to stay the night, but Hamish was very tactful and said the children would not sleep in a strange bed. When it was time to go we went back on the track to get a taxi down again. It was getting dark quickly, but we managed after a 20 minute wait in the clothes workshop. I was given firm instructions by Hamish not to admire any of his work or he would feel obliged to give it to me. There is a plan to tarmac the mountain road and then traffic will be much busier and the tourists will flock up the mountain and they will need hotels and restaurants.

Statistics about Yemen

Yemen is a country with a population of about 20 millions doubling every 20 years but with life expectancy just 45, so I would be living on borrowed time here, and a size of .5 million square km, approximately the same areas as Britain, but one third is uninhabited desert. There is an English newspaper, the Yemen Times, surprisingly, very anti government, but a beacon of the realtively new free press. It has a considerable circulation outside Yemen, but was most annoyed when mail orders never seemed to get through, so they put an investigator into the post office and witnessed the dumping of their papers, 3 weeks ago, so that was a good story. Next week they printed a story about the forthcoming elections. The gist of this was that the main parties had come to an agreement about how many seats they each should have. The assumption was that actual elections would be rigged, so it was better to decide beforehand, so at least there is a reasonable balance of representation! The big issue in Yemen is whether Aden should be given free port status. This should attract much needed foreign investment and a flourishing trade, (perhaps another Hong Kong), but the downside is that customs duty in a country with no income tax is a considerable proportion of revenue, and the North does not want to loose revenue. The Times says that 'Aden as a free port' could either become the goose that lays the golden egg, or a mini timebomb. Hamish thinks that Aden is too unstable to attract foreign money. In the recent civil war all the smart oil company flats and houses were ravaged and looted and they don't want a repeat of that. In the Yemen Times of 22/7/96 there is a curt reminder to the editor from the President, that he will be expelled to Cyprus if he does not report more favourably about the beloved republic. This week the lead story is how Yemen is top of the league in the world for sex discrimination in primary education with 70% of girls being absent from school, so we are rather wondering what is the future of the 'frank' commentaries and the gutsy editor. Young girls seem to have a rotten time in poor families. One sees them aged 4 in the streets struggling with 3 litre water containers, carrying them home, resting every few yards.

Monday - visit to the Immam's old Palace in Taiz

Hamish is the wonder guide and off we set to see the Taiz museum, which is the old Immam's Palace, as occupied before the revolution of 1962. The outside of this building is traditional and ornate; the interior is rather ordinary and shabby. The successor regime regarded the rebels as martyrs and so what is on show is intended to rubbish the Immam and discredit him with as much conviction as possible, so on display is the state sword of execution, with the comment, some sword, some justice! And there are vivid pictures of the martyrs. Inside the rooms of the palace are many but small. There are lots of relics of his state visits, presents from King George VI, and pictures of the interior of Buckingham Palace. There are lots of rooms with his personal possessions in cases or hung in wardrobes, masses of swiss watches and clocks and Parker fountain pens. He loved giving visitors up market Western gadgets. There were masses of old valve wirelesses, and 1950 gramophones, and a western bathroom, which was really very modest. The hand rails going up the stairways were just old plumbing pipes! His bedroom was stuffed with huge boxes of shoes on display. The ladies rooms had their best clothes and lots of golden shoes and gold braid on their costumes; there were children's toys and a rocking horse and trike! From the windows there were superb views over Taiz. In the top room was a mass of medicines and bottles of morphine used after the attempt on his life in 1961 by the 'martyrs'. Another room was stuffed with old bottles of wines and spirits to suggest that he was a decadent drunkard. How odd to rubbish a former king!

Yemeni architecture

This is very distinctive. Whereas England was once described as a nation of shopkeepers, Yemen has been described as a nation of architects. One town, Shibam, has had 6 story mudblocks as skyscrapers for 500 years! Around Taiz there is stonework galore from the mountain and also lots of redstone quarries and the stones are hand cut to shape. The older houses are completely made of stone. A block will typically have 4 arched windows, as half moons richley ornated into about a 100 more half moons decorated in coloured glass. The houses today are constructed with central pillars of reinforced concrete, the sides infilled with breeze blocks and then faced with traditional stone. In the villages the houses blend beautifully with the mountain terraces. In the large blocks a whole extended family lives. The domestic animals live in the ground floor, the patriarch in the top storey, others in the intermediate floors. The roofs are flat and generally sustain a large red tank to store water, and now in recent times a 2 metre sky dish. The Yemenis like to have their window on the world. The more elaborate houses in towns have balconies and fancy windows showing the Turkish style, a remnant of the two occupations by the Turks.

The tourist guide and the Japanese girl

When we came out of the palace we paused at a fountain and Hamish quickly got into an animated conversation with his neighbour who worked on the tourist staff at the palace. Afterwards he translated the conversation. "How's things Abdul?" "Oh dear Hamish. I am in awful trouble". "Tell me more". "You see Hamish, there was this georgeous Japanese tourist and she was on her own and I made such an effort to be hospitable to her and showed her around many of the sites of Taiz over several days". "And of course, it was a romance?" "Oh Hamish you read me like a book. I was over the moon in love with her and wanted to marry her, but the hotel owner where she was staying reported me to the authorities, as I was not an official guide with an agency, so I got into dreadful trouble and the girl was so very upset too. She thought that I was the cat's whiskers". "Come on Abdul, you would do far better with a Yemeni wife". "Oh no, I wouldn't, they cost $2,000 in dowry, and here was this georgeous Japanese girl I could have got for nothing". "But Abdul, you don't understand, what it would mean to get a cheap Western or Japanese wife. They would expect far more from you after marriage than $2,000;

you don't know what you could have been up in your neck for!"

Markets in Taiz

Hamish simulates his weekly shopping run. Amazingly, women hardly ever go into the supermarkets, the fruit market, the fish market. I can understand why. The supermarket was about the size of the one on the Isle of Arran at small town Brodick, with typical groceries and hardware leading to one checkout point only. (In Edinburgh Safeways has a 62 checkout superstore in the Gyle). There were two trolleys in the shop but neither were for mothers and todlers. None of the customers was female. The fruit market was so very crowded, like pressing through to the bookies at a racecourse, but the motorcycle taxis were roaring by, and the middle of the walkway muddy and stenchy from the previous night's rain. Most of the produce was stacked high on barras and there was a huge variety of Yemen fruit and vegetables. Occasionally we came across a huge stack of live chickens clucking and squawking, looking rather miserable having chewed most of the feathers off one another's backs and not much enjoying life in a market cage. We thought we were buying a globe artichoke only to find that it was a particular variety of guarva, delicious but full of huge black seeds. Nicola had never eaten one before. Next we were next confronted with a band, making the most enormous commotion. "My goodness, Hamish, I never expected to see an Orange parade in Taiz"! (Sorry, Johnny, for the windup)!

Taiz post office

We go to Hamish's mail box number. It is checked once / week but today is a blank. Outside on the balcony there is a man sitting at a desk, smart in a full zana, (long white shirt). "Hamish what does that official do?" "Oh he's the one that writes the letters for those who are illiterate, and reads them too". Some 50% of the population are illiterate in Yemen, so his job is secure as a house.

And a little about post Gorbachev Russia.

Next stop was an electrical shop. Hamish knew the proprietor as he had bought gadgets there for his house pump. We were given a terrific welcome by another Abdul and taken to the back of the shop and given large glasses of cold limeade, the top soft drink of the market place. Abdul was like Hamish, an engineer, and they had a terrific rapport with one another. My joke was that when Hamish was 60 he would be tubby like his Dad. Abdul spoke fluent English and also Russian. For 15 years he had run a business in Russia, but after Gorbachev things got really difficult, and the mafia quite impossible, so he had no option but to quit and return to Taiz.

A little influence

A really modern 1994 4by4 passes us in the street, and the driver waves frantically at Hamish. "That is the sheik's driver. He knows me from the private English tuition given to his 17 year old daughter". The sheik also has a 4 year-old son, who likes to play with Jonathan, and the big attraction here is that he has a toy car with an electric motor for riding around the garden.

And the Taiz bank - a French Bank

There was no paycheck to pay in today, but Hamish had a Moroccan friend who opened his account, yet another Abdul. "My Dad tells me that he teaches a class of bankers in

Scotland on their professional studies. Do you have to face professional examinations here?" "Oh, no that would be an awful imposition. We just have to satisfy the authorities of the bank in the capital Sanaa that we are okay". More banter about tubbiness and some more delicious limeade drinks. Hamish is a great tour companion to travel with, a friend in every street and drink in every home.

Bumper Cars galore

Tuesday we join another family, Stephen, (he teaches mathematics and computing in a school in Sanaa) and Susan, and Hannah aged 4 and Norah aged two, and make a family trip to 'The Park'. This is a pleasure ground 20 minutes drive away from Taiz in a 'Land Cruiser'. Hamish has borrowed the car from Pamela of the Swedish Trust, and how the children do love this fun park. There are lots of swings and merry-go-rounds, and bumper cars, shoots, ice creams. Jonathan lets Grandpa take him in the bumper cars. The sceenery, once again, is spectacular. We are in a lush plain, but all around are the mountains rising to 12,000 feet with jagged peaks, all lush green almost to the tops, and of course masses of Yemeni children and their mums. Women don't wear the veil till they are about 10, and as children, they wear very brightly coloured clothes. It is enchanting seeing them all playing together. The Yemeni mums think the blonde Western children are cool too, so it is a very friendly afternoon. 'The Park' is a favourite weekend destination for Jonathan and Timothy.

Trek across Yemen

Wednesday is my last day in Taiz. Early in the morning the two families and Pamela load up the Land cruiser and Hamish and Stephen take it in turns to drive the 5 hour journey to Sanaa. Every hour or so we stop and swop seats; front is comfortable, middle is middling, back is very bumpy, and some passengers have a tendency to car sickness in the back. All luggage for 3 families is on the roof, so we are travelling in typical Yemeni style, but much more comfortable than the 1970 Peugeots! And with 4 children under 4 this journey is quite a challenge for them. The car has air conditioning and is comfortable. When you get out it is like walking into a 'greenhouse'! There are 3 mountain passes on the journey and chances to take photographs, and in the villages to buy figs, cacti fruit, pepsies etc, and sweeties for the children. They all have hiccups at some time, but no serious rifts, just the stupid little tantrums to be Mummy's girl or Daddy's girl etc. Air conditioning is turned off half way through the journey. We are about 5,000 feet and the temperature is cool. When we reach 'pumpkin' village we know it is only 1/2 hour from Sanaa.

Home schooling

Denis and Brenda Cox, (he is an engineer), are our hosts in Sanaa and give us a light lunch. Pamela is an authoress, having a book about 'Talking funny', a book on language and dialect and she is mega interested in my reference to the 'snob' corncrakes of Coll, and the branch of research opening up about dialect among our feathered friends. Brenda and Denis have 4 children and the pride and joy of her life is the 'home schooling' she has delivered up to the last grade of secondary. She is a leading proponent of the 'home schooling' movement. The home educated children are delightful, and she can tell me all the curricula she has introduced them to.

Apparently, in America, 'home schooling' is a boom industry. In Britain the 'Open University' is just that for adults, so I was intrigued to listen to Brenda.

The Old City of Sanaa

The rain comes down in Sanaa, but Hamish and I are determined to see the old city, and out we go with umbrellas and a plastic raincoat. The water is cascading down the main streets, but we get a taxi to the impressive entrance to the old walled city, and the roads are drier. At first hand you see how these 6 story blocks are built in mudbricks, and some are 600 years old, all with arches and some with ornate decoration. There is a 'tourist hotel', a conversion from a sheik's house, with coffee house on the 6th floor. We trample to the top. The steps are 18 inches high; the doors at each floor have elaborate brass embossments and carvings, at least 300 years old and at the top the view is a gorgeous panorama, of spires and domes, ancient houses, 3 miles in every direction. Sanaa is now the capital city since the revolution of 1962 and has a population of about 1 million. Downstairs we buy post cards and chat up the guide. "How the Germans and Japanese would like to buy up old Sunaa, but we have a rule in Yemen; foreigners cannot buy real estate". The nice thing about Yemen is that the tourists do not come here in large numbers. The traders are all so relaxed. They will chat you up as though time were no object, so unlike the West, with queues and telephones. There is a visitor's book and I am very interested to read the delightful comments of other travellers. There are no mortgages in Yemen. Old property just passes on down the generations. When marriage occurs the new wife moves into the husband's extended family.

A bulging pocket to take home

All the Yemenis want to know what I will take away with me about Yemen. I would like to take its sceenery, its architecture, and my lovely family all home with me in my pocket! There are some wonderful and rich memories of this week with Hamish and Nicola and the two little boys. The great watershed on Tuesday was when Jonathan agreed to go on a bumper car with Grand-dad, after going with Dad but at least an acceptable second choice! Nicola was so very welcoming and fed me and looked after me so very well. Timothy is just as very 'cute' as he is described in Nicola's family letters. I loved the companionship and love of this little family of four. They live a life of interest and adventure, are well and cheerful, have friends in every street in Taiz, and in some of the mountain villages too. What more could one ask of life? I feel that I have had a ride in a time machine and gone back to biblical times. I am amazed to see this land of architects, and the blueprints of 'high rise' buildings 600 years before New York. Sheik rule and mediation is so much cheaper than the impossibly expensive British law courts. The progressive consumption tax is so simple to administer. I am amazed to find a nation with a 'no courting' cuture, very little hooliganism, no drink problems. The week in Yemen has been for me a voyage of discovery.

*End

Author in Taiz, Yemen

4.3. Long weekend in South Africa.

Family letter from week beginning Sunday 23/10/94

Drama in the countdown days

All this week I am getting psyched up for Lucy's countdown. On Tuesday I ring South Africa, promising to fax the wedding speech, just in case there is a hiccup. I don't know why I had an instinct that travelling always has some element of risk! All my university friends and students think it a great joke that I am going for a long weekend to the Cape, leaving Glasgow after lectures on Thursday and returning for lectures again on Monday afternoon at 3.00 pm. Naturally, I would have gone for longer, perhaps at least a week, but the university is preparing for an important assessment at the end of its second birthday as a university, and there is a three line whip not to take time off. When I get back on Monday I have had 7 jumbo jet meals and 7 delicious Cape meals; no need to say which were best! I had had two breakfasts, the first at sunrise over Mont Blanc at 39,000 feet, the second over Birmingham!

On the flight deck of a 747

The highlight of my return trip was at 1.00 am in the morning. I am rather thirsty and go and get a drink and see the stewardess; 'I have just acquired a nephew, Patrick, who is a jumbo jet pilot and I am longing to know what he does. Could I spend a little while on the flight deck?' Anyway two minutes later I get ushered forward to see the captain and co-pilot at the controls of a 747 Jumbo Jet. It is just like something out of a 'Jim will fixit' programme for me. I am about an hour talking to the two of them. That night there were 384 passengers on board from a possible 400, so it was very heavily loaded. There was also 300 tons of fuel, and 15 tons of flowers for the London market. The jumbo jet cost $600 million, a massive figure. We were flying over Brassierville on autopilot, but there was a lot of communication with the ground, and the navigation system was operated on lazers so all that was required was to key in your destination position and autopilot would get you there to within a few hundred yards from an 8,000 mile trip, quite incredible what high technology does today.

Southbound

I slept like a log on the trip to Capetown, and found a most congenial colleague during the last hour's flight early in the morning. He was enrolled for a PhD at the London Business School for doing a dissertation on entrepreneurship, so we chatted and swopped lots of references and experiences and contacts, including the entrepreneur of all, Paul Bristol! Philip was at the airport to meet me. I was almost first off the jumbo jet, but made a b-line for the gents to have a shave thinking that it would be sometime till the luggage could be collected, but this was a tactical error. I was then at the end of the queue for immigration, and they took nearly an hour to process the 400 passengers, and I was almost last. A tactical error.

House guests.

Philip was as usual as large as life and in cracking form. This wedding was being organised like a military operation, I should say a mega operation, like Trooping the Colour for the Queen's Birthday parade. Indeed for two years he had to do just that as Adjutant of the Scots Guards. Ida's Valley was a houseful of guests; Anne and Michael Caruth, bridegroom's parents; Camilla, Patrick's sister and bridesmaid; Lorna, Lucy's best friend and bridesmaid; Edward and Debby Erskine, brother and sister-in-law to Lucy; Rupert and Alida also brother and sister-in-law were around but in a local B & B; Val Arthur, wife of Philip's friend John Arthur from the Scots Guards. She had come to help Fiona with the flowers and we called her RSM flowers. Ida's Valley looked absolutely stunning as we went up the drive. Early summer is the best time for the Cape. The colour in early morning is a sensation. Philip has some 16 acres of garden and some very fine specimens of trees, gum trees, eucalyptus, oaks, elms, stinkwood, bamboo, and an enormous 60 foot jacaranda up the gable of this Cape Dutch homestead.

Robert's gaff

Philip goes to have his breakfast outside in the vorcamer of the homestead, and a young lady arrives, blonde and Africanse and to me rather indistinct in speech. I ask her what I can do to help and she murmurs about a harp. I immediately think that she is a journalist from Harpers Garden magazine and whisk her round the garden pouring out Philip's cv etc, and she looks so enthusiastic, I feel that I am being such a help. When Philip has finished his breakfast I take her back and say I have given her a very full briefing. Then she says to Philip, 'Where am I to play the harp for the wedding party'. Philip collapses in laughter. No she is not a journalist, she is a harpist and she is playing at the reception under the oak tree for the tea party then in the marquee for the wedding breakfast.

Everything is in control

On the lawn is a huge marquee. It is the size of those you see at Chelsea Flower Show, with a capacity for 250 sitting at 23 tables. That morning the tables arrived and I helped Philip get them perfectly positioned ready for laying with table cloths and flowers. Outside the kitchen door of Ida's Valley is a wall with 23 wreaths all prepared to go on the tables. Philip has such fun directing this operation; 'everything is in control' is the watchword for this weekend, no matter what the crisis. The ladies of the house are all working in a team at the church, St. Mary's Stellenbosch. Oh dear, Edward comes back to report that Saturday is really super busy in the church. There is a wedding of a coloured couple at 2.00 pm. Oh dear, will the church be available for Lucy's wedding just an hour later at 3.00 pm? How could they schedule it so close? Edward will have to have a brief to be in Stellenbosch at the church and report through wireless when it is possible for the Erskine bridal procession to leave Ida's Valley. Anyway, 'everything is still in control'.

The ladies appear for lunch on Friday after their flower operation in the church. This is the first time I have seen dear Fiona. She is in wonderful form, just like Philip, and so very welcoming and sweet. Val Arthur has emerged very much the RSM of the flower arranging party and also in cracking form. Of course my leg is pulled unmercifully about the Harp incident!

Friday's Brai

In the afternoon I am enrolled to help Edward prepare for a brai that evening. There are 80 people coming for the pre-wedding celebrations. A brai is a barbecue, and Edward and Rupert are past masters at organising this. We use the 'buckie' to get the food and logs to the barbecue site. I am rather amused to see bucket loads of strawberries being transported. Philip has arranged a small 'umpah band' to give us some music for the evening. Apparently, they always have this band at Christmas and all Philip's garden boys and Fiona's girls and children come and enjoy the evening. This brai starts at 7.00 pm and continues till 11.00pm. It is a wonderful way for me to meet Philip's friends. This weekend trip to the Cape is my third visit. I came first for 10 days at Easter 1986; then for a week in July 1992, in mid winter.

After my jumbo jet night I slept like a log in Ida's Valley in a room next to Lucy and Lorna and Ted and Debbie, and woke up to the dawn chorus. This is quite a sensation in its own right at Ida's Valley. Philip has Muscovies and geese, there are hundreds of doves and there are many exotic birds, paroquet, heron, owls. How the bird watching Andrews would have loved this. Dear Lucy comes in and chats to me on the morning of her wedding day. She had slept well and literally glowed with happiness.

The Commissioner General offers Robert an alternative career

On wedding morning the ladies of the household disappeared to have their hair done and then the make up ladies arrived for the bride and bridal party. I helped Ted get lots of ice from Stellenbosch. All members of the house party went off for lunch with a local Dr Billy Trengrove, who had a lovely house in Stellenbosch. We go straight from there to the church and I am on point duty standing on a parking space nearest to the church to keep a space for the bride. Both Philip and I were dressed up in Scottish clothes. Philip wore a red and green Erskine tartan suit and I wore a kilt complete with glengarry, and capercailzie feathers and a beaver sporran. I noticed another guest wearing Erskine tartan tie. My goodness, it was Anthony Erskine, 5 years the Commissioner General from de Klerk to Chief Buteleze, the head of the Inkata Zulu movement. He told me that he was not a party member and de Klerk respected him for an independent judgement. I was intrigued and said I had heard that Anthony was one of the key nation builders of the new South Africa! I was amused by Anthony's remark to me when I said that students are often asked to write an alternative career profile for the members of faculty in the university. You, he said to me would be a good 'praise-raiser' or bongo-bongo man, the one out front who prepares the audience for the big one to come! Anthony told me one or two hair-raising instances when a meeting had been fixed with the Zulus but the atmosphere was so threatening that his party members had warned him not to go out on to the platform as he would be fair game for being lynched. What did Erskine think? Erskine said he must go out, as the Zulus despised any form of cowardice, and no further progress would be possible. De Klerk took the advice and got the crowd on his side. When elections were held Anthony was given a chance to address the Zulu assembly, the only non member ever given that privilege by the speaker, so he was very well thought of by both sides.

The bride and tiara

The bride arrived and that was the end of our point duty, so we took our places in the church, absolutely packed. Lucy went up the aisle on Philip's arm, veiled in the de la Rue veil from kind Aunt Diana. Her dress was another sensation made for her by her friend and cousin Zara (Piercy) Digby. She wore the Radcliffe tiara and a lovely diamond and pearl necklace. Her two grown up bridesmaids were her best friend, Lorna and Camilla, Patrick's sister, and she had a large group of pages and little bridesmaids, children of her South African friends. These outfits had been made by Val Arthur's daughter. The Rev Andrew Hunter, who had grown up with Lucy, took the service. He had a wonderful multi-coloured cape and a charming presence. As Philip gave Lucy away he turned back the veil and Lucy's face was all smiles and her diamonds shone. Later in the service the Rev Barrington, a former rector, sang an anthem. It was wonderful, and the rest of the hymns were sung by the coloured choir of Stellenbosch. Philip and Fiona both looked so very pleased and happy at this marriage and after the service the two families went down the aisle together.

Tea at the reception

The reception at Ida's Valley started at 4.00 pm. Car parking was at the top of the 16 acre garden by the huge gum tree, and the guests had to walk through the delights of Philip's rose garden passed the line up for tea and champers for the next two hours. Philip press ganged me into the line up. Everyone got told how his alsation, Dishy, had nearly had my sporran for breakfast, and my gimmick was that of the two brothers Philip was the good looking one and I was the ugly duckling! Anyhow this Laurel and Hardy show was the order of the day and I felt I knew so many new people by the end of the day. The guests loved my beaver sporran, and it was so tight on me its eyes moved when I laughed. Philip's number one society guest was Princess Lotte of Lichentstein, a granddaughter of the last Emperor of Austria and like many others she was intrigued by the beaver sporran! The children were fascinated by the dirk in my stocking. The harpist gave a great rendering under the oak tree by the house. As light faded we were all called into the marquee for the wedding breakfast.

Wedding breakfast

The harpist moved into the marquee. All the food was at one end of the marquee and the guests went up table by table. Philip had been very careful in the table seating. He kept families together. All his museum friends were together; all the historical housing members were together; all Fiona's Red Cross friends were together; all her Church ladies were together; all the widows were together. After the first course, Ted and Philip did their bongo bongo bits for me to do the bride speech. (See verse 1.9). Lucy had been so helpful and given me her cv. Anyway to my utmost amusement as we went for the second course a lady on the widow's table said to me, 'I am only 83 but I would so like to be your honorary niece'. I could not have had a nicer compliment! Lots of people on the various tables sang the praises for Philip and Fiona for their contributions to various aspects of Cape life. Patrick gave a charming speech in thanks for the lovely bride and for all Philip and Fiona's arrangements for this wonderful occasion. Julian, best man, shared some experiences with Patrick flying and rally driving and there were jokes about how long he took to propose to Lucy!

The party lasted till about 10.00 pm. Then the cry went up that Patrick and Lucy were going away. Otto, Lucy's long haired dachund, wanted to go too on honeymoon, jumped into the car and had to be taken out. Meanwhile Yum Yum, Fiona's dandy dinman, lay in front of the car legs in the air, and much appreciated the confetti.

An hour in Philip's studio

Next morning I enjoyed the dawn chorus for a second time and then went off for an early church service with Philip and Fiona and managed to take some photographs of the abundant floral displays in the church. After breakfast Philip took me round his studio. Huge extensions have been made into what was previously a piggery. Philip has a mini factory and sawmill to make his frames, and painting boards. They are painted over some five times and then scratched so that they absorb the paint. He tells me that he uses 40 brushes / picture, generally finishes a picture in a morning. In the main dining room at Ida's Valley was on display his picture of Thursday morning. On wet days he stays in the studio and does 'still lifes'; in the height of the summer he prepares his boards and frames. The idea is to make 500 boards at a time. This is no mini business. On a really good day he will paint a picture in the morning and sell it over lunch that same day!

I try to persuade Philip to exhibit in the UK market and also suggest a fortune is to be made from calenders and postcards with his range of Cape pictures, but he does not want to divert time for business away from his basic painting. The commercialisation of his work is another 'alternative career' for me, sometime. Maybe with the hotspot of my recent encounter with the university principal, I will soon be looking for an alternative career, and now there are two possibilities, a professional bongo bongo man, or as Philip's commercial manager.

More Erskines

On Sunday lunch we all go up a mountain pass to Dunkeld for a party given by the Wilson family. Yvonne is a charming Swedish lady. Derek a farmer / business man. The setting of the house is another Stellenbosch sensation, and inside the rooms, wow there are hanging pictures, both painted by Philip Erskine and Lucy Erskine, which of course are a sensation in their own right! I make friends with another Erskine cousin, Petal Allan, daughter of Derek Erskine of Kenya. I remember Denis, her uncle, well. He owned the Kensington Palace Hotel in London and started the firm Securicor with Keith Erskine.

An unforgettable long weekend

The clock strikes 3.00 pm and I have to depart to my return flight at Capetown. This must have been the most memorable long weekend of my life.

A break in honeymoon

On Monday evening Lucy and Patrick return briefly from their honeymoon. The tradition in South Africa is to bring presents on wedding day, so there is a vast pyramid of presents in the downstairs bedroom at Ida's Valley all waiting to be opened. How nice for Lucy and Patrick to come back and enjoy all the fun again at Ida's Valley.

On Monday at 3.00 pm I am again lecturing in the University. My students are amazed at the description of the jumbo jet flight deck.

end

4.4. Robert and Susan's Bank holiday trip to Arran September 1993

In Scotland for the autumn holiday we have both Friday and Monday, and with four days there is a temptation to go off on a jolly. This year we chose the Isle of Arran. It is less than two hours to Ardrossan, and an hour on the ferry with cars stacked on two decks, and there are six ferries a day to choose. Susan remembers coming to Arran in the 1950s on a garden cruise in the Meteor with her Mother and the magnificence of the rhodidendrons of Brodick Castle, now a National Trust Property, formerly owned by the Duke of Hamilton, whose daughter married the Duke of Montrose. Susan was keen to come again for a longer visit. Johnny Andrews said he thought that we were just doing a re-run of our honeymoon but with a different island. Arran is so different to Coll. It is dominated by the high ground in the North and Goat Fell, just short of 3,000 feet but part of a ridge of other peaks, and with plenty of wild red deer which one can see from the car at Lochranza. Arran is much larger than Coll. The population is now about 4,500, and it is 170 square miles, and with 7,000 deer. Like Coll and other parts of the Highlands Arran went through the traumas of being cleared to make way for sheep. In the 19th century it supported 7,000 souls but many of them were obliged to emigrate to Canada with some partially assisted passages by the Hamilton family. Apparently they took with them very strict sabbatarian principles but were non-plussed to find in the cold Canada climate water would freeze on a Sunday and no amount of preparations on a Saturday could keep the cattle unattended on a Sunday. Others were cleared from their small holdings and rehoused in a line of houses known as the 'Twelve Apostles', built by the Estate. But the small holders were annoyed at having their land taken so refused to occupy this line of houses and they lay empty for a few years. Now they are very popular and we noticed one was for sale with an asking price of £60,000. The main road round the island is a proper double track road. There are also two roads which go across the middle of the island, and a embarrassment of riches for choice of B & B.

B & B Kilmichael House

Inevitably, after the Cornwall experience we find for the first night from the tourist office an up market

Jamie Robertson small country house style B & B, Kilmichael House. The core of the house is 300 years old. We have a lovely ground floor room, known as the 'garden room', which is most convenient for the yorkies, and looks out onto a garden with a gorgeous view, and my goodness, there are some of those tropical plants and gunera just like the Nansidwell experience. Our bedroom is beautifully furnished and the double bed has a huge cannopy in bright yellow and with a surround of flowers. On the table by each side of the bed is a mini palm tree, live and watered in large cubical Japanese decorated pots. The room is full of Japanese pictures, but the overall effect is very pleasing. We are about a mile up country from Brodick, but there are stunning views of Goat Fell and the ridge. At the bottom of the garden is a bridge over a burn which leads to a track to a pony trecking farm. In our bedroom is a book which signposts the delights of 42 walks in Arran, which are highly recommended. Perhaps we should have come for a month! We met a couple over dinner from Minnesota, a doctor and wife, and they knew all about Honeywell in Minneapolis, and with 8 children and 3 grandchildren they had quite a family to talk about. Another guest, about my age from the Lake District, had just climbed Goat Fell and could relate the joys of getting to the top with some cloud on the mountain. "As the cloud moved it opened new windows below. Sometimes it was to Bute, then to Mull, then to Islay, then to the coast of Ireland, then to Ailsa Craig and the Ayrshire Coast, then to Ben Mor in Argyll". What a wonderful description of a climber's delight.

B & B Sannox House

Next day we have to set out and find B & B for the next two nights. Kilmichael House is full on Saturday. We set off for Lochranza on the Northern tip of Arran, past Brodick Castle, and then up on to high moorland, where we expected to see red deer but no, we were disappointed on our first visit, and then back onto the coast with fantastic views both of Bute and the Mull of Kintyre. Lochranza Castle was a ruin, but had a history from the 13th century when Arran was part of the kingdom of Norway. We had a delightful pub lunch and made friends with a young German student who was coming to study soon in Edinburgh, so we swopped addresses. We then backtracked to the village of Sannox, and entered the back drive of Sannox House, which displayed a modest B & B sign, but looked a gorgeous house. Lucky, first time. A lovely lady Mrs Sloss came out of the byre and said that she was not full. They only took a maximum of 6 and there was just one other couple apart from us, a young couple on a BMW m/c. ... and the terms were much cheaper than Kilmichael House, but the charm was no different, and yorkies were most welcome, they could sleep in the bathroom. We soon found that we had got digs in the Estate shooting lodge. Next week a shooting party was coming for a week to cull the deer. Mrs Sloss was the house keeper / cook and I immediately identified her with a 'Mary Lang' role (she knew all about the Hamilton / Graham family for the past six generations and all the properties on Arran), and we had complete run of the house with this other BMW couple, who were obviously courting hard and led a very low profile. The house was full of the most charming Hamilton pictures and a huge marble bust of the 12th Duke graced the stairs. A statue of the same duke was in Brodick outside the

Primary school. We had the principal room of the house with two huge double beds and sensational views from the windows. In the evening we had freedom of both the drawing room and dining room, again full of charming Hamilton pictures, and a gorgeous carpet, surplus from Brodick Castle, and we enjoyed the cullinary skills of this very charming and versatile Mrs Sloss. The garden was protected by a goose, much to the joy of the yorkies. On the staircase up to our room was a charming print of three foxes by Samuel Carter, just like one I remember at Normans. I wonder whether Aunt Diana still has it? In the garden there is sometimes a red squirrel. Grey ones never got to Arran, and a week ago Mrs Sloss said that in the morning a stag and two hinds were on the front lawn of the house, and she had heard the stags up the glen roar, as the rut had begun. I wondered whether we would share in this particular delight during the rest of our visit. Sadly, no red deer, but we got a beautiful eyeful of a red squirrel by the Craft Centre in Brodick on the last morning.

Genuine Brodick Castle

On Saturday afternoon we toured Brodick Castle, swelling the number of visitors to over 60,000 this year, the third most popular stately home in Scotland, and since 1957 managed by the National Trust for Scotland. We could have spent far longer there, as we only saw a fraction of the gardens, but we did get an impression from on high and to see the vivid autumn colours from the chestnuts, the glimpses of Goat Fell through the trees, the giant rhodidentrons on the drive up to the castle, the light tinges of yellow on the palm trees and the colourful borders, all looking magnificent in the sunshine. In the car park was a sycamore planted by the Queen in 1947 on her visit to Brodick. As we entered the castle by the main hall and looked up there were three stories of walls all covered with heads of deer. There must have been nearly a hundred heads in that one eyeful! Susan found this rather putting off. Hughie C R would have loved this sight of trophies galore. We then go through the rooms. None of them are very big, but they have fine proportions and much charm with fine portraits, and pannelling and racing trophies and very intricately carved ceilings with mountings of coats of arms of Hamiltons and Grahams and of the families which they married into, and a two elegant chandeliers. There is a photograph of Edward VII and Queen Alexandra, and (?) and Edward VIII, George VI and Princess Mary as children. Susan immediately thinks that (?) is her great aunt Mrs Kepple, but the guide firmly puts her in her place. The (?) is Princess Victoria. "Mrs Kepple was never photographed in public with the King, anyway at Brodick"! In one room my eye is caught by seven small one foot sketches, all in a row, of Brodick landscapes, all by Thomas Gainsborough. I said to the guide that I had thought he always did portraits, and she replied, "Gainsborough painted portraits for his living and Arran for his pleasure" The library was decorated with many fascinating racing pictures, all painted in the old style galloping with front legs forward and apart. The first Epsom derby, the first 1,000 guineas at Newmarket fought as a match, the first three St Legers at Doncaster, also matches, and some gold cups at Ascot, all won by Hamilton horses. I am sure that the Hamiltons must have battled it out with Thomas and Warren de la Rue in the 19th century on the race course. And the room displayed some silver racing tropies, the most impressive of which was the Chesterfield Cup, a huge equestrian statue with a maiden about to mount, very Uncle Ericish! From the rooms high up you could look out of the windows on to stunning views of Brodick and the southern peak of Holy Island, and down on the terraced garden and borders and rhodidendrons. On the corridor on the top story there were masses of other styles of sporting pictures, mostly prize fighting with bare fists; one of the Dukes of Hamilton was an olympic boxing champion. The tour ends with a passage through the original kitchens and a wide range of copper saucepans and bowls are on display, and finally we take a cup of tea outside onto the terrace and drink in the sunshine and look up at the 100 feet or so of the red sandstone of the walls of this glorious place, and then hurry, hurry, the castle is soon closing and we want to buy more tea towels in the gift shop for decoration at home with Arran scenes. Brodick is charming and everything there is genuine and interesting. How Philip and Lucy would love this island and its natural treasures.

Bogus Holyrood

The previous week with Barbara we had taken her round Holyrood House and we were most amused to see there the long gallery. On one side were the genuine portraits of kings since Bruce, but on the other side were 40 bogus portraits for the previous 1,000 years. James V had wanted to give the impression of continuity in the divine right of kings, and the artist simply replicated 40 portraits with nose and face of James V all in slightly different positions!

The Sabboth on Arran

A lot of the churches on Arran seem to have been closed and made into private houses or festival halls or just open in the summer for the visitors, so choice was not that great. There was an Epsicopal Church in Whiting Bay, which we failed to find, and a Church of Scotland with a lady minister, The Rev Elizabeth Wilson, BD (Hons). Naturally Susan wanted that one, so no more argument! Whiting Bay is opposite Holy Island in Arran, which has a lighthouse and a 600 foot peak, dominating the bay. Rev Elizabeth's church has 17 pews each wide enough for 20 to sit in and is 3/4 full. They are celebrating harvest festival and the baptism of a little girl, Abigale, 3 months, so the congregation is bigger than usual, but with all the good things on Arran it seems so natural to celebrate in thanks for all the bountiful fruits of the lord! There are hardly any men in the congregation, just a few in kilts. But anyway Rev Elizabeth seems popular and has lasted 12 years in the parish. Her diction was good and she preached well.

After the service our yorkies had a wonderful run on the beach and we had a bar lunch in Whiting Bay. In the afternoon we continued our tour around the South and West of Arran. There were stunning views of Ailsa Craig, then of Kintyre, a deep blue in the light of that afternoon. We could just make out the outline of the Irish Coast beyond Kintyre. We found Dougarie Lodge on the West Coast, which used to host the parties which shot 5,000 brace of grouse in a season and was visited by Ranier of Monaco a cousin of the Hamiltons, and Edward VII and Mr and Mrs Kepple, (so Susan's great aunt did get to Arran after all). When the Shah of Persia stayed in the Lodge he blew his nose on the curtains! We were later to find out from the knowlegeable Mrs Sloss that

Dougarie was sold by the Arran estate to a Mr. Gibbs in the 1970s, and he is the brother-in-law of Susan's first cousin Antonia Gibbs. Oh dear, we missed an opportunity of going in to see a little Victoriana, the former principal shooting lodge of the Arran Estate, and those curtains.

*End

Susan, author's wife on the Isle of Arran

4.5. Autumn Bank Holiday in the Isle of Bute, 1994

Mrs Watson, as promised, sent us directions of how to get to Ascod Farm and assured us that her West Highland terriers, Rogie and Rowan, were in a state of ecstasy in anticipation of entertaining two yorkies, and now Susan too has caught the bug of ecstasy. Thursday is a lovely sunny autumn day, so the long weekend augurs well. The weather holds on Friday, so we decide to go the long way to Bute via Strachur and Colintrive. It is about 30 miles longer than the Glasweigan route 'doon the watter' via Wemyss Bay. There is something rather special about a mini autumn holiday in the Highlands just as the trees are turning to a gorgeous golden. We stopped for lunch at Luss on Loch Lomond. Now the road has been vastly improved around Loch Lomond and there is a by-pass at Luss, but the shore side restaurants and bars are still doing a good trade. The weather was very calm, too calm for the wind surfers, who kept toppling over, as we watched them eating our lunch. Next we negotiated the 'Rest-and-be-thankful' road coming down on to Loch Fyne. All down the shore there were super gardens with gladioli and nastershams, all in resplendent colour. I was rather amused at one B & B with its name 'Fyne view', a nice pun! We ended up at Colintrive, 125 miles from home, the same distance as Oban. On the route over the hills one got a spectacular view of the Kyles of Bute. The Bute ferry from Colintrive is just 5 minutes and once again we are on a magical Scottish Island. Initially the ferry road is single track, but after a mile it opens up to a normal A class road and we are soon in Rothesay Bay.

Rothesay

We might almost have driven in to Cape Town! There were huge grass bowling greens between seafront and shore and almost a forest of tropical palm trees, then two huge pavilions (now a little like Brighton), advertising a show by the well known comic for Sunday the Johnnie Beatie Show. The bay is vast and the architecture is bold Victorian with masses of very up market hotels and expensive shops, but rather too many empty shops in the main street. On Saturday morning we found the shops did not open till 10.45 am, all so very relaxed! Until the 1960s Rothesay had 400,000 visitors a year from the 'Doon the watter' trade, but this year this has dwindled to a mere 100,000. Cheap European holidays have spoiled the Rothesay trade. The population of Bute has shrunk from 14,000 to 7,000 in 20 years, but it is still a popular retiral place. Selina Scott, the well known tv star, was information officer for Bute for three years early in her career, but when she gave up the Naval Submarine Base moved to Faslane, and population shrinkage escalated. Perhaps they had better get Selina back! We had a pub lunch one day with the manager of the MacBrayne's ferry. What are you called if you come from Bute? - A Butey, a Buttock, no none of these, a Blannech, so called after St. Blane, who brought Christianity to Bute in the 6th century. Our friend told us that at its peak Bute would get 100,000 visitors on one weekend. On our trip to the South of the island we saw the remains of St. Blane's chapel, still very well preserved and in a super spot on high ground overlooking the hills of Arran and the other islands of the Clyde. In the modern St. Blane's churchyard we looked for a tombstone in remembrance of the parents of one of my University friends. We found the stone and to our surprise we found that his Mother was an Erskine, so perhaps my friend is a cousin. What a funny way to find out! I could not help noticing that most of those who died in Bute reached their 80s or 90s. It must be a very healthy island!

Bute B & B

Ascog Farm is just 3.5 miles South of Rothesay. It is a large white farmhouse up a steep farm track, some 200 years old built originally for a Chrichton-Stuart lady who married an officer in the Greys. A huge Bute palm tree with multiple trunks dominates the gable end of the house. Everything is spick and span. Mrs Irene Watson is such a cheery landlady. Before she retired she had worked for a land agent in Hexham Northumberland and her portfolio was the really up market houses. She loved going to work and visiting beautiful homes and fantasising on what she would do to her own home one day! She told us that she had painted up every room in the house, using extensively Laura Ashley wallpapers and furnishings. The previous owner had let the farmhouse deteriorate badly. He had been a director of ICI, and never brought his wife here. He used the house as an escape, but without a wife's loving care and attention the house had suffered badly. Susan and I had the main B & B room, sometimes let as a bridal suite, with a huge double bed and vast canopy and curtain. The West Highland terriers, Rogie and Rowan, the giants, were there on the front drive to greet us, and immediately Yorkies and West Highlanders made friends with some very enthusiastic sniffing and tail wagging. Susan gave Mrs Watson an address book embossed with a West Highland Terrier, which she had bought in the Luss gift shop, so all relationships were so very warm and the Yorkies had the freedom of the conservatory at night! On the drive there were also a charming pack of 12 muscovey ducks, lots of hens, two geese, a peacock and a peahen. Further up the track were hen coops occupied by two broodies. A lot of young cattle were on the hill above the farm. After having a cup of tea in the conservatory we climbed the track from the farm on to the ridge to get the most wonderful view of Bute, Kintyre, and the Ayrshire coast. The cattle were rather too curious at the yorkies and we had to withstand a stampede. Susan grabbed the precious Yorkies and dropped the mushroom we had picked up for breakfast. I am not sure that I really appreciated Irene's bathroom taste. There are plants there in profusion, giant violets; they are there to absorb the moisture. There are also fancy tiles and a ladies hat with dried flowers. Then there is a huge mirror the whole length of the bath. The last thing I wanted to be reminded of is how tubby I have become! Perhaps the mirror acts as a disincentive to consume hot water, very subtle! Next morning Irene gives us a super breakfast including bacon for the yorkies and makes no fuss when they sit on the sofas, a really perfect B & B lady if ever there was one.

'Free' Bute farming the easy way

Mr Watson said that in the summer he let the keep to other farmers for a very good rent, of £65 / acre. In the winter months he bought sheep and fattened them up for spring, (the Bute climate is so mild grass grows all the year round like in Uganda), no hassles of lambing and clipping and dipping, or haymaking or reaping and sowing; the only capital needed was a good fencing mallet to keep the place stock proof. A minor irritant was that the red deer would often roam into the farm and eat their roses. One afternoon we saw a pair of roe deer slipping into the wood as we went down the drive. 'A geriatric could run the place with no ties; and Irene loves to show off her decorating talents and enjoying the company of new visitors. The farm is like money automation.', he said. The farm was one of the very few independent Bute farms. Nearly all the others were owned by the Marquis of Bute with huge rents, except the North of the island which was an estate owned by Sir Richard Attenborough. The present marquis (6th) is reputed to have inherited a £12 million overdraft on the Bute farm account. No wonder the rents had to go up! I could not help feeing that this B & B was the bastion of 'free' Bute. However, you never see 'old bangers' on Bute. The farmers all run about in smart 'Shotguns' so all this thing about high rents is perhaps just crocodile tears. Ascog Farm was an amazing husband and wife business; both throughly enjoyed doing their own thing; they could supplement the earnings with two pensions, and lived a fulfilled and rewarding life.

Sunday on Bute - hill climbing and music-hall

We found a little Episcopal church in Rothesay tucked next door to a disused bingo hall. It was Harvest Festival at 3.00 pm. There were about 25 in the congregation. The rector was helping out from Dunoon. Most of the year Rothesay does a do-it-yourself service. They have a nice church hall for tea afterwards. The organist takes her King Charles spaniel to sit under her feet as she plays, right up Susan's street.

In the morning we had bought sandwiches in Rothesay, then drove to the most northerly point on the Attenborough estate and climbed up 800 feet to the top of the ridge, for a fantastic view of Arran, Kintyre and the Cowal Peninsula. We didn't see any grouse or deer. The climb helped me take off 2", but Susan said that I had been so greedy on Irene's breakfast sausages, that it was a 'no change' situation! On the way back to the digs we drove through Mount Stuart estate and got a glimpse of the huge Bute red sandstone mansion. Apparently the house and garden have just been made into a trust and from next year the house will be open to the public.

Sunday evening was the Jimmie Beattie show at the Victoria Rothesay Wintergarden. The place was packed and we had Alexander Morrison and Annie Grant as support singers. Jimmie was the comic and also a singer and the other two offered a wonderful and varied programme of music-hall songs. We had Harry Lauder, Vera Lynn and the war time songs, lots of Scots sing along songs, a little opera and masses of rather corny jokes from Jimmie ... 'the snooty man from Edinburgh who had turnups in his underpants'. This was Victorian Music-hall at its best, with the audience joining in the chorus and how they loved it. We never hear music-hall now, but Rothesay is full of retired oldies with concession tickets and they loved music hall. Jimmie Beattie has a house on Bute and does 3 shows / year. The September weekend one is the last. We must have been lucky to get tickets on Saturday before it was sold out.

So now you know what is involved in 'going doon the watter'.

*End

Susan, author's wife on the Isle of Bute

4.6. A mega tour of the Highlands, May 1996.

On Sunday 5/5/96 we begin our week's tour of the Highlands. First stop is West to Loch Awe; tea with Mary and Eddy and a glimpse at their gorgeous garden; then supper and bed with Jamie McGrigor in his super home. He has just opened a new drive entrance, so you no longer have to approach the house through the farm. We are given the conservatory room, which has steps and is so very convenient for letting dogs out of. Jamie is in spiffing form, full of the joys of life, just back from jetting to London for the Caledonian Ball. He has some charming pictures of his two delightful girls, Sarah and Sibylla, and he is working so hard up at dawn to get to the sheep and cattle at Upper Sonachan. Determined to offer the best of 'highland hospitality' for our dinner he goes out on the loch to catch a trout for our dinner and gets soaked in a downpour, but this trout is beautifully cooked, sliced into four and wrapped around in bacon, for the fish course! This is 'cordon bleu' plus treatment. But oh dear such a sad story too. Those wonderful Campbell-Prestons, who run the Inverawe Smokery and a fantastic mail order business, have just lost their 18 year old daughter on 'Gap'. She was in Tanzania and got taken by a crocodile while swimming in a water hole. The crocs had come in after heavy rain unexpectedly. Her friends had swum every night there for months. This was a story which was the 'headlines' in the Northern Press on sale next day on the Orkney ferry.

Route to Loch Maree

On Monday we set off from Loch Awe about 10.00 am with a route of 180 miles to Loch Maree, which is about 30 miles short of Ullapool. Most of the country is new to us, and the day being bright the colours of the hills and lochs are enchanting.

Glen Orchy

The first delight is the route up Glen Orchy on a single track road which connects with the main road to Glen Coe. The Orchy is full of rocks and falls and trees just coming out with buds bursting. 15 miles of winding track and hooting over every hump was a small price to pay for this lovely bit of Argyll. Susan thought that she saw a volcano erupting! The clouds were coming over and rising rapidly and it really did look like an eruption. How Lucy would have loved to have had her paints - she would have painted a Royal Academy picture in no time!

Glen Coe

This is wild and spectacular. The hills are still covered with snow, but not enough for skiing. We stop at the top of the Glen at a beauty spot where there are 3,000 foot hills on both sides of the road and they look sheer and very difficult to climb. We find two ladies from Yorkshire. "Much more impressive than the Yorkshire Dales?". "No not one bit, we love our Dales". "No exciting massacres down there?" "The Scottish ones are very over-rated. In Yorkshire we had Scargill; you cannot beat that". My brother Philip writes that Scargill is now in South Africa trying his best to organise a national strike.

Fort William

We crossed the Balahulish Bridge. When we did this bit on our honeymoon in 1964 we had to go over a ferry. My goodness, there has been a lot of property development on that stretch by Fort William. It rather reminded me of the front at St. Helier in Jersey. We were now looking for a pub lunch and stopped at Spean Bridge where there was a Woollen Mill and Restaurant and outside tables so we could remain with Cheeky and feed her too. The mill had some georgeous tea towels too.

Urquhart Castle

The next stretch of our journey takes us over the Caledonian Canal at several places and then the long run up Loch Ness, with a stop half way up the loch at Urquhart Castle, and hot dogs from the snack bar. From this high point you get a good chance to see 'Nessie', but today with a brisk wind and white horses everywhere on the loch there are a 1,000 'Nessies' if you only have a little imagination.

Loch Maree

We next turn for the Ullapool route and that is via Beauly. Suddenly we are in rolling country and lush green fields for about 20 miles and then all change again. The hills go a deep black and we are in the wilds till we eventually get to Loch Maree. Gwen used to say that it was the loveliest loch of Scotland. We stop for the night at the Loch Maree Hotel. There is a huge memorial stone by the front door. Queen Victoria stayed there for a week in 1877 and laid the stone in appreciation of her visit to the district. We had the room immediately below where she slept. Inside the inn there were lots of pictures of the loch and the strange shape of a scabbard, 'Slioch'. This amazing hill is partly obscured by cloud that evening, but we find a pleasant walk along the shore of the loch. Inside the inn is stuffed with fisherman's memorabilia, fishing nets, and so very many stuffed salmon and stuffed trout, no doubt to inspire plenty of fishermen's tales. We find an Irish couple from Belfast who says that I am 'Murphy's double'. He had a friend who ran the distillery in Comber and he knew all about the quality of the Andrews linen yarn. Two sisters, one from Canada, one from London, were playing rummy in the bar and we taught them the delights of two handed bridge. I wonder whether Queen Victoria would have been amused! Our breakfast is in a dining room with a sensational view across the loch. Lake Geneva would not have given a better offering.

Gardens of Inverewe

From the delights of Queen Victoria's hotel; she stayed a week; we could happily have stayed a month, we make our way about 15 miles to the famous gardens at the mouth of Loch Broom. There are 130,000 visitors / year to this 56 acre extravaganza. Because of the Gulf Stream this garden is host to many plants normally only grown in the tropics. The gum trees and Eucalyptus are magnificent, the tallest trees I have ever seen. It stretches some 1.5 miles along the shore and there are pathways on about 5 levels, so it is ever so easy to get lost in a garden maze. Luckily there are posts which guide you to the way out. May is probably the best time to see the camellia and rhododendrons out in their glory. Some are very high about 30 feet, and then there are gorgeous burns and ponds and a profusion of enormous buttercups. In the distance are the snow capped peaks of Wester Ross. There is a walled garden with peaches in blossom and a strawberry patch fed with Loch Broom seaweed. Nine gardeners tend this place. It was started by Oswald MacKenzie in about 1850 and eventually gifted by his granddaughter to the Scottish National Trust in 1956. Bits of it were like Ida's Valley, then like Upper Sonachan, but 56 acres is a huge area. Some of the plants and views were a little like the Cornwall tropical gardens. No-one seemed to know the origin of the expression being stuck up a gum tree. Everything was so very tidy and most of the species were labelled with tags, so the rhododendron snobs could have had a field day here. One of the gardeners told me that they suffered the -10 degree C frost in December and a lot of the medium sized plants were killed off and then removed. Today you would not know of the frost save a few rhododendrons not flowering this year, the buds all rotten. Some of the leaves were about 14 inches long, quite sensational. We could have stayed a day, even 2 days to absorb this garden, but we had 140 miles to make, so after an early lunch we were on our way. A couple from Nottingham told us to look out for the wild goats and deer on the way to Ullapool.

Susan, author's wife, in the gardens of Inverewe.

Ullapool

This is another fantastic drive around the West coast, passed the Summer Isles and sometimes in sight of two or three gorgeous peaks. They are all so individual in shape and size and colouring, and so photogenic. Some of the road is covered both sides with gorse in flower, a brilliant yellow - kissing is definitely in season as we progress on our second honeymoon! We were through three reels of film in no time and then were out for replenishment at Ullapool. This is a town planned as a fishing centre by Thomas Telfer in late 18th century, and for many years prosperous on the herring trade, eventually hosting the klondikers from Eastern Europe, but there is also a bitter history of clearances in the area when sheep were introduced. Over 100 left the town to found a settlement in Nova Scotia, and the ones left behind lobbied for the Crofter's Commission of 1876, and a place in the political history of Scotland. The town has a beautiful museum sited in a redundant 'Free Church' building and in the gallery is a video sequence of the town's history. There are many tourist shops and a population of about 1,000. Half are 'incomers', and very little Gaelic is spoken, though all street names are in both.

Tongue

We did not quite make Tongue. We stopped at 7.30 pm at a fishing hotel Altnaharra Hotel, which looked delightful. Yes , we did see the wild goats, about 10 all together snoozing by the roadside, one with a little kid and another fearsome beast with just one horn, a unicorn lookalike. Later on we saw the deer, a half dozen hinds, which just looked at us from a gully. From the bedroom window you could see a lovely silvery loch Naver. Inside the decor was excellent and the food excellent - we had stuffed quail as starters cooked Danish style by our hosts a Danish couple, and a dining companion a Dr Monro from Boston America descended from an 18th Century Sutherland Monro. He must have been a cousin of our friend Donald, ex neighbour from Cliftonwood. He was retired with his wife. He told us that he had 10 children and 16 grandchildren and aged just 63, so that is prolific anyway. The hotel was very comfortable and full of fishing and birdie pictures. A fishing guest told us she had a house 30 miles South, also in Sussex and that she came up always by flying to Inverness with the dog in a crate - quite docile, never minds a bit going in the crate for £5! She left heating on and didn't get frosted but her local hotel had 80 bursts even after putting anti-freeze down the loo and they had 28 degrees of frost C. Our breakfast companion was an engineer all the way from Inverness, about to close a 'General Wade' bridge a mile North crumbling from the frost.

Orkney ahoy

On Wednesday we were up at crack of dawn, no not to hear the dawn chorus of the birds, but to get to Scrabster by 11.00 am for the Orkney ferry. The day was showery, but the rainbows were brilliant. A few more peaks to be seen including Ben Hope, conquered by another of our hotel companions. The road for Tongue to Scrabster was mostly single track for 50 miles, all over moorland country, rather like the Lammelmuirs in the Borders but much longer, but then we got a few lovely sights of bays with pure white sands and various sights of Orkney. We passed Dounrea, the nuclear power station which is soon to close. Probably Sandy will be involved in its de-commissioning. The St. Olav is on time. We have an arresting two hour journey past the Old Man of Hoy, a stack 450 feet high and then past the cliffs of St. John's Head, 1,100 feet all in brilliant red sandstone. This is quite an eyeful.

Digs in the Palace among the 'Thatcher clearance victims'

We search for B & B out of Stromness and head North till we get to the village of Birsay. This has the ruins of the old Earl's Palace, a telephone and the 'Palace Stores', and we find digs for the next two nights. Chris and Fran Whitley, our hosts, are a couple from Yorkshire. He is ex Royal Navy, Ark Royal, petty officer electronics, now county planning officer in Orkney, and his director got the chop the day we arrived, so Chris is the most powerful man in the place, and how he does hate solicitors. In Orkney, population 20,000 they customarily represent both buyer and seller and some deals are reported as real rip-offs. This is the place the Southerners flock to as a farm of 300 acres is about the same price as a Yorkshire 100 acres, but there are also masses of 'English cleared by Thatcher in the recessions' and with golden handshakes and no job at 50 the appeal for self sufficiency and £30,000 house with 5 acres is irresistible! Anyhow Chris knows the planning regulations like a walking computer. They have a large and comfortable house, a cockerel and 8 hens. He wakes us up in the morning with a crow like a bird having its neck wrung. Outside our window is a links and then the shore. There are hundreds of bunnies on the links early morning and seals on the shore. To the right is the Brock, with an ancient settlement and 11th century church. The earl's palace is a ruin. He moved to Kirkwall after a squabble with another earl and built St. Magnus Cathedral, but Chris with all his planning power has more clout than the original earl.

Birds galore and two lamas

On our first afternoon we explore all round East Mainland of Orkney. This is a very green lush island with houses everywhere and rolling hills and lots of inland lochs. Most roadsides by the houses are brilliant yellow with daffodils. Off the main roads there are steep banks, mostly covered in primroses. There is lots of evidence of building new houses, but they are rather dull like prefabs with just a 30 year guarantee, not the traditional stone Orkney house with slab roof. Apparently, for a new house a purchaser recovers VAT, whereas for a renovation of an old stone house you have to pay the full price. Sadly, that means that no-one renovates the old and there are an awful lot of recoverable ruins about, and bungalows which would be more compatible in the South of England. There are birds everywhere, sea birds and the curlew and its striking shriek, and masses of oyster catchers. Orkney is a bird watcher's paradise. There are also lots of puffins and fulmars, though these were on Hoy and a ferry distance away. In two days we had time to explore no more than East and West Mainland of Orkney. No sign of the Albatross which John Andrews asked about, which got lost up here from the Southern ocean. On Thursday morning Chris is off on a ferry to a small island. Someone has been dumping in the Council quarry and he has to go and put a stop to this. That evening he tells us that he has found out more than he wants to know about the place. A couple are there as self sufficiency fanatics, also Thatcher clearance victims. The man is 60 plus and nearly died. The nurse aged 30 took pity on him as she nursed him back to health and left her own family for him and gave him another 3 children. They farm 30 acres by a cliff which is constantly sprayed by the rollers and all his cabbages are stunted. He has two lamas and 6 chickens and lives off lama milk, and was dumping rusty cars in the council quarry.

Exploring - memorials - ancestors - friends

On Thursday our first stop is the 'Kitchener' war memorial tower about 5 miles from the digs on an impressive hill top. We climb about 300 feet from the road through the fields. The rich laidback Orkadians have 4 strands of plastic barbed wire and then an electric top wire so fences take some negotiation. This is a very impressive monument. Kitchener was Secretary of State aboard HMS Hampshire, a cruiser, which perished on a German mine at Marwick Head on 6th June 1916. There were only 12 survivors. The monument was erected by the islanders. We then had a delicious lunch in Kirkwall, and then spent an hour in the St. Magnus Cathedral. This is really a most moving experience. The red sandstone gives this building a resplendence of colour to compliment its grandeur. The pillars inside are beautiful, though three of them are perceptibly now out of true! The Cathedral is very well kept and maintained and owned by Orkney County Council, so no obligation on the Church of Scotland. I was amazed to find a tomb of John Rae, a native of Orkney, the one who found the final remains of the John Francklin expedition to the North West passage. The guide on duty that day was a descendant of John Rae and amazed when I was to tell her that John F had been my grandmother's uncle. When we left there was an address book and amazingly the Dalmahoy organist Jane Gilmour, had been there just the previous day. How odd that one should have followed our friend to St. Magnus. She had taken a party of boys from Watson's, where she teaches.

Italian Prisoners of war

Our next turn was to go South down East Mainland and over the 3 'Churchill' barriers to South Ronaldsea. These were built after the Royal Oak was sunk by German u-boat and built mostly by Italian prisoners, some of whom were probably captured at Tunis by General Erskine. Anyway Father never knew that they built the most beautiful Italian Chapel out of their nissen hut and used plasterboard and concrete. This is a gem of a work of art, and much appreciated by the Orkadians. Our final destination was a stack on Yesnaby, and a cliff with a large hole, the oddest formation I have ever seen.

John O'Groats - more relations

On Friday we are up at the crack of dawn for the ferry home. First stop is the Castle of Mey, but this is an abort. The Castle is not open to the public. So we set off East for John O'Groats. The 'Last House' is a gift shop and restaurant and there is also an industrial site and museum. Now it was Susan to find relations. Lord Beatty, her Mother's first Cousin, is shown receiving the surrender of the German fleet in November 1918. The next picture shows the fleet in Scapa Flow, where it was scuttled.

Dunrobbin Castle - more but remote cousins

Two hour's drive South is Golspie, the site of impressive Dunrobbin, home of the Dukes of Sutherland. The hill overlooking Golspie is dominated by the memorial to the first duke, better known in history for the highland clearances in the 19th century. He owned a million acres and introduced sheep to his land and most of the tenantry were sent to the colonies or sent up to the coast to do factory work which they rejected. Earlier in the week we had been in Ullapool where they celebrated the heroes of the crofting acts passed because of the horrors of the clearances. Anyway the family home is the most impressive of the great houses of Scotland. It overlooks a formal garden with fountain and topiary yews, a copy of Versailles. There was much French influence in the architecture and furniture of this castle. There is a most impressive portrait of Queen Victoria and one of the treasured relics is her handkerchief which she left in 1880 after staying. Outside there are hundreds of feet of embankment, which are covered in daffodils and banks of primroses, quite lovely in the May sunshine. There were many portraits of the family including marriages with the Argylls, so Susan once more finds her cousins, a little more remote than the Beatty's! At the bottom of the garden is a converted summer house, now a museum. The main exhibits are stuffed animals from Africa and India shot at the beginning of this century, lots of impala, buffalo, a camel head, an elephant's head. We enjoy the garden rather more than the museum.

Digs in Dornoch

We end our drive on Friday in a beautiful 19th century house next to Dornoch Cathedral. It has a delightful garden and hosts. Mr MacKenzie is a retired policeman served many years in Stornaway coping with Spannish fishermen, and very knowledgeable about island life.

Hunting for friends and cousins

On Saturday we had a short viewing in Dornoch Cathedral, consecrated in 1259 by the Bishop of Caithness. Outside there was a no dogs sign; inside there were gorgeous windows in dedication of animals, dogs, a hedgehog, and there was a full length stone of a saint with a pug at his head, and still they would not allow dogs in the cathedral! Our next destination was Jenifer Cameron who lives by Bonar Bridge. We found her home but alas, she was away that day. Our next target was Strathdon the home of Hamish Forbes, Susan's first cousin once removed, brother of her godfather Ian. We went through en route Granton-on-Spey and had coffee with Margaret MacMillan who now lives in the old station master's house. The railway was one of the victims of the Beeching cuts, and there are railway lines in the garden instead of edges, very original! Margaret gave us a super warm welcome. She was a member of the Dalmahoy Congregation. The next leg to Strathdon was over the very high ground of Aberdeenshire, the Lecht ski centre, and up and down 20% gradients through the heather, the steepest I can remember. For a short time we were in the snowfields. We eventually find the home of Hamish. He is now the 6th baronet and lives in a modern miniature castle. It is built in the style of the old grand castles of Aberdeenshire but much smaller and has its completion date embossed in Roman numerals, MXMXCII. This is 1992! He built it himself aged nearly 80. That does show some spirit does it not? Unfortunately no-one is at home. We did, however meet on the Newe Farm the daughter of the 5th baronet, a second cousin, so the cousin hunts were not completely abortive. We next drove over the military roads over the hills to Crathie, saw Balmoral Castle and stayed the night in a B & B in Ballater.

The very popular dog

Sunday was the last day of our mega tour of the Highlands. Our route was down Deeside from Ballater to Banchory, and a stop at 10.45 am. We both saw so many smart Sunday hats we could not resist the town Parish Church on their Sunday service, particularly as the outside notice had a picture of a lady minister, Rev Susan, described as a partner. Later we were to find that she was a Hungarian and that Banchory was twinned with her parish, so there was no Rev Susan in Scotland! This was a large church and we sat half way up rather surprised that there was no-one in front of us. But, of course, there was a reason. At 11.00 promptly 60 children came in from the front, the biggest Sunday school I have ever seen, and they occupied all the front pews. After the minister had given the children's address, (it was an excellent one), they all trooped out, but could not resist giving Checky a friendly fondle, and this created quite a queue and delay, she was so very popular!

House of Dun - Erskine National Trust Adam House

Our next destination was just South of Montrose, the House of Dun. This is an amazing Adam house belonging to the Erskines of Dun and gifted to the National Trust in 1980 with all its contents, and was opened to the public in 1989 after the spending of a £1 million of restoration money. The Queen Mother presided at the opening ceremony and spoke to all of 30 children lined up to greet her at the front door. This is an Erskine Mecca if ever there was one. Every room had its share of portraits, and some of them were of excellent quality, Romneys and Raeburns and of course there were plenty of stories about the family. Inside was a portrait of John Erskine of Carnack from which the Erskines of Dun and Cardross are both descended. There was also a portrait of Lord Mar, the 'Regent. One Erskine of Dun was a Scottish judge and had the life peerage 'Lord Dun'. Another married a daughter of Lord Cassilis, head of the Kennedy family and Culzean Castle in Ayrshire, and then the family became known as Kennedy-Erskine. Another married Lady Augustus Fitzclarence, a natural daughter of William IV and actress Dorothy Jordan. Apparently William had nine children by Mrs Jordan, 5 sons and 4 daughters. If they had been legitimate then Queen Victoria would never have succeeded the throne! Anyway William made the eldest son a Duke and the other children were given precedence as a marquis or marshioness, hence Lady Augusta, who was a very merry lady and created much of the present garden. In the dining room there is a picture of the nine children at Windsor. There is also a fine portrait of Lady Augusta and her 3 Erskine-Kennedy children in the National Trust guide. I think I will have to find a place for her next to Susan's Great Aunt, Mrs Keppel! In their heyday the Dun Estate was 80,000 acres, but now the National Trust has a more modest 1,500 acres with the house. So ended our 1,100 miles mega tour of Scotland.

*End

Susan, Author's wife at the House of Dun

4.7. A Bank Holiday weekend in Ghiga.

On Saturday Susan and I set off for a short trip to Ghiga, mainly to see the gardens at Achamore, having been rather fired up by recent experiences at Inverewe. We set off just after midday and first stop was Inveraray on Loch Fyne. The weather was sunny; the town was incredibly busy with bank holiday and also the "Series 4 Rover Yachting event", next biggest annual event after Cowes. Lochguilphead and then Tarbert were also packed out with this jamboree and all rooms booked. From then on we were on the lookout for digs and everywhere was booked, over booked. We even tried a caravan site, but no luck. When we got to Tayloanin, the ferry point for Gigha at the hotel, we tried the hotel and they were fully booked too, but "Wee Mary over the road might oblige". Indeed wee Mary was fantastic, right in the tradition of Highland Hospitality landladies, and not a bit wee, a large jolly lady with home ever so spick and span and cheery. Cheeky was welcome and promptly saw off her labrador in her own home. That was a bit cheeky wasn't it? We had a lovely breakfast of porridge and then caught the 11.00 am ferry to Gigha, the first run of a Sunday.

Some interesting connections

Gigha is a narrow island 7 miles from top to bottom with just one main road. The village and pier are in the middle of the island and they had a nice church, and German Minister, small choir, no children, but pleasant Whit Sunday service. We had previously rung the hotel for digs. They were fully booked but Mrs MacSporran of the Post Office would oblige. Even she was fully booked but she had a wee Mary too so all was well and our lodgings were with the semi retired Island teacher, who loved telling us all the Gigha politics and history. We met the man who had previously lived in her house and amazingly he had once courted the ex Coll teacher Louise, who then married Alistair Oliphant. What funny connections we were to make. We had lunch in the Gigha Hotel, run by the son-in-law of the Island proprietor Mr Holt of Holt Leisure. The fisherman's dish was fantastic - king prawns, mussels, clams, herrings galore - I have never made such a pig of myself before! When we were waiting for our meal in the bar we chatted to a couple staying. Michelle had a South African accent. "Did she know Stellenbosh or Swellendam? We have a nephew Rupert who is the swell of Swellendam, with lots of flats from the Auld House." "Yes, indeed, my brother Henri Veldman, is one of his tenants"! "Is Rupert a good landlord?" "Yes, he is so very kind and helpful. They are the nicest couple in Swellendam!"

Gigha gardens

In the afternoon we made a 3 hour trip to the famous Achamore Gardens. It was raining slightly but the beauty and variety made us want to go 'singing in the rain'. This was the prefect time of year for a visit. The rhododendrons and azaleas were in their glory. There must have been 100s of varieties, both hybrid and pure species. There were also acres of woods, carpets of wild hyacinths and on the banks. The paths were ablaze with primula. The garden was a maze of paths, and ponds, palm trees, and exotic Australian plants and trees, birds everywhere with the nesting opportunities so much available. There were lots of peacocks, and their wild squawks, a cage of golden and silver pheasants, masses of courting doves, seemingly miles of gorgeous borders. This was a strong rival in beauty to Inverewe, about 30 acres of Garden of Eden species and colours. As 6 pm approached we were lost and we were rescued by a blond lady and two children. She was the proprietor's daughter and gave us a very sympathetic appreciation of the estate and gardens. There are 3 gardeners, one is supported by a Trust, but Mr Holt is determined to build on the tradition of Sir James Horlick, who did the original development. Susan had seen the garden in the 1950s and confirmed how much development had taken place since then.

Gigha hospitality

The postmaster's wife, Mrs MacSporran, gave us 'high tea' and then there was time to do more exploring. We went on the central track to the North of this narrow island, past 'Queen's Bay', so called as HM usually stops Britannia there for a picnic on the way from Oban to Aberdeen and summer holidays. The North of the Island is more wild and overgrown with bracken and brilliant yellow gorse, but the banks of the hills suddenly a-blaze of blue with hyacinths, lovely beaches and stunning views. There are no ruin crofts here. There is no 'prefab development' like on Orkney. The reason is simple. Gigha has one proprietor. All the farms are tenanted. Most of the land is lush and green. Mr Holt disappears in our winter to manage his South African interests.

Climbing the peaks

On Monday sadly our holiday came to an end. We were up at the crack of dawn and finished breakfast by 9.00

am, just time to do some more exploring, so we climbed the 'Mount Everest' of Gigha. It was a brilliant day and once we had got a little height the view was a sensation. Islay and Jura and the rugged paps were all glinting and blue. We could see the Arran peaks and the coast of Northern Ireland. It was an easy path at the beginning then on the higher slopes there was a mass of hyacinth, bracken and brambles and some high heather, but we were soon on the top and I reckon I had lost the inch of expansion from the previous day's gourmet fisherman's lunch at the Gigha Hotel. We returned home via Inverary, and a gorgeous outside lunch under sunshades at picnic tables in the azalea gardens. Susan kept singing the Tom Stewart song 'I have fallen in love with Jean from the Inveraray Inn'. At home lying in the porch was this year's edition of the Coll Magazine and my article on Farming Memories of Coll. We had enjoyed a long weekend of indulgence once more with the delightful B & B landladies of Scotland; no regrets.

*End

Susan, Author's Wife, on Isle of Gigha

Chapter 5 - Family and special events.

The wedding scene was taken from the House of Lords, and the author lost his hat; it turned up in the 'Bishop's Bar'. Did anyone know that the Bishops had a special tippling point in the Palace of Westminster?

The newsletter about the Queen's visit to South Africa contained a remarkable conversation between monarch and subject. The subject was the author's brother, and managed to put HM into fits of laughter. The newsletter also put into context the healing process which brought South Africa back to the Commonwealth. The author also had a cousin, Anthony Erskine, who held a crucial post during the transfer of power from de Klerk. He was Commissioner General to the Zulus, and the main go-between linking de Klerk to the Inkatha movement.

Special edition of 23/4/95 Family letter

5.1 Philip's account of the Queen's visit to South Africa

This is the story I had been awaiting for eagerly for several weeks now, and at last when we returned from Coll, there were three pages from Stellenbosch, but oh dear, Philip's photocopier has a gremlin in it and the copy is readable but not of good enough quality to reproduce again. Thus, I am forced, to select out the main items of interest, and play a rather low-key role as an editor and give it an an introduction to the characters in the narrative.

Introduction

Philip is well known in the Royal Family. He commanded the Guard at Balmoral in 1968, and had ever so much fun mobbing up Mrs Harold Wilson when the PM came to visit the sovereign! Anyway he got into the good books of the Queen Mother by doing an enormous mural for her in the hunting lodge. It was a very vigourous wall extravaganza of stags and birds in rugged glens. Lanseer would have been fascinated by this remarkable work of art. Anyway, the Queen Mother was absolutely delighted, and asked Philip and Fiona as weekend guests as a thankyou. Shortly after being captain of the Balmoral guard Philip served the Duke of Gloucester for about two years as a crown equerry. He would often be sent on representational duties on behalf of his royal master and during those years he made many friends in the Royal Household, many of whom were like Philip, ex Brigade of Guards or Green Jackets etc. Furthermore he knew several of the Bowes Lyon family through the Scots Guards connection. When he went to South Africa in 1971 he became a prominent member of the 'Guards Association of South Africa', and now for some years has been its president. Every year they have an annual dinner and send a loyal greeting to HM. Two years ago the young Kents did a 'feeler' royal visit to South Africa and made a helicopter visit to Ida's Valley, and spent the afternoon enjoying the magic of Philip's beautiful home and garden. Six weeks ago Lord Strathmore went to lunch at Ida's Valley. He was doing a business trip for Polly Pipes, selling in miles of pipes for the new SA housing mega plan. Last year Philip kept a 'hot line' with our Cousin Anthony Erskine, who was de Klerk's Commissioner General for the Quazulu movement of Butelezi. This was a Dr Kissinger role. He witnessed the final acceptance by Butelezi of the new constitution. I met Anthony at Lucy's wedding in November on my never to be forgotten long weekend in Cape Town! Kent Durr was SA ambassador in London for several years. As a friend of Philip in SA he had opened an exhibition of Philip's paintings in Cape Town. Now you know all the characters of Philip's drama.

Philip's text

The Queen's programme was predictable stuff ... the Cape Times headlines 'Curiosity Not Hysteria.' In 1947 a quarter of a million blocked Adderley Street. The City was brought to a stand still to see the Royal party. I drove round Cape Town on Tuesday and there were no crowds; life in the City was normal. She addressed Parliament, lunched with the Speaker. There was nowhere large enough to accommodate 700 so they had a party in the Southern Suns Hotel. There was a return match on Britania in the evening. On Tuesday, she visited various projects that the British Government has been involved in. She attended a service in St. George's Cathedral. Tutu, in his element, I gather preached for 8 minutes and very well. Later in the day she visited some Black church near Cape Town.

High Commissioner's Reception

The Cape Times said in this morning's paper, "There was a reception at the High Commissioner's Residence, for prominent citizens and decision-makers." I am not sure under what heading we were asked! When we arrived Wendy Smith said, "I have a message that the Queen wants to see you; could you catch the eye of Sir Robert Fellowes, (Private Secretary), at the entrance of the marquee".

A conversation about Commercial plumbing

As it turned out Fiona and I were the second couple to be presented, after General Constant and Mrs Viljoen. The Queen talked away without drawing breath. "How many years was it, you did the Guard?"

"28 years ago Ma'am ... is the mural still alright?"

"Perfect, it still gives us great pleasure, Alwyn lets us have the moor for two weeks".

"Do you remember Ma'am Mary Wilson was provoked by me into writing a poem about the Scots Guards?"

"Yes, a right doggerel piece of verse it was too! We thought it so funny".

"I was given a photograph by Lord Strathmore when he came to lunch the other day ... he told me that he was now a commercial plumber. I think the problem was Ma'am you didn't pay him enough as Captain of Yeoman of the Guard!"

"Yes, it's very difficult with cousins. They do get greedy!", she laughed.

"He told me he could now afford to fly first class. What amused me Ma'am, he had with him his boss, Mr Kevin MacDonald of Polly Pipes. In a very strong North Country accent he said as an aside to me 'I have told Mickie he's not on the board to look decorative, but to get the Buckingham Palace contract!"

The Queen roared with laughter. She asked me about the Guards Association, how many members and what did they do. She asked me if I still painted, and so on. It was quite delightful to be able to talk to her.

New role for Philip - an entertainer?

After she had passed on, Jannie

Momberg, an ANC MP, tapped me on the shoulder, "Man", he said, "you should be on the stage. I never saw her laugh so much"! Fiona noted that she was wearing her Rhodesian lillies, a huge spray of diamonds. In fact all the South African sparklers have had a good airing.

Looking prosperous

I talked to Prince Philip later on. His opening remark was, "You're looking a lot more prosperous since I last saw you"!

"Well Sir, I think you would put on a little weight if you stayed a little longer in this lovely country". We talked about the Guards Association.

The end of republicanism

The band then played on the terrace. They played 'God save the Queen', tunes from 'My Fair Lady', naval tunes. Of course it may seem old hat in London, but not here, where even the faintest whiff of Royal nostalgia has been frowned upon for 30 years! Many said they thought they would never live to see the Berlin wall collapse. I never thought I would live to see the Queen back in Cape Town, welcomed with such delight by everybody. There was something dejavu. The memories of Verwoed's campaign for the Republic, leaving the Commonwealth in a painful and sad way, we had been carried by determined Africaner nationalism through the long years of isolationism. It has evaporated; it all seems to have been forgotten ... or at least we were forgiven. The Queen's visit brought that moment of magic back into our lives.

Kent Durr told me when Alistair Aird told the Queen Mother that South Africa was re-applying for membership of the Commonwealth, she cried. Alastair told Kent he had never seen her so visibly moved by any news before.

Churchill, in his 'History of the English Speaking peoples', caught the magic of the Queen's visit, in different times and different circumstances, when he wrote of Charles II's restoration in 1660 ... "General Monk received the King with profound reverence when he landed; his journey to London was triumphal. All classes crowded to welcome the King home to his own. They cheered and wept in uncontrollable emotion. They felt themselves delivered from a nightmare. There were scenes of reconciliation and rejoicing without compare in history. It was England's supreme day of joy".

I don't think there was a dry eye last night - with the magnificent backdrop of Table Mountain, in fading light, the band played the second 'God save the Queen,' the Queen departed. I don't know what it all adds up to ... but right deep down in my heart, I feel profoundly happy, after 34 years of Republicanism, we had the Queen in our midst again.

Durban and more Erskines

The Queen's visit was over last Saturday. It ended in a blaze of glory in Durban. Ian Crowther told me that it all went very smoothly in Johannesberg; he attended a reception at the High Commission in Pretoria, more or less like the one down here, very well done. Cousin Anthony Erskine rang me and said that he and Diana had attended the final State Banquet on Britania. He was over the moon with excitement as he hadn't seen any of his old chums since the election last April when he finished his job as Commissioner General to the Zulus. He told me that both de Klerk and Buthelezi were very warm and pleased to see them again. Prince Philip said to him, "This part of the world seems to be full of Erskines.

Are you anything to do with that prosperous looking character down in the Cape"? If only he knew my swollen face is cortisone related and has nothing to do with my bank balance!

A hard tour

As you can imagine, the Press has chewed over every detail of the visit. Every aspect has been subject to intense scrutiny, and I think it has been a remarkable success. The Queen just never stopped. It must have been one of her hardest tours in terms of effort, but she never flagged. It was a wonderful performance. She carried all before her. There was awfully little criticism. Winnie accused the government of wasting money on the Queen's visit, which should have been used for the homeless, but I don't think anybody took her comments seriously, sour grapes!

Part of the healing process

One of my trolleyboys outside Pick and Save, (they are often artists models for me), said we all love the Queen. Billy Trengrove, who lectures at Stellenbosch University on journalism, asked his students to write about the Queen. They were all Africaans youths brought up on Republicanism. He said almost all were enormously curious; she had made a great impact on them, but they couldn't see how she fitted into the relevance of the new South Africa. I do think that many Africaans people do have difficulty digesting the wave of royal euphoria. The current visit has destroyed the Republican myth in much the same way as Maggie destroyed socialism.

There has never been a tour of its like. I tend to think the Queen's visit helps to give the new leaders confidence and the weight of her support and the strength of her encouragement are abstract factors of great value. I think that she has played an important part in the healing process this country has to go through. There is no doubt about it; the Queen gave untold pleasure to millions of people and across the whole of South Africa. Anyway in personal terms ... Fiona and I derived a great deal of happiness to think that she came here at last, and her tour was an outstanding success.

*end

5.2. A family wedding in the House of Lords May 1997.

A morning down memory lane

Polly was ever so welcoming at 5 Grafton Square at 10.00 am. In minutes we are off on a jolly for two hours - destination Westminster Abbey, wedding church of us both, now cleaned up and sparkling white. We have a lovely walk thru London, past Smith Square. (Tory Central Office) and then into Westminster Abbey, past the lines and lines of Prime ministers, and poets and kings and queens eventually to Henry VII's chapel ablaze with the very colourful banners of the knights of the Bath, and vast new stained glass window donated by Canadian, Templeton and put up by Harry Cardross' firm of stain glass makers. This was our wedding chapel, in memory, dark and rather forbidding with Henry VII's tomb taking up a lot of space, now bright and sparkling. We found the coat of arms of Dean Abbott who married both Polly and Paul and me and Susan. The abbey was very busy and a guide lady priest stopped the moving throng with some well articulated intercessions, yes, a lady priest has got on the staff of

Westminster Abbey. It was all rather a rush but we soon got back to Grafton Square, time for a quick change, delicious lunch in the garden, and off to the wedding.

The marriage service at The Chapel of St. Mary Undercroft

The entrance in the Palace of Westminster was via St. Stephen's entrance, down some stairs, past the great Hall in Westminster, famous for the trial of Charles I, and then down under to the chapel of the Palace of Westminster. There to our delight both families were gathering for Mony Erskine's marriage to Rachel Prior. This was a very ornate chapel, low roof, but lots of gold engravings around the religious pieces, and soon one could spot the leading family figures, but the bride's side had not one bride's mother's hat, but over half a dozen. Every lady seemed to wish on themselves the honour of being Rachel's Mother. In the pew in front of me are the Bristol ladies Mum and Sophie and Pollyanna, all looking their very best and smiles all round. Sophie has an exhibition of her works in just a few weeks and is full of beans. Current fashion is very short dresses and the Bristol ladies are very much following fashion on wedding day. Lovely Rachel comes down the aisle on Father's arm and immediately she is passed to Monty, he picks up her veil and tosses it back to reveal the sparkle in her eyes. No, he certainly, was not going to marry the wrong bride. The choir of St. Margaret's Westminster was at the back of the church and gave its all for beauty and dignity in this marriage ceremony. Rachel had two small bridesmaids, one was Monty's niece, Seraphina's little girl, the other a Prior relation, both about 4 years old. The service was beautifully constructed. Rachel enters to 'Crown Imperial'. Her two friends did the readings, the first a passage from the song of Soloman, the second about loving your neighbour. There were three hymns, a psalm, an address, two anthems of love, and a final exit of the bride to a resounding trumpet tune. It would have lifted the roof off a normal church, but it would have been pushing it to lift off this chapel roof with three stories of the House of Lords above.

The reception - finding my hat in the Bishop's Bar

The reception was in the Peer's dining room. It is a real pleasure and excitement to get there through the long corridors of the House of Lords with all those super portraits of the major figures of history and events of the past, for instance, the Lords debate of the bill for home rule for Ireland. Anyway my glengarry is hung up on a peg in a side room. Stupidly, I forget to check the name of this room and 2 hours later I am slightly non-plussed in trying to retrieve it. Goodness me this room turned out to be "The Bishop's Bar"'. My free church friends in Stornaway would have had a fit to even contemplate the bishops of England getting tidley all on their own in the Palace of Westminster! Susan loved this part of my account. "I suppose you were tidly too looking for your hat. It must have taken you hours to find it." Needless to say the reception was a great family occasion. Malcolm and Hilary looked wonderful, so pleased to have their last child married off. I chatted to Malcolm about my Blair initiative and he suggested that I progress it thru Mr Peter Mandelson, minister without portfolio, MP for Hartlepool, Blair's chief election campaign strategist, the man for progressing an intervention. All the speeches were very short. The bride's brother was delighted to be the one brother selected to toast his sister the bride. I much enjoyed meeting Monty's army and Edinburgh University friends. He is such a charming young man, so very popular with his friends. The Scottish relations rallied to me in the kilt and I met a delightful couple from the Isle of Skye, MacDonalds. Also Arabella Erskine and her new husband.

Getting mobbed by the tourists

After the reception Lucy and I had an awful job getting a taxi outside the Palace of Westminster. We walked half way down Parliament Street but no luck, and all the tourists kept mobbing us both for photographs. Lucy looked a peach in resplendent red outfit, (the christening suit), and the biggest red hat you have ever seen. Any horse at Ascot seeing such a hat in the crowd would immediately gee itself up to win the gold cup. I think the tourists also loved the kilt and the sporran and the cappercailzie feathers on the glengarry! Anyway we retreated and returned to Polly's via the underground and got rather mixed up with football supporters returning from their winning Chelsea match.

*End

Chapter 6 - Biography and book reviews

There are six newsletters in this section relating with biography. The first two concern the author's father, General Sir George Erskine, GCB, KBE, DSO. The profile is developed from family documents, and covers his career and achievements. To the author he was an outstanding hero, knighted 4 times, decorated in the field at the battle of el Alamein, and with an impressive set of post second world war appointments. A bundle of 6 letters written immediately after the battle of Tunis to the author's Mother are also included. They carry the spirit of the allied victory; 30,000 allied troops took 150,000 axis prisoners; this was the turning point of the second world war.

The biography newsletters continue with reviews of other author's works, and are selected for the interest of the character, and usually read as part of a university research programme. Pamela Digby Churchill was a sister-in-law of the author's cousin, Lady Digby, and grew abundantly in talents throughout her life, finally sponsoring the candidature of President Clinton. This newsletter is used in university to form the basis of discussion of management development issues.

The review of the 'House of Thomas' was an analysis of the founding de la Rue family. Robert Erskine is a grandson of Sir Evelyn de la Rue, and was curious about the circumstances in which the family lost control of this public company. This newsletter is used in university as the basis of discussion of life cycle issues of companies.

The review of the Carpenter Biography of Archbishop Runcie was triggered after Robert Erskine had completed an academic investigation into the property gambling of the Church Commissioners and found that they had underperformed by £5 billion.

The review by Helga Drummond into 'escalation' was triggered by Robert Erskine's curiosity into how £400 million could go down the plughole in the Stock Exchange computer project, 'Taurus', for getting electronic settlement.

6.1. General Erskine Profile of General Sir George Erskine, G.C.B., K.B.E., D.S.O. 1899 - 1965 (Father of Robert Erskine)

This is an edited collection of material from family archives of the military life of General Erskine beginning with experiences in the trenches in the first world war and with his ending as a figure with four knighthoods and achievements in military, political, diplomatic fields. The story is interwoven with the incidents from family folklore. The main sources were extracted from Major Philip Erskine's collection of family archives which Robert had access to in August 1996 on his trip to South Africa. Early in the year Robert had circulated some of his father's letters written in the period immediately after the fall of Tunis by his division the Desert Rats. 30,000 allied forces accepted the surrender of 150,000 axis forces. These letters were very enthusiastically received, so this is Robert's next attempt to get into the Box Office of General Erskine memorabilia.

First world war in the trenches

From Sandhurst Erskine was gazetted into the 60th Rifles, K.R.R.C. and he went straight into the trenches on the Western Front in March 1918, in the height of the last German offensive. He survived, many didn't, but he was soon a victim of the 'flu epidemic that took more lives than the combined offensives, and was evacuated home to recover. He was always known in the army as Bobby Erskine; latterly he was called General Bobby.

Service in Germany and Ireland and India

As a young officer he served in Germany immediately after the armistice at Cologne, then in the troubled provinces of Ireland, which he always said was most unpleasant, and irksome, never knowing who was one's enemy and being shot from any direction. He served in India, on and off for 12 years between the wars and said that he thoroughly enjoyed this sort of Regimental soldiering, being Adjutant or having his own Company. There were polo tournaments, which on a very limited income was possible. The 60th Rifles were a very closely knit regiment and almost like an enlarged family. He was devoted to his Regiment and he had many dear friends.

Staff College and marriage - India

He returned to the Rifle Depot at Winchester, partly to prepare for the Staff College and to be training officer at the depot. It was during this period of his life that he met Ruby de la Rue in 1928. They were married in 1930. Ruby was the eldest daughter of Sir Evelyn de la Rue, a former Chairman of the de la Rue Company. Apart from bringing him into a huge new family their marriage gave him some financial stability which hitherto did not exist. After two years at the Staff College 1929/1930 Erskine was given a grade III staff job in Rawalpindi, in India and he remained in India until 1937 and then he returned to his Regiment and commanded a company, also in India and then went to Burma.

Brevit Colonel at 38 in the London Division

He was made Assistant Quartermaster General at Houndslow in 1937 and for four years the family lived at 10 Thurloe Square. He was promoted to Brevet Lt. Colonel at 38, the youngest in the army and was given a grade I staff job, GSOI of the London Division. This was an important administrative position as he was the senior regular officer in the London Territorial Division, and he had the responsibility of preparing this division for the developing crisis, and he took the division on the outbreak of war to the South coast as England's first line of defence against invasion.

War Service

Raising the Regiment

The family moved first to Eastbourne and then to Charing in Kent. By May 1940 the fall of France had changed the situation, with the loss of so many regiments at Dunkirk and Calais. Erskine was then charged with the task of raising a new battalion of his regiment at Tidworth.

Promoted to Brigadier and off to the Middle East

Within a year he was promoted to Brigadier and given the command of a brigade, and in May 1941 he embarked for the Middle East, from Basra in Persia to the defence of Cyprus after the fall of Greece and then to the Western Desert as Brigadier General Staff 3 Corps. He took part in several of the advances and retreats of the 8th Army.

Decorated at Alamein

He was awarded the D.S.O. for his part in the first battle of Alamein, generally called the Battle of Alam Halfa. He was BGS to 13 Corps after the second Battle of Alamein and for a period of several months was acting Chief of Staff to General Montgomery.

Major General Erskine greets King George VI 1943

Commander of the Desert Rats

After the capture of Tripoli he was given the command of the 7th Armoured Division, the Desert Rats. He was described as a brilliant armoured divisional commander and the reputation of the division was a household word. One battle which he master minded, Medinine, General Montgomery has written 'it was the most perfect and classic tank battle fought during the whole war'. The Desert Rats captured Tunis. 30,000 allied forces accepted the surrender of 150,000 axis forces. Rommel had been soundly beaten. Erskine led the division in the Salerno landings and this was followed by the capture of Naples. He fought with the division up to the Volturno Rover in Italy and then was withdrawn to England to prepare for the Normandy invasion.

He was awarded a C.B. (Commander of the Bath), for his part in the German surrender in North Africa. He landed on D Day + 3. His old division was a shadow of its former self; many of the key personalities had been given to other divisions to bolster up some weak teams; many had left for a variety of other reasons, and it was generally thought that the division disappointed expectations in Normandy. The old veteran tank crews were thought to be over cautious in the close boakage country of Normandy. Progress was too slow for the super charged nerves of the senior commanders, and in mid August Erskine was relieved of his command. He was extremely tired. The division deeply resented losing its commander, but Montgomery needed a totally reckless commander who could force a break out disregarding losses, and the consequences. Many commanders who are relieved of command in battle never have another command. It speaks highly of his reputation that his career was not affected, and he continued to serve in the army till 1958.

Reporting to General Eisenhower

In September 1944 he was appointed Head of the Allied Mission (SHAFE) in Belgium and Luxembourg, and was virtually military governor of these two countries till June 1945. This was a political appointment requiring a whole new set of skills not only heading a joint British and American team, but also trying to re-start every aspect of civil administration, to disarm the resistance, re-establish the Police Forces and the Army, encourage industry and business to start again, and not least to handle a highly sensitive political situation of a divided and humiliated country and the king refusing to return and the country split on every aspect on his return. Erskine's measure of success can be judged by the fact that of all the occupied countries Belgium made the quickest recovery. The period was not without its difficulties, as during the winter of 1944 the Germans launched their last great offensive through the Ardenne, and their initial success caused panic in many parts of the country. Wiley Erskine had a strong political instinct. When the resistance leaders demanded the right to march through Brussels and establish their case to assume the role of government he joined them the evening before the big parade and celebrated with such verve and whisky that the leaders became paralytic. Next day without leadership the parade quickly disintegrated much to the relief of the provisional government.

Awards galore from Belgium and the United States

Erskine was awarded Grand Cross of the Order of Leopold. His appointment had required diplomatic and political talents of the highest order, and his contribution as one Belgian was to relate, was part of our history. It was during this period that he became friendly with General Eisenhower, who was his immediate superior. He was awarded the USA 'Order of Merit' by Eisenhower.

The Orders and Medals of General Sir George Erskine, G.C.B., K.B.E., D.S.O.

1. Knight Grand Cross of the Order of the Bath.
2. Knight Commander of the order of the British Empire
3. Knight Commander of the Order of St. John of Jerusalem.
4. Knight Grand Cross of the Order of Leopold, (Belgian).
5. Commander of the Order of the Oak Leaf. (Luxembourg).
6. The Congressional Order of Merit. (USA).

The medals from left to right:-

D.S.O., Two first war medals, known as Mut and Jef. Four campaign stars, including Home defence, North Africa with an 8th Army bar, Italy and North West Europe. Two defence medals with a mention in dispatchleaf. East Africa medal (mau mau). Queen's Coronation medal. Medal Militaire (Belgian).

They kept in touch and Erskine visited Eisenhower when he became President of the United States. Lady Erskine, as a widow, was an official Government guest at President Eisenhower's funeral.

A copy of the citation follows:

CITATION FOR LEGION OF MERIT - DECREE OF COMMANDER TO:

MAJOR GENERAL GEORGE WATKIN E.J. ERSKINE, BRITISH ARMY

"For exceptionally meritorious conduct in the performance of outstanding services as Head of the Supreme Headquarters, Allied Expeditionary Force, Mission (Belgium) from 12th September 1944 to 30th June 1945. General Erskine was primarily responsible for the close and friendly relationship that existed between the Belgian Government and the Allied Expeditionary Force. Many delicate problems which would have adversely affected the allied military effort were effectively solved by his tact, understanding, foresight and energetic leadership. The great confidence and respect which he commanded as a result of his brilliant leadership and strength of purpose enabled him to influence affairs favourably to the Allied cause. The distinguished service which General Erskine rendered has been of such an outstanding character as to have been of inestimable value to the military and diplomatic effort and has reflected great credit on both the American and British Forces."

Writing the Constitution of post war Germany

In June 1945 Erskine was given command of the 43rd Division at Celle in Hanover and after a short period he was appointed to be Deputy Chief of

Staff of the Control Commission in Berlin. His skills as diplomat, politician, and soldier were tested once more, and it was a highly interesting and exacting work at this level while close contact was maintained between the Americans, British, French and Russians when many of the decisions on post war Germany were made including her constitution. He established a friendship with Sir Robert Birley, Headmaster of Charterhouse, seconded to the Control Commission, to make a blueprint for primary and secondary education in post war Germany. When the family joined Erskine in 1946 in Berlin they travelled in a special coach - Goebles' coach. What fun the family had in Goebles' bath and using his inter-com telephones in the different compartments. The train stopped en route to Berlin at Brussels and the family were summoned to meet with the Regent, Prince Charles. They were given tea and then played ping pong. The Regent swiped the ball hard and it hit Mrs Erskine in the eye. Prince Charles was ever so courteous and apologetic, a prince charming if ever there was one.

Erskine's post war career

Director General of the Territorial Army

Erskine always rejoiced that he had not been promoted to the dizzy heights of 'Corps Commander' in the second world war with a rank of Lieutennant General, as after the war he would probably have been retired. But there were still plenty of appointments available for a 46 year old Major General. At the end of 1946 Erskine was appointed Director General of the Territorial Army. It was at a time when the British Labour Government wanted to re-establish the Territorial army in the face of considerable opposition. His work brought him into close contact with the Labour leaders and especially Mr. Shinwell.

GOC Hong Kong

18 months later he was sent to Hong Kong as General Officer Commanding. He held this appointment during a very unsettled period when there was great anxiety over the Communist takeover in China.

GOC British Troops in Egypt

Article printed in the Strand Magazine

(Vol 116, issue 697 1949)

'Erskine the Uncommon Man'

'"Mental robustness", Lord Wavell declared in his wise essays on Generalship, "is the first attribute of a good general." There in a phrase, is the quality of Lieut-General G.W.E.J. Erskine, C.B., D.S.O., who headed the Territorial Army drive, and has now been appointed G.O.C. British Troops, Egypt and the Mediterranean Command. (He was a Major-General when our drawing was made.) He looks robust. An ample frame carries strong features, curly blond hair, clipped moustache, and a sometimes ferocious eye. Not a man, one would say, lightly to slap on the back ... In reality, less formidable: a friendly man of tact, with gentle manners, a rich voice, and a humorous mouth. Given the choice of four Christian names - George, Watkin, Eben, James - his friends invented another and call him Bobby .... In 1940 he left a staff job to rebuild the second battalion of his Regiment, the 60th, lost at Calais. Read the citation to his D.S.O. won as Brigadier General Staff to XIII Corp at Alamein. "For the complete success of the operation", said his Corps Commander, "Erskine was a tower of strength, throughout the battle, and remained quite unmoved during the frequent shelling and Stuka attacks". He took over the 7th Armoured Division, the "Desert Rats", and cracked them through to Tunis, on to the Salerno beaches; and in mid 1944 - he led them in the first outbreak from the week-old Normandy bridgehead. ... He switched, imperturbably, from soldiering to diplomacy. As British head of the Shaef Military Mission in Brussels he remained cool in the more disturbing atmosphere of champagne and celebration which surrounded Brussels' early days of freedom. He handled politicians, disarmed the Resistance, gained a new reputation for administration, which made him, for a time General Robertson's number 2 in Berlin.'"

In 1949 he was appointed to command the British Troops in the Canal Zone of Egypt. It was initially a very enjoyable peacetime appointment. There were ceremonial and social events and scope for interesting military training and tattoos. There were annual visits to Cairo and to other more remote parts of his command. Transjordan and Libya were linked by defence treaty with the British. He maintained respectful contact with the Egyptian Government and visited and shot duck with King Farouk. In October 1951 the Egyptian Government abrogated the 1936 Anglo Egyptian Treaty and there followed a period of tension and terrorism. Under Erskine's leadership the pressures failed and the Egyptians were forced to make a reasonable settlement, (which was later cancelled after the 1956 Suez debacle). A newspaper at the time ran a headline 'This is the General who gets beautifully angry'. "Erskine says we will not be kicked out, pushed out or shoved out of Egypt". The Egyptian Government put a reward of £1,000 to anyone who could bring Erskine to book. He immediately garrisioned the key bridge over the Suez Canal to control supplies getting to the Egyptian army on manoevres in Sinai. His soldiers took charge of the water supplies for the town of Suez. Erskine had his finger on the windpipe of the Egyptian Army and a major city. The Egyptians soon found that terrorist activity against tactical Erskine was a demoralising 'no hoper' cause. They appealed to the British House of Commons for intervention by Labour MPs against his strong tactics and the British Embassy sent a diplomat, Hamilton, down from Cairo to 'steady him down'. "Hamilton was white with fear and trepidation at what Erskine would do next and the possible political consequences. But Erskine, who had dispatched Rommel with such panache, merely said that he would control the water supply of Port Said too, if terrorist acts continued"! His leadership in times of crisis was of a very high order, and ensured the total failure of the Egyptian war of attrition to remove the army from the Canal Zone. He was made Knight Commander of the British Empire, (KBE), and promoted to the rank of 'Lieutennant General'. and later made Knight Commander of the Bath, (KCB). However, as usual in times of conflict Erskine became a close friend of Hamilton, and was persuaded by him to send his son, Robert, to King's College, Cambridge, the College of Hamilton, and many other distinguised diplomats, the first prime minister, Sir Robert Walpole, and the world economist John Maynard Keynes. A year later General and son were on the Backs of Cambridge, and Robert had set his sights on passing the King's College entry examination.

First knighthood - what to call knighted Erskine?

(Poem written by Mrs Miller with addition from Eileen White.)

When at the font the parson mild
Asked Godmama to "name this child".
She answered with a string of names,
George, Watkin, Eben, James.
*
The child grew up became a man,
Who didn't stick to Godmama's plan.
Thinking to make a better job,
He always answered just to Bobbie.
*
And now the Sovereign as is right,
Decides today to dub him knight.
But which to choose of all the names,
Sir George? Sir Watkin? Eben? James?
*
Despite official Christenings,
Gazettes and patents and such things,
By all the common soldier mob, he,
Will be known as Bold Sir Bobbie.
*
(A message arrived on the nursery table from Ruby Erskine, what is nanny's answer?)
*
Eileen
*
"As to the quandary I find you in,
I'm sure you'll call him 'Bold Sir Bruin'.
*
(Husband and wife pet names for one another were Puss and Bruin).

Hosting politicians

From time to time Erskine would host his political masters when they visited his command. While he was in Egypt he entertained Michael Stewart, the Minister of War. In the evening he introduced the minister to his secret weapon, his chess playing son, Robert. Minister and teenager set up a board for battle, and in 15 minutes flat the Minister for War was checkmated by the teenager. Doubtless to say the general teased the minister and won through this a psychological battle. There is usually some rivalry between soldiers and politicians! Erskine thought that when on home ground he should always win.

GOC Eastern Command

On return to England Erskine was appointed to Eastern Command, following General Templer. The family had a happy year at Walton-on-Thames and in 1953, Coronation Year, Eastern Command acted as host to the many thousands of Empire and Commonwealth troops who came to London and required accommodation. Erskine rode with other generals in the Coronation Procession.

Churchill's briefing for Commander in Chief East Africa.

Three days before the Coronation the Prime Minister sent for Erskine and told him he wanted him to go as soon as possible to Kenya, where the internal security situation was getting out of control due to the activities of Mau Mau. Erskine, a wily tactician, having been primed by the War Office, had prepared carefully for his meeting with the Prime Minister. He had thought about the situation in Kenya and what needed to be done and he was determined to be given terms of reference which were suitable, so he drafted his own. He was ushered into Churchill's briefing room and biden to sit down on a large sofa. "Erskine, do you have any bad habits"? "No Sir". "Well I am going to corrupt you". Winston reaches under the sofa and pulls out a large bottle of whisky and two glasses. The briefing proceeds. Erskine, "Prime Minister, I have drafted terms of reference for the defeat of Mau Mau. I do not want to assume the powers of a Colonial Governor as the first phase of this job is to get an operational victory against the Mau Mau, and I need a unified command of troops and civilian police. Apart from having the police under my command I do not wish to erode any authority from the Governor". Churchill glances at the notes, takes a deep gulp of Johnny Walker, signs them without quibble and says "I have always respected a general who knew exactly what he wanted to do and the resources required to do it. Good luck."

Recovery of law and order

This appointment was the climax of Erskine's career. He was now promoted to the rank of full General. He had direct access to the Prime Minister, and faced formidable problems. The army had been making no progress against Mau Mau; Sir Evelyn Baring, Governor, had assumed power after a damaging 3 months of vacancy in Governorship. The local white settler population was hostile and un-cooperative; the colonial administration had been ineffective for too long; the native population was ripe for revolution; the local police force was totally inadequate and badly led; the British Government wanted a quick solution. Kenya was in chaos. Erskine treated his task as an operational one. He set up a compact Headquarters, and lived in a small house in Mathanga, on the outskirts of Nairobi, which he used as an officer's mess. Apart from two ADCs, he had Peter (Gllette later a Major General), as his Military Assistant and Michael Carver, as his Deputy Chief of Staff, (later chief of the Defence staff, Field Marshall Lord Carver). Erskine found that there was no strategic planning in Kenya, nor any concept as to how to deal with a deteriorating situation.

Third knighthood G.C.B.

When he handed over command two years later Mau Mau was a defeated threat and confined only to remote mountain areas, which would take another two years before the last few terrorists could be hunted down. He had to use every talent to persuade and convince the settler population to co-operate. He had developed a general military strategy which was highly successful, which welded together all the regular and local forces, military and police, into the general plan. The terms of reference signed by Churchill were decisive in an initial brush with the governor, Sir Evelyn Baring, over who had jurisdiction over the police. Erskine was awarded the

Knight Grand Commander of the Bath for a highly successful tour of duty.

Queen's representative in Jersey - a fourth order of knighthood.

From 1955 till 1958 Erskine was Commander in Chief Southern Command at Salisbury. He was then then the senior General in the British Army. This was followed by 5 years as Lieutenant Governor of Jersey in the Channel Islands. The last appointment was supposed to be a reward for a lifetime of service to the Crown, but even this one had an awkward beginning. Erskine's predecessor had rowed with the Bailiff of Jersey and recommended to the Home Secretary that the office of Bailiff be abolished. The Bailiff, Sir Alexander Coutanche, veteran Bailiff from war occupied Jersey, had recommended also to the Home Secretary that the office of Lieutenant Governor be abolished, so that was a potential wasps nest to fall into! However, Erskine, on hearing of his appointment, invited Sir Alexander to stay and dine with him at Southern Command. Coutanche brought two gifts. One was an official Jersey seal from King Edward I and the second was the seal of a former Lieutenant Governor, Sir Walter Raleigh. The two leaders immediately established a sound rapport with one another, and that paved the way for a very happy and enjoyable 5 years in Jersey. Coutanche eventually retired and was ennobled as Lord Coutanche. There were two Royal visits during those years, the first from Princess Margaret. On leaving Government House she presented the family with a signed portrait taken by her favourite photographer, Anthony Armstrong Jones. The second visit was by Queen Elizabeth the Queen Mother and her last evening she held a large dinner party on board Britannia for her Jersey hosts. Erskine was given his fourth knighthood, Knight of St. John of Jerusalem.

A short retiral

After Jersey Erskine and family returned to their small farm in Somerset in 1963, but ill health was already beginning to limit his activity, and within a few months cancer was diagnosed and he died in August 1965 in his Somerset home. At the funeral in Horsington Parish Church there were over 120 wreaths and a church packed. His widow, Lady Erskine, refused to see this as a sad day but one of thanksgiving for the life of a hero. She ordered that the flags be put up at full mast, such was her defiance at his death. A month later there was a large memorial service for him in Westminster Abbey. Many of his friends and colleagues from his many and varied appointments attended a most impressive service, next to the Chapel where the banners of Knights of the Bath were hung. Sadly, he never lived long enough for his own banner to be hung in the Chapel. The Queen sent her representative to this service. The band of the Royal Greenjackets were in attendance in the Abbey and with a full choir and to the sound of the Regimental buglers, whose predecessors had rallied the British army at the battle of Waterloo, the roof of the Abbey was nearly lifted off.

Devotion to friends and Regiment

General Bobby Erskine was devoted to his Regiment, 60th Rifles and was Colonel Commandant for 12 years. He was largely responsible for the larger Regimental concept in the British army into Divisional groupings of the infantry. He had served as a subaltern with Anthony Eden in the trenches in the first wold war, and kept up this friendship for the rest of his life. Anthony Eden, ennobled as Lord Avon in 1957, and then as ex-premier, visited Erskine at Southern Command with his wife 2 years after Suez. Amazingly, the Suez Canal seemed to run down the middle of the drawing room of the Erskine home, Bulford Manor. A huge bitterness was still apparent at the luke warm support of Dulles, the US Secretary of State, leading to the withdrawal of Britain's forces from the Canal. Eden looked to a brother officer for a sympathetic ear to unburden his sense of frustration.

Hobbies and interests

In retirement Erskine became an enthusiastic gardener, adored his roses and fruit trees and reorganised the garden at Government House in Jersey. He also loved poultry and guinea fowl and loved hearing them screech when visitors came to sign the book. They screeched at Queen Elizabeth the Queen Mother, much to her own amusement, when she did her Royal visit to Jersey. Erskine was an avid reader of the 'Poultry World' and back numbers would be stacked in his official interview room at Government House. He took great interest in education, having been fired up by his friend Birley in Berlin, and was a governor of Millfield School in Somerset.

Local Government and business

He served on the local rural district council for two years. He was Vice Chairman of Securicor for seven years. He was an admirer of kinsman, Keith Erskine, Securicor's founder.

Erskine in the family

He was utterly devoted to his wife and family and he had a very wide circle of friends, from taxi drivers to Dukes. At Christmas time in Jersey he hung his cards on strings on a wall in the entrance hall. There were at least a 1,000, which was a very colourful sight. He was a man of great warmth and stability, yet he was humble never wishing to take any credit for himself only for those with whom he worked. He never wrote memoirs as he was sure that they would cause conflict. His papers are all lodged with the Imperial War Museum and open for public inspection. As a father he was a major figure of encouragement to his children believing soundly in the principle of playing to their strengths. Philip, the eldest, willingly followed his father's footsteps and went to Sandhurst after leaving school. Robert, his second son, never showed much enthusiasm for the army. When he was in Hong Kong he made friends of naval officers and persuaded them to take him on operations in a submarine, which meant missing two days of school. The General was invited to go on the flagship with the Admiral and it was only then that it was revealed that junior was also on exercise in a submarine! Anyway Robert secured a place at King's College Cambridge, and his Father supported this education, knowing that the son was destined for a career in industry after 2 years of National Service in the 60th Rifles and university. Polly, the youngest in the family, nearly found herself enrolled in the army too, but quickly assured her Father that she wanted to specialise in a girl's thing, interior decorating, and was encouraged to follow that path.

Winning the Peace and building Commonwealth

General Erskine holds a position in post 2nd world war history as one of the military figures who through his competence as a military commander combined with his skill as a diplomat / statesman was able to control the fires of nationalism that were sweeping the old empire. By successfully controlling and succeeding in his missions in Belgium and Luxemburg he helped the Allies to win the Peace, and in his missions in Egypt and Kenya helped to nudge Her Majesty's Government in the tortuous process of converting the

Empire as it was in 1945 into the Commonwealth of the 1960s.

*End

6.2. Tunis letters

Fall of Tunis - 6 letters of General (Bobbie) Erskine to his wife 8th May 1943 - 13th May 1943.

Preamble on a first hand account

Presented by Robert Erskine

My sister, Polly, recently send me these 6 letters from my Father to my Mother after the fall of Tunis in May 1943. They really do make rather interesting war reading. Tunis was the final battle of the African campaign and over 150,000 Germans and Italians surrendered. Father had commanded the 7th armoured division from January 1943, taking over from General Harding. In the final battle 7th armoured was attached to the American 1st army, but led the assault on Tunis. I cannot help smile at Father's aspirations to get round Monty for leave to tour the Mother's Unions to tell them about the great victory! Tunis was the Erskine battle of the second world war and General Bobbie, as he was known, was decorated C.B.

The strategic position of Britain in the Middle East

Britain's strategic position in the Middle East was dependant on securing victory in North Africa. If we had lost the battles of the desert we could not have supported India and the Far East. Italy initially was our adversary, as Italians had colonised Libya in the 1930s. In the early periods of the war the British laid havoc with the Italian army, but when it was reinforced by the Germans with the desert fox Rommell they sent the Brits packing back to El Alamein, only a few miles West of Alexandria. Montgomery was sent to command the 8th Army and then sent Rommell on the run.

Churchill said that El Alamein was the turning point of the war. "Before Alamein Britain had seen no victory. After Alamein Britain saw no defeat"

First Letter 8th May 1943 7th Armoured Division

M.E.F.

My Darling Puss,

My letters have been very few and I have been unable to tell you anything because we have been making various moves and plans for the capture of Tunis. Now that we have done it security does not matter and I can tell you something of this phase of operations.

Tactics for the taking of Tunis

It was clear that the easiest way to Tunis was from the S.W. We had pushed the enemy as far back as we could into the hills opposite us, as the hills were very considerable obstacles. On the S.W. of Tunis the country was much more favourable for my tanks and although the enemy was holding a fairly strong position it was in every way more favourable country. So I moved over from the 8th Army to the 1st Army. The decisions were taken very quickly. I had my orders at 11.00 am and was on the move at 3.pm with my leading people who arrive in their new area (170 mile journey) by 10.00 am next morning. The rest followed on and in a very short time we were all complete in a new area and under a new army. There was very little time to prepare the plan of battle and get to know the country or the new people with whom I found myself working. But there was just enough time working at top pressure and doing about ten things at once.

The plan was a very simple one, and in fact it had to be, as there was no hope of carrying out anything complicated in the time available. A very heavy infantry attack was launched supported by about 400 guns on a front of about 2 miles. When this attack had finished, whether it was successful or not I had to go straight through to Tunis with another armoured division on my right doing exactly the same. We started about 25 miles from Tunis as the crow flies. Nothing could be more simple. We did not know a great deal about the enemy's positions - how they were held or how much they had mined themselves in - we thought the going would be fairly good at this time of year, but I was not at all sure I was not going to meet uncrossable wadis and obstacles. Everything went absolutely according to plan. The infantry attack was terrific and the Germans got up and ran as the shells rained down on them.

Sweeping into Tunis after 36 hour advance

I was lined up on two tanks pretty nearly head to tail for 25 miles on each track, with my head ready to go through at 7.00 am on the 6th May. We went and swept everything in front of us - fairly slowly to start with and then gathering speed. By 3.00 pm yesterday 7th May, I had my leading armoured car in the centre of Tunis - 36 hours after the battle had started. By the evening we had a close grip on Tunis and were virtually in possession of the whole place. This morning we have been rounding up prisoners in thousands and all organised resistance has completely packed up. It was a thrilling 36 hours and I will write separately describing other parts of the battle in detail while events are fresh in my mind. I am terribly pleased that this division that started at El Alamein and has pursued the Germans ever since, was the first into Tunis. The troops are in terrific form.

All my love darling, your devoted, Bobby.

Second Letter 8th May 1943 7th Armoured Division, M.E.F.

My Darling Puss,

The softening up bombarment

I have written to you separately giving you a general account of the battle, but I thought a few other notes might interest you. On the evening of the 5th May we were all driven in our right places for the morning. I spent the night sleeping outside my tank which was almost in the infantry front line. At 11.00 pm we bombarded the German positions we were not going to attack till 3.00 pm, then we bombarded the ones we were going to attack. It was the most intensive bombardment I have ever seen. As I was in between the guns and there the shells were landing you can imagine the din. This Pandemonium went on till about 7.00 am when we started to move forward. The R.A.F. joined in with terrific bombing from 5.30 am. My chaps were splendid. They were quite determined to be in Tunis first and also determined to show the 1st Army the way. On we went steadily over the cornfield driving right across it on about a 3 or 4 mile front treating it just as if it were open desert. It paid us everytime as we must have looked a most formidable force to Germans.

Collecting ourselves before the final push

By nightfall on the 6th I had got all the objectives I had expected and there had not been a hitch. It was tempting to go on even further the first day, but I thought it would be better to collect ourselves for a really long day on the 7th, so I steadied down about 2 hours before dark and got properly collected. This was very necessary as we had passed in single file through two narrow tracks and the immense amount of transport I have takes a lot of sorting out. The next morning we were off again with most of the people fresh after a bit of a night's rest. We started at 5.00 am and went straight ahead. We knocked the Germans terribly hard and they ran in all directions leaving burning tanks, lorries and guns all over the country. I have never seen such a sight. It was not very fast but it was absolutely relentless. By 10.30 am I was on a very commanding hill overlooking Tunis. I then brought up my tail behind me as we were miles outwith the middle of the German Army by then and I wanted to be ready for any counter attack, which I thought was bound to come. We got ready for the German dash into Tunis then only about 7 miles away. I sent my armoured cars (11th Hussars) on first and they nosed their way round and into the town. My first armoured car was in the centre of Tunis by 3.00 pm. We then dashed in to cut the North side with my tanks and I sent in an infantry battalion in case there was any street fighting. We completely surprised the Germans and the whole thing was then in complete confusion.

Combat with guns and garlands of flowers in Tunis

The boy in the 11th Hussars who first arrived in Tunis was most amusing about it. He found Germans walking about the street and completely taken unawares. When they saw him they rubbed their eyes - turned quite white bolted in all directions. The population went quite mad and threw flowers at him and half the population climbed on his car. In the middle of all this the Germans started to throw hand grenades and shoot at him. A proper party. The next twelve hours were taken up with a battle of flowers and rounding up the local Germans some of whom indulged in street fighting. This morning I drove round Tunis in my tank. I have never seen such hysterical enthusiasm. We were deluged in flowers. Everyone seemed completely mad. This was the end of the German rout which could not have been more complete and absolute.

Your loving, Bobby

Third Letter 8th May 1943 7th Armoured Division, M.E.F.

My Darling Puss,

6 months of winning battles

I have written you two letters today describing our recent battle which may amuse you. I don't see how much of his army can get away now. The prisoners are countless - there are several thousands walking past me now in sight of my caravan and stretching miles and miles away down the road out of sight. Some may and try and hide themselves in the countryside, but they have little chance of getting back to Italy or Germany. I am sure the Royal Navy and the R.A.F. will see to that. It is rather wonderful to have reached Tunis after this long, hard struggle across Africa. It has taken me exactly 6 months. On 7th November we started the pursuit from El Alamein and on 7th May we captured Tunis. The only division who had been all the way, Matruh, Tobruck, Benghazi, El Ageila, Wadi Chebia, Tripoli, Medenine, Mareth, Wadi Akait, Sfax and finally Tunis. Three quarters of the time and about half the distance I have led the Division. We have never gone a step back, and we have gone a good many steps forward.

8th and 1st Armies combined for victory

My casualties have not been heavy and although my chaps are damned tired they are all the better for such a wonderful experience. Their morale and confidence has to be seen to be believed. I have indeed been lucky. We thought this 1st army we are now with was very inexperienced. They acted just like you do on manoeuvres at home - all very tidy and clean and polite. We are just so untidy you can hardly believe it but we do get on with the job. These other chaps just don't know what it is to get a move on and all the things which seem to me to be automatic are a business for them. But the 1st Army (from the USA) is a fine army and it is only because of their lack of experience we think them slow. We have become so accustomed to moving every day and great distances that is no problem. We never have a telephone and live entirely on the wireless. They don't at present start to know how to use their wireless properly. It is all so interesting comparing the two and I do so in my own mind out of interest and not for the purpose of making an invidious comparison.

I would like to have seen Monty entering Tunis, he would have done it so wonderfully. I have met Anderson several times. I should say that he is a first class General and I am very glad that he will get the credit for this last show. This success will also do the whole of the 1st Army good. They wanted a really big success to give them self confidence.

The general wants some leave

I really think they might give me some leave now! I shall tell them I could give some very good lectures in England. I would visit every mother's union and my lecture tour would take a very long time!

Blessings and love my precious darling,

Your devoted, Bobbie

Fourth Letter 9th May 1943 7th Armoured Division, M.E.F.

My Darling Puss,

Prisoners galore and the spoils of war.

Today has been rather like the mad hatter's tea party. I went round this morning to count the spoil. I found that we had taken over 7,000 prisoners yesterday - another 10,000 by mid-day plus 30,000 which I could not bring in and handed over to the Americans. This included old Borovitch, who commands 15th Armoured Division, and I am sorry that I could not have seen him to kick him in the pants myself! The stores which we have captured are conservatively estimated at being worth £100 million! It includes 100 new aeroplanes, complete tank base workshops, all the German photographic aeroplane equipment, two complete field hospitals, so many guns and so much transport that it cannot be collected. Huge stores of supplies of every kind, almost everybody is out collecting prisoners, who seem to be only too thankful to give themselves up. The roads are a crawling mass of men utterly defeated. It is an astonishing sight to see 10 miles of road solid with prisoners marching along to cages and to know that this is only a fraction of what is to come along behind them.

Revenge for Dunkirk

We have killed a great many. My chaps are quite relentless and are on the look out for opportunities. We found a place where they were embarking in rafts and shot them to ribbons on their way out to sea from our field guns. At another place their only road passed in front of a low hill where I had 50 tanks hidden. When the German transport came we waited till we had about 100 vehicles 300 yards away and gave them everything we had from 50 tanks. I have never seen anything like the confusion and destruction - I think that it should satisfy anybody who was at Dunkirk. My chaps are very funny - they say it was such an easy party that they can't understand why the 1st Army could not have finished it off months ago. They are of course delighted at having come in at the end, and their morale is quite extraordinary. They are so pleased with themselves that simply nothing could stop them. They feel that they have had a really good party and success of this kind enormously strengthens my own hand. I am looked upon by them (quite wrongly) as the chap who gave them the chance. It is the most terrifying position to be in as one is at once regarded as something almost supernatural! As I arrived in command of this Division with practically no experience of commanding armoured forces it is a help to have had so many successful battles. In this last battle my casualties were under 20 men and 5 tanks knocked out by the enemy.

Blessings my love, Your devoted, Bobbie

Fifth Letter 10th May 1943 7th Armoured Division, M.E.F.

My Darling Puss,

More prisoners galore.

I have written you several letters lately describing our capture of Tunis and you must be getting rather tired of hearing about the place. There is still a little fighting going on in the Cap Bon peninsular and at one of two isolated points but virtually all resistance has collapsed. German prisoners are just pouring in and they look like the crowd walking back from Goodwood to Chichester after the last race. At the beginning there were a good many Italians but now they are nearly all Germans.

Congrats from Monty

I had a nice telegram and letter from Monty, which I will send by ordinary mail. The B.B.C. gave the division a bit of a "write-up" last night. I am glad they did it as it pleased the troops immensely. I had to go and stand for my photograph under the direction post outside Tunis which said to Cairo 3133 K.M.! There I was photographed in all positions by the press.

Carnage not culture

I paid a visit to Carthage today which was most disappointing as there was nothing much to see and I had expected all kinds of interesting relics. However, you do get a wonderful view as it is on a hill overlooking Tunis Bay and La Goulette. It was a lovely day and we sat and had our lunch on Carthage Hill with the Mediterranean and Cap Bon beyond with Tunis at our feet. The port is smashed to pieces and the airport must have had 500 smashed aircraft lying in all positions. The town is hardly damaged at all.

Pride of being first

The troops are very naughty and have labelled the town with "8th Army welcomes the 1st Army" - The French have chalked up everywhere "Tour a 7th Armoured Division au passage".

A bath for all. Mice on the mudguards.

I am giving the men a chance to get clean and washed and tidy. Most of them have not had a proper bath for a year or more. I am going round to inspect every unit, present their medals and have a talk to the men. This will keep me busy for some days but I think it is a good thing to do. I have started a club for the men in Tunis so that they have somewhere to read, listen to the wireless, and write their letters. It is not very ambitious as these things never last very long, but always worthwhile even for a few days to make some effort. We have a concert party which I have not seen yet but I expect it is pretty vulgar. I do hope that you have got my letter with the drawing of the Juboa sign? Somebody in the 1st Army was heard to ask who was the formation with mice on the mudguard!

Oh to get some leave

Give the children my love - I would love to be with you all for a few days. I think if Monty is really got at the right way he might send me home for a few days. We can't have a job for a little while. Blessings and love to you all. I would love to hear how the mighty British public react to the Tunisian victory. I have been looking at some of the stuff we captured today. It is immense.

Your devoted Bobbie.

Sixth Letter 13th May 1943 7th Armoured Division, M.E.F.

My Darling Glorious Puss,

150,000 prisoners from unconditional surrender

We heard last night that the whole German army had surrendered unconditionally in North Africa. So that is the end of this campaign. I can't describe the masses of prisoners everywhere. They numbered 103,000 yesterday morning and can be hardly less than 150,000 in the end. They fill all the road, many of them marching along, and others driving their own lorries and cars off to captivity. They are quite demoralised and exhausted.

It's my battle

It has been a most satisfactory end to the campaign and my Division are very pleased that they were in at the death. I believe the B.B.C. gave out a bit of talk about us and the 11th Hussars, who are my armoured car regiment. Of course everybody in the division regards it as their own battle and are frightfully funny as they refuse to admit anybody else counts at all! You ought to see the smile on their faces. It really is most heartening. I have written an account of the operation as far as we were concerned and will send it to you by sea mail or quicker means if I can find any.

No escape by sea

Pascoe turned up to see me yesterday. He is with the American forces. Pascoe and Lionel and I took a few hours off and drove all round Tunis and sat on the hill at Carthage which overlooks Tunis Bay and contemplated the scene. It was rather fun. You could still see a bit of fighting on the Cap Bon peninsular - huge fires and smoke where the Germans were burning their equipment. Tunis below is returning to normal but the harbour absolutely flattened by the R.A.F. The La Goulette aerodrome a tangled mass of smashed German and Italian aeroplanes - the port of La Goulette also smashed to pieces. Some Germans had obviously tried to get away from here as there were a large number of German vehicles which dived straight into the docks. I don't think many did in fact get away as the Air Force covered every inch of the sea and I saw them myself diving down on rafts and boats trying to get away to sea. It was a hopeless proposition for them and they soon realised it.

Culture at last, but I could sleep for a week

I have felt very well and on the top of my form during the operations but after these battles are over one feels desperately tired. I don't know why, I feel that I could sleep for a week or more! Also one wants to get away from military affairs. Robert took me off to see some Roman ruins at a place called Douggan. I believe they are famous. Most lovely Roman amphitheatre, Capitol, Forum etc., all in pretty good order. Robert was an excellent guide and his command of the French language and classical education stood me in good stead.

11 miles a day to secure a sweeping victory

Now what? I don't know. I suppose a new campaign, but where and when. That must be what everybody is wondering. This last party really started on 7th November when we broke through at El Alamein. Since then we have covered over 2,000 miles in 180 days - an average speed of advance 11 miles a day! I don't suppose many people realise that was our average advance per day over the whole period. I don't suppose the German and Italian Armies have ever suffered such a defeat in their history and I doubt if the British Army has ever won such a complete and sweeping victory.

Lucky to be there

I was very lucky to be in it - Blessings my love. We are at the moment camped in the most lovely scenery. I am longing to get your letters.

All my love to everybody,

Your devoted Bobbie.

Postscript

General Erskine (Bobbie) continued to command the 7th Armoured Division (the Desert Rats) in the next three campaigns which were the invasion of Sicily, followed by the invasion of Italy followed by victory in Italy. Only then did he get his spot of leave! The Division then returned to Norfolk, England to prepare for the Normandy Campaign. They finished the war in the Baltic. Bobbie held command of the Desert Rats for the longest period (January 1943 - August 1944). His next job was Head of the Supreme Allied Commander's Control Commission to Belgium, reporting to General Eisenhower, with responsibilities to aid Belgium in the aftermath of liberation. He ended the war as Chief of Staff to General Robertson, in the military government of Berlin. He was on the group which drafted the constitution of Post War Germany. Post war he became Director General of the Territorial Army, GOC Far East in Hong Kong, GOC Middle East in the Suez Canal Zone, GOC Eastern Command England, GOC East Africa (Mau mau rebellion of Kenya), GOC Southern Command England, Lt. Governor of Jersey. Tunis was probably the most exhilarating period. Normandy and Kenya were the hardest gruelling periods of generalship. Jersey the most relaxed and enjoyable - at last with his family. Death came a year after retiral at 66.

He had no regrets about being a soldier. He loved 'walking around' the units meeting his men. He won a reputation of being the soldier's general, determined to minimise casualties, but deliver the results. He said of 'high command'. "A general can make and break the careers of others, and sometimes sacking decisions are done on the flimsiest of evidence and regretted later. You cannot take risks of having unsuitable officers in high command".

Fate of German General Rommell

Romell was lucky enough to get out of Africa before the final capture of Tunis, and returned a hero to Germany. He later became involved in a plot to assassinate Hitler. (He wanted to negotiate terms with the Allies). He was executed for his plotting, but given a State Funeral. Hitler could not admit publicly that his hero general was a traitor.

*End

General Erskine decorated DSO on the field of El Alamein by Montgomery

James Gunn portrait of General Erskine

6.3. Review 1997 of Biography by Christopher Ogden *'Life of the Party'* Pamela Digby Churchill Harriman

Abstract

The book takes us quickly to Pamela's adulthood, with 'finishing' in both Paris and Munich, and launch on the British debutante circuit of 1938. She was bored at home but soon got swallowed up in the Leeds Castle set of Lady Bailie and was a very attractive participant. At 17 with parents in Canada she turned the head of a press baron and was bunched much to the irritation of her parents. From Leeds Castle she met Randolph Churchill. In one month he proposed to 5 girls. Pamela accepted him. He wanted an heir before going off to war and she obliged with young Winston and was attracted by the name Churchill, for all the doors it would open . The Churchill marriage was really short. Randolph had no money, gambled, expected Pamela to pay his debts from her modest allowance, and wenched his way around Cairo. Pamela, homeless, soon lost her loyalty to Randolph, but moved in to number 10 Downing Street with her in-laws and like Randolph started 'playing the field'. For Pamela it was Averill Harriman and almost all the top generals of US and Britain who she met at Chequers or number 10. At the end of the war her major lover was Ed Murrow the broadcaster, and she wanted to marry him, but Ed's wife outsmarted Pamela and Ed's marriage was saved. Pamela stayed in Europe hunting out the rich and famous but they would not give her more than highly elevated 'mistress' status and substantial financial reward. After about 8 years as freelance she went to America and at lightening speed moved in on Leyland Hayward, the Broadway Producer, outfoxed his wife Slim, and was married a second time. Pamela's second marriage lasted 10 happy years and she outlived Hayward and was widowed at 51. Six months later she married her old flame, Averill Harriman, 79 and also recently widowed. She had another 13 years of happy marriage and emerged as a political operator in her own right raising $13 million in funds for the Democratic Party, masterminded the funding support for President Clinton, and was rewarded with the post US Ambassador in Paris. The book review works through the main incidents in this story and ends up with a short analysis of Pamela the person, an assessment of her management skills and roles, and a short assessment of this book. Pamela died in office in 1997 and her funeral oration was made by President Clinton.

Introduction

This book was a 60th birthday present book from my sister-in-law Fiona about Pamela Digby Harriman. It immediately gave much promise of being a mega good read. The opening chapter gave a scene of her hosting a party in Washington. Clinton is the President Elect and she has lined up about 60 leading members of the Democratic party to meet him. Many have expectations of getting jobs in the new administration. He toasts Pamela as the First Lady of the Democratic Party. Hilary is standing there applauding. Next day Pamela was offered the position of US Ambassador in Paris. The biographer then moves to a more normal chronology and begins with a brief summary of Digby history, West Country gentry since 1066, with marriages previously with the Churchills, and with considerable riches earned from Royal Naval booty of Spannish ships. Admiral Henry Digby was one of the Nelson band. Pamela also had a very wild ancestor, Jane Digby, who died in Arabia after a final 20 year marriage with an Arab Sheik. She had previously married Lord Ellenborough, divorced him, and then had a series of affairs with courtiers and kings, but a real zest for life. The theory was that Jane was Pamela's role model.

Digby Background

Pamela was the eldest of the family, a very competitive horse woman, winning rosettes by the time she was seven, and noticing, by the time she was 12 the 7 foot erection of the 'Old Man of Cerne', the huge Ancient Briton fertility figure carved out of the chalk on the hill near Minterne. At 16 she was 'finished' in Paris, but she hated closely supervised regime. Then her parents took her with them on tour of America and Canada and at 17 she got noticed out hunting by a Canadian newspaper proprietor, George McCullagh, who got his newspaper to take photos of this plucky English girl cavorting over the jumps and leading the hunt. To her parents irritation she received bouquets of flowers and invitations from this 35 year old whizzkid. Mum and Dad Digby were thankful to get Pamela home to England. But Pamela had already acquired a taste for attracting older powerful men. This was a skill she was to develop to perfection. Her education had one more piece, a spell in Munich, being polished in German culture. In 1938 she met Hitler, but he did not make a very great impression on her. She was more aware of the Nazi threat than her parents had been.

Into Leeds and Clieveden sets

Pamela was a popular young lady and soon a regular guest of Lady Baillie (Olive) of Leeds Castle set, a leading hostess of her day. Pamela often met Boudoin , the Interior Decorator par excellence, who had done the renovation at Leeds Castle. She absorbed the techniques with which Olive arranged house parties, the positioning of the chief butler, the seating plans, and all the finest points of etiquette. She absorbed the taste and designs of Bouoin, and made him a life long friend. She met and befriended David Margesson, Chief whip, also on periphery of Cliveden set, to which she went often for house parties.

First marriage

Pamela was introduced to Randolph Churchill, by Lady Mary Dunn, another London Hostess, as a blind date. She persuaded Pamela to accept the date. This was followed a lightening courtship. Lots of her friends and her parents warned her of Randolph's wenching, drinking, gambling - a real high risk young man and for a few days she wavered then went through with the marriage. This was followed by motherhood, but then the posting of Randolf to the Middle East and no proper matrimonial home. As soon as Randolph got to Cairo he was promoted to major and made the Middle Eastern War Correspondent. He sent cables to Pamela to settle £3,000 of debts, much to her mortification. Pamela went to Beaverbrook, godfather to young Winston and explained the problem of the gambling debt. Meanwhile she had weekly meetings with Lady Cunard, another London hostess, and met Averill Harriman, distinguished diplomat, Rosevelt's London representative for the wartime lend lease programme, the windpipe from America to Britain's stand against Nazi Germany. Pamela had an immediate hit with him . She sees him at his flat, and 4 weekends out of five at Chequers, and plays hostess often to relieve Clemmie of the strain of being hostess to all these military and diplomatic staff. Pamela became the best informed woman of Britain, constantly going between Beaverbrooke, Churchill and Harriman to cement the Anglo American relationship. Averill goes on an official visit to Cairo. His daughter is sharing a flat with Pamela in London. Randolph is a major, press secretary to GHQ, and hosts Averill on his visit. Anthony Eden writes home to Winston 'that Randolf has the bottle of spirit in his eyes'. Later is embarrassed and blames the cypherist for putting an o instead of an a in the vital word! Randolph meanwhile enjoys the ladies of the Cairo fleshpots, and goes off with the general's wife. Later Randolph does heroic feats with Fitzroy MacLean in Yugoslavia with the commandos, and proves that he is as brave as a lion. He injures his back and is sent home, but by this time his marriage is sore. Averill then gets posted to Moscow, and is in some trouble back home with his wife Marie. Pamela continues to correspond with Avril. She divorces Randolph. The last straw was the request from Randolph to settle his gambling debts from Cairo with Digby money!

Jock Witney, Charles Portal, Fred Anderson, Ed Murrow - War time flings

Pamela was not lonely for long in London without Averill. Soon she was hosting parties for diplomats and generals and she had a very winning way with them. Jock Witney was the special US representative in London, Fred was a US Airforce general and Portal Head of the Airforce Staff of Britain, a solid clutch of heavies in war time Britain by any standards, and the attraction of Pamela? She was a very attractive young woman, but with the wheeling and dealing at Chequers, in Downing Street, with Max Beaverbrooke, and now with the generals and diplomats she was probably the best informed lady in Britain. Those who had access to her could use the information. In particular she helped the Americans and British to understand one another through the very close personal contacts which she forged. She got converted to socialism, (for a short period), by broadcaster Ed Murrow. She had a heavy affair with him after Averill went to Moscow and wanted to marry him but his wife soon saw off Ed's promise of a divorce and left Pamela stood up. Through her friendship with Averill's daughter she made contacts with the Kennedy's and went on a trip with Jack Kennedy to Ireland and helped him when he was ill, diagnosed as having Anderson's disease, an ailment of the back.

Aly Khan, Gianelli - mistress 5 years

Pamela was introduced to Aly Khan by the Kennedys, and was immediately attracted to him. But she was not Aly Khan's only lady friend. After about a year and a half Rita Hayworth moved in and even Pamela could not cope with such competition. But just as things were getting difficult Gianelli, playboy bachelor, the heir to the Fiat Empire came and swept her off her feet on his boat to Capri. For the next 5 years the romance blossomed, then Gianelli one evening went home early after a party and

Pamela caught him in bed with a glamorous 17 year old. She was very hurt. He got up and drove the girl home but he was on cocaine, and drove very fast and had a nasty accident. Pamela was superb in a crisis and arranged for him to be taken to a clinic and was present while gangrene was cut away from his legs with just a local anaesthetic. A general anaesthetic was not possible because of the cocaine. She could feel his tears as she covered his eyes with her handkerchief. The romance continued for another two years. She converted to be a Roman Catholic and got her marriage to Randolph annulled so as to be free to marry Gianelli, but no, his family were against it and he did not want to give up his independence. Pamela had managed his life and brought taste to his several homes. She began a pregnancy and then realising that still he would not marry her, she went to Switzerland and had an abortion. The Digby's heaved a sigh of relief. They were furious about her conversion to Catholicism. So was Sir Winston Churchill, once again Prime Minister. He could not condone a possible marriage with one who had fought on the Axis side in the war and who had put the formidable Fiat war machine into the production of munitions. Pamela had wanted to marry Agnelli. He was an eligible bachelor, but when the chips were down his sisters vetoed Pamela and that was it, convert or not, she was not considered husband material for Gianelli.

Elie Rothschild - mistress 6 years

Pamela went to Paris. Soon she was going out with Elie Rothschild, a banker and owner of a substantial vineyard. He was married but his wife was rather neglectful. Pamela spotted the vulnerability of Elie and took advantage of the situation, but ever so discretely, never being seen with him in public. She seemed to have the best of all worlds, her own freedom, a life with very high standard of living from all her rich beaux, time to enjoy the culture of Paris. She made friends with many of the connoisseurs of the arts, also studied wine making so that she had a good rapport with Elie and his direct interest in the Rothschild vineyards. She made friends with the Duchess of Windsor and studied carefully her skills at being the top Paris hostess. She mixed with lots of the intellectuals, writers and artists. Pamela absorbed a fantastic post graduate education in culture and enjoyed every minute. There was one cloud. After medical tests she found at 36 that she had to undergo a hysterectomy. The period in Paris ended when her affair with Elie collapsed. He would not divorce his wife for a Catholic divorcee. His brother had done this amidst huge recriminations in the family and Elie did not want to repeat the mistake. Anyway as a jew indeed a leading member of the Jewish community in France there was little mileage for him in marrying a Catholic. Pamela eventually knew that all was up when her dinner party butler supplied by Elie did not show, and his office left a note that Elie was no longer supplying that service. Pamela had had a varied 10 years in Paris, soaked up masses of culture about good furniture, pictures and the best of the racing bloodstock lines, lived in a luxury Paris flat paid for by Elie Rothschild, with flower bill alone £10,000 / year. My goodness if Andrew's Knightsbridge Plants had a Paris branch with this contract alone, he could soon retire! She observed the hostess skills of the Duchess of

Windsor and studied the wine making techniques of the Rothschilds to become quite a connoisseur of good wines, but she could not achieve marriage with Elie. Young Winston could not stand Elie, but liked Gianelli, the head of Fiat. After Elie's butler failed to show up Pamela realised that marriage with him is a no hoper and she goes off to USA to look up her old war time chums and other contacts.

Leyland Heyward - marriage 10 years

Pamela decided to go to America. She already had lots of US contacts from the war days in London and her affair with Averill. Within a few days of arriving in New York she was a guest in a first night party for one of Heyward's productions and invited for the dinner party. She sat next to Leyland and they immediately hit off with one another. He took her back to his flat and wow they spent the night together, but this was not just a quick fling. Pamela was overwhelmed with this Holywood giant producer, and knew that his third marriage, now in its 10th year was on the rocks. Here was a man she really did want to catch and marry, and Slim, the current wife, had been neglecting him badly for a few years now, and deserved to be replaced, so rationalised Pamela. Slim was waiting in Switzerland for a second honeymoon trip with Hayward, who never showed. She was furious when she realised her mistake in offering Pamela an introduction to hubby and went for the biggest settlement possible. When the royalties on 'The Sound of Music' were being considered she took a mere 10%, thinking this was a silly little story, leaving Pamela with 90% as a marriage settlement, (now worth £1 million / year alone). Pamela had a sharp eye for a bargain, even better than Branson, and her battle tactics would make even Montgomery blush! She never let Hayward out of her sight till the divorce settlement was through and she was married. Pamela was a very determined lady and knew exactly what she wanted. In a few weeks she had set up her appartment in a New York hotel, shipped a lot of her priceless pictures and possessions from the Paris flat, provided by Elie, and was plotting with Leyland Hayward to secure the divorce from Slim. Pamela's pressure worked and within 3 months she was married to Leyland Hayward. This was a happy marriage for the next 10 years and Pamela adored Leyland and looked after him beautifully. Leyland's career however, went into a decline. He never had any real success after 'Sound of Music', but had enough capital to live well. He died rather suddenly and Pamela was left a widow at 51. She had major problems with her step children in winding up the will. He had no capital left, but two houses. She could not afford to keep them both going. Daughter Booke accused her of selling off her valuable pearls deposited in Father's safe for safe custody. There was war between Pamela and two of the Hayward step children. One even wrote a spiteful novel about the wicked step mother and it became a best seller.

Technique

Pamela had known how to move in with all her big guns in man management - home organisation, good taste, brilliant party management, knowledge of all the sybaritic flourishes that rich men appreciate, good contacts, agreeable conversation, being a good listener and able to absorb quickly the core interests of the current man and adapt to his tastes, a good rapport with the leading writers and film stars of the day and lots of experience of sex. Hayward had wilted under all this pressure.

Short Widowhood

Pamela was soon off to stay with Frank Sinatra. He had been a friend and admirer of Hayward and was happy to console his widow, but needless to say Pamela wanted romance once more and this was a relationship which was one sided. He eventually threw Pamela out and for a short time she returned to Europe, was bored in London after 2 weeks, and got an invitation for a yachting trip in the Mediterranean with the Guiness family, but even that bored her, and getting wind of an invitation in Washington to a ball to be attended by widowed Averill Harriman, she jetted rapidly out of the Mediterranean, picked her finest ballgown and attended the ball sitting back to back with Averill. This strategic positioning was intended to be the 'hard to get' trump card to make him turn and notice her. She had some tactical sense. In romance she knew all the tricks.

3rd Marriage Averill Harriman 14 years

Within hours Pamela had moved in to comfort Averill on his widowhood and it was romance all the way. His daughter, Kathleen, disturbed them late one evening smooching on a sofa in the drawing room and a few weeks later there was a modest wedding in a catholic church followed by a reception for 100. Averill was 79 and Pamela was determined to marry him before he was 80! She quickly set to redecorate his 2 homes and take complete charge of his life. Friends and relations of his former wife Marie were deliberately excluded from the new inner circle. Pamela did not want any more trouble from step children / grandchildren. Averill gave Pamela a quick grounding in world politics with visits to Moscow and other European Capitals, and then a complete immersion in the Democratic Party machinery. She initiated the movement of setting up Political Action Groups primarily for fund raising, but also for disseminating political ideas and stimulating debate in the country. As Averill aged and his hearing deteriorated Pamela became the active political member of the team and with her ever widening contact base she became a political force in her own right. Averill was so proud of his political wife and so contented with the abundance of the care she poured upon him that he openly stated that his 13 years with Pamela were the happiest of his life, and she became almost the sole beneficiary of his will which disposed an estate of $100 million, much to the miff of his two children by his first wife Marie. She had known Kathleen since war time days when Averill brought her to London and she and Pamela had shared a flat. Kathleen had been Father's cover for his London fling with Pamela, and then years later Pamela, not Kathleen, was the big heiress to Averill's fortune. She was ever so skilled in out foxing step children and their possible expectancies.

Pamela's Political Action Groups for the Democratic Party

"She treated every guest as an honoured friend. The only difference was that as you came in, there was a card table in the front hall and you would be asked to sign the guest book and, if the money had not arrived, to sign the cheque right then and there. It was $1,000 and Pamela did not take chits. The invitations went around the country every month in Pamela's name, advising that the speaker would be Senator Muskie or Congressman Richard Gephardt or somesuch and the moderator Clark Clifford, the party's silky eminent grise or Bob Strauss or former Lyndon Johnson aide Harry McPherson. After accepting the invitation this is what happened.

The welcome

Mr. Smith would arrive with his $1,000 and taken down to the hall facing Van Gough's *White Roses,* (worth $10 million probably), and major domo Michael Kuruc and two hired butlers in black tie would greet him with a tray of drinks. He'd walk down two steps past the Degas sculpture of '*The Dancer*' and the Derain and Matisse on the wall into this beautiful, soft lit room with bouquets of fresh flowers placed just right, and there would be Governor Harriman in pinstripes and Pamela in a perfectly tailored Bill Blass suit and diamond earings greeting you with exquisite grace. It didn't matter if you were a car dealer from Ohio or the king of England, you got the same treatment. And there seriously would be several of the Senate or House leaders, because Pamela only went straight to the top, and a smattering of younger House members, who she thought should have a higher profile. There would be 10 people standing there you would give your right arm to meet under *any* circumstances.

The party

The party would consist of about 40 people, and you'd schmooze around drinking and nibbling molded canapes of ham or tuna and mayonaise, iced carrot rounds. After one full drink Pamela would say, 'Averill and I are so thrilled to have you in our drawing-room'. Then Governor Averill would say hello and turn it over to Clark who would introduce the big banana of the night for an address of 20 minutes. Then Michael would announce dinner and you would sit at round tables on the sun porch overlooking the terraced gardens and in the dining room, eight to ten at a table, with the Digby ostrich place cards with the green border, always everything green, written by the secretary with the best finishing-school penmanship.

The dinner

You would be served with a beautiful dinner, entirely prepared by Pamela's cook Gretchen, and her sous chef, beginning with smoked trout or creamed lobster. Absolutely first class. It was exactly as if you had come to Pamela's for an exclusive private dinner. That was the secret. That you had just signed a cheque for $1,000 had nothing to do with fact that you were being totally enveloped in this beautiful world. There would be six decorative ladies to keep the tables from being too male, as well as wives along with the schnooks from Wisconsin or whatever. Then it was filet and fiddle ferns and a salad course with cheese and English water biscuits, three wines. Desert was a bombe of some sort, then champagne and coffee.

The toast

Pamela would clink her glass and make a little toast about how necessary it was to get the Democratic Party's juices flowing, then ask everyone to return to the library, where little gold chairs had been brought in. There the discussion was opened up to everyone. Stuart or Sandy would make some remark to get things started and by 10.30 everyone would go home.

The money raised

Pamela hung in with these dinners for 10 years and raised $10,300,000". Pamela's Political Action Group was the most successful of several thousand which sprung up in America after the debacle of Carter's defeat. Her final thrust into the fund raising game for Clinton's election was to open Hayward's estate for $10,000 for a whole day trip, which makes the fee our punters pay in London for viewing Buckingham Palace look a bit modest!

Young Winston's view of Pamela

Young Winston eventually writes his own autobiography during mid career. He had been a journalist then MP, married Minnie, but the marriage was not particularly happy. Winston never made it to the front bench. His political career was a disappointment. But anyway he committed his life to autobiography. In this his father still figured a hero, but Pamela his mother, was almost totally ignored. It seemed as though he had been brought up motherless. In the early war days, Randolf was away fighting in the Middle East, Pamela dumped him with a Nanny at the home of Lord Beaverbroke, (Winstons's godfather), and then he was packed off to boarding school as soon as he was old enough, and teased to death for being the grandson of the great war leader. In the holidays he went to join his mother in France but invariably she passed him off on friends while she concentrated on her men. Gianelli, the Fiat boss, was really nice to Winston, and he enjoyed all the fun life of skiing and yachting with him, but Elie Rothschild was a real cold financial fish, fond of cavorting with Pamela, but treating Winston as though he were surplus baggage and just a nuisance. Luckily both grandparents, the Churchills and Digbys were excellent and took enormous trouble to fill this gap. Winston rather resented his lack of mother support and even late in life with her success with Averill Harriman and American politics never considered her a real politician as she never stood and won elective political office, just knew a lot of politicians and was married to one. But Young Winston had to watch his Ps and Qs financially. Along with many friends of his generation he had a position with Lloyds and was obliged to look to Mum with all that $100 million inheritance to help him out with debts. Oh how he was like his Father, Randolph, who in the 1940s was cabling Pamela to help him out with gambling debts.

Second widowhood

Never without a man Pamela turned to Clifford Brown, the chairman of the American National Gallery, but he was only a friend. By this time of life she was independent and well provided for and she began a new phase in her life. From being essentially a facilitator to a powerful man she wanted to become her own woman with a leadership role in its own right. She set her mind on specialising in foreign policy with a view of ending up as an ambassador to a major country. And by the age of 73 that was it. She had taken up her appointment as US Ambassador to France, living in a sumptuous embassy a mansion bought from the Rothschild family, a cousin of Elie, his erstwhile mistress. But now she was master of this house; the mistress days being part of history. And how did this transformation from facilitator to leader take place? She befriended every member of the Foreign Relations Committee. She undertook missions to China and Moscow. She ran seminars on foreign policy. She wrote up newsletters in the influential '*Washington Post*'. She developed a friendship with the Speaker of Congress. She maintained her fund raising activities for the Democratic Party and directed its fruits to the Clinton camp, a cool $3 million. She entertained Gorbachev and Raisa, (miffing the Regans who thought the First Lady of the White House, should be the first to welcome Raisa, not Pamela, who by this time was called the First Lady of the Democratic Party). Clinton was elected President in November 1992. Within a week he was entertained by Pamela at his triumphal entrance to Washington. By the following March she had been nominated Ambassador to Paris. In May she appeared for 45 minutes before the Senate Confirmation Hearings. All the Democrats of that Foreign Affairs Committee she had funded into office, so this was to be a mutual admiration set of exchanges for Pamela, and with her impressive bearing, her knowledge of the issues of foreign affairs, even the Republican members of the Committee fell like a tree to her charms. Her confirmation was unanimous with a final standing ovation. At last she had arrived as 'Madame Ambassador' in Paris. She shipped the best of her Harriman collection of pictures to the Embassy, and soon imported the famous Pamela style into its functions. She knew all the other US ambassadors in Europe and quickly set up a hot line of communication with them so that she was entirely on top of the big issues. In the first week she was visited by the British Ambassador, Sir Christopher Mallaby. (He was a contemporary of mine in King's College. Sometimes he gets my newsletters. I must ask him about Pamela!). She also set up a hot line of regular telephone calls back to Clinton, the Speaker, and her cronies on the Foreign Affairs Committee. With this network on the US front and her entree into all the power corridors of Paris on the home front she could put up a formidable performance as ambassador.

A final black cloud

While Pamela was enjoying her ambassadorial honeymoon in Paris, Kathleen and Mary, her Harriman Step Daughters were no end miffed by a cessation of their trust income and they brought a lawyer's suit for $30 million alleging trust mismanagement. She had delegated trust management functions to a wise fool, not all that unlike Sir Douglas Lovelock of the Church Commissioners case study, and he had gone into property speculation and put the step daughter's trust up as collateral, and bang as the property development glitched, the step daughters, saw what little they had also going down the plughole. Pamela offered $10 million, and there the story ends.

Assessment of the book

This book is a compulsive read. Every phase of Pamela's life is sympathetically researched. How any biographer could have got his mind around such diverse fields and people is amazing, but the narrative is fast moving, and arresting. Pamela's life was so much more enjoyable than the one I recently read on Runcie by Carpenter. Runcie just fell into every hole in life that was there, whereas Pamela makes the agenda and the holes for the other participants, but she is a very naughty and unscrupulous operator. Runcie would win in the moral game, but Pamela would win in the achievement and management game. She has a remarkable list of achievement skills. She goes through life listening and absorbing ideas, taste, technique, decor, racing bloodlines, vineyard management, theatre production, the skills of facilitation, finally the skills of statesmanship out in the front line. She is a vibrant, well informed lady, learns from her failures, no wonder the Senate Confirmation Committee, gave her a standing ovation on her appointment of Ambassador. Her greatest contributions were probably in the war time period, bringing the thoughts of the higher commands of Britain and US together to defeat Nazi Germany, and her final years as kingmaker for President Clinton. Pamela was the flower which never seemed to stop growing in capacity and charm. But she did have enemies, particularly other wives who saw her as a threat, and step children, who were ever so cutely disinherited at her hand.

Postscript

Pamela died in 1997 after taking a seizure after swimming in Paris. Two presidents paid tribute to her at her funeral in America - President Chirac of France, and President Clinton. Clinton delivered the funeral oration.

*end

Portrait of Pamela

6.4. Book review of '*House of Thomas*', Lorna Houseman, 1968, Chatto and Windus.

The author is daughter -in-law of de la Rue director; the reviewer is the grandson of Sir Evelyn de la Rue, penultimate family chairman of the de la Rue Company.

Abstract

This book covers the period 1820 - 1939 in the life of what became an international company de la Rue plc. It covers the 4 generations of family ownership and control followed by one generation of professional management under Westall and

Lambert. Thomas, the founder, began with making straw hats and playing cards. He was very entrepreneurial and sent his brother, Paul, to Russia to set up a monopoly for the Czar. Thomas had a scientific bent which enabled him to register key patents and then develop a portfolio of stationery products. Thomas, founder, had two sons, Warren and William. Warren established an international reputation for science, and developed the technology to get into adhesive stamps and banknotes. William was the supersalesman who secured the contracts from kings and finance ministers. He was very market orientated. The next generation, Thomas, changed the firm's status to a public company, was made a baronet for the work done in the Chest Hospital. He became complacent with the long term contracts, and lost the British stamp contract through lack of customer orientation. In the next generation the three brothers Evelyn, Ivor and Stuart don't get on and failed to win back the stamp and banking business though they did attempt some diversification into boilers and plastics. Stuart, the youngest, was the only one not going to war, but in 5 years he cleaned out the reserves and accumulates £90,000 debt. In 1923 Lambert followed by Westall gradually filled up Bunhill Row with orders for stamps and banknotes. Westall was the brilliant salesman, like Colonel William de la Rue. And they managed to turnaround the boiler business and plastics business, and re-established the Onoto fountain pen. By 1933 the de la Rue Company was once more profitable.

Guernsey de la Rues

The de la Rue family in Guernsey had a modest beginning with agricultural small holdings. Thomas, born 1793, was 6th of 10 children. Thomas began adult life in partnership for making a local newsletter, but the partnership lasted just a few months. Thomas continued in printing but diversified into straw hats.

London prospecting

In 1818 Thomas uprooted his family and went to London. He brought with him the straw hat making business in boom as a result of war in America. Soon he was experimenting with coloured printing as well and taking out patents for playing cards, and in 1830 begin a partnership with Cornish and Rock. The hat business, the cash cow, lasted till 1835, after which printing was the core business. Thomas bought out his partners in 1835 .

Foundation difficulties

In 1837 a financial crisis was triggered by the failure of the bank, Esdailes. For a short time Thomas was in prison for debt, but as his bankruptcy would have not been in the interests of the creditors he was soon rescued by Sedgewick. Thomas then developed a patent for white lead and sold it for £9,000 thus clearing most of the outstanding debt. In 1938 Thomas printed commemoration copies of the Sun in gold for the Queen's coronation, and they were a wild success.

A solid base

Young Warren de la Rue was educated in France till the revolution of 1830. His school reports were glowing, particularly for science subjects. He started work with the partnership at 18 and was made a partner at 23. Already by the age of 21 he had registered his first patent, 'the Daniel electric battery'. Meanwhile young Paul de la Rue was sent off to Russia to manage the

Imperial card making monopoly. The Czar had had word that de la Rue card printing was the best in the world. Four years later in 1847 the Russian monopoly was making 4 million packs / year. The English production never reached a million till 1873. Paul's daughter, Maria, met Walter Winans, elder son of Ross, the US railroad maker magnate, who had commissions to build railways across Russia. Ross Winans had huge influence in America and Maria was soon to give Uncle Wiliam de la Rue an entree into the contract to print the 5 cent postage stamp of the Confederate States.

Products and contacts

There was very rapid growth in the foundation years. As a printer de la Rue's were perfectly placed to make playing cards and a large portfolio of the elaborate Victorian stationery that was coming into fashion. The rich loved eating their way through 14 course meals and taking home the menus with ever such fancy de la Rue printing. Warren de la Rue was rapidly establishing his reputation as a scientist and engineer. He was elected to the prestigious Royal Society and befriended the scientific superstar Michael Farraday. Can anyone who studied physics not recall his fundamental contributions? Warren offered Michael the use of his laboratories for the famous experiments into electricity. Warren was elected secretary of the Royal Society, He was on a select group who planned the Great Exhibition of 1851 with Prince Albert and was a juror for the awards. De la Rue exhibited 289 items including the star attraction, a machine making 2,700 envelopes / hour folded and with gum in the right places with just one operator. De la Rues then exhibited in New York in 1853 and in Paris in 1855. They had a flair for publicity. Thomas de la Rue was made Chevalier d'Honneur after the Paris Exhibition.

Into stamps and banknotes

In April 1853 Rowland Hill awarded de la Rue the contract to print adhesive stamps for fiscal documents using the new high productivity typographical process, developed for making playing cards. Soon de la Rue was also printing stamps for the East India Company. Stamp contracts for the colonies in the 1850s were awarded by Penrose Julyan, of the Crown Agents. Perkins Bacon had received the early contracts but failed on one occasion to have their design approved, and slighted and aware of the de la Rue success with fiscal stamps de la Rue was offered the chance to bid, and they did so successfully. This opened the way to a mass of stamp contracts for the colonies and the first contract to print the £5 note for Madagascar. In 1862 as Italy united Warren and William went to Turin, made contact with senior official, Cavaliere Perazza, and in no time they had secured orders for stamps and railway tickets and an agreement to help the Italians set up their own plant in Italy. Whenever a new nation was to be formed, or a new king ascended the throne they were quick to make engravings of the new ruler / monarch and secure the stamp contract. This generationn of de la Rue's were proactive and customer orientated.

Confederate stamps

Colonel Billy de la Rue visited his American cousins in Paris, the Winans, and with the help of this influential contact got into the bidding for the 5 cents blue for the Confederates. The first shipment was delivered as planned but the second was lost on 'The Bermuda' as it failed in running the blockade.

Growth

Growth was rapid with founder Thomas senior partner, and with two very able sons, Warren and Colonel William De la Rue. Warren was the ever credible scientist and research and development boffin, William the brilliant salesman. He negotiated the contracts to print stamps for India for 71 years, for Ceylon 73 years, for Great Britain 55 years; these were the solid long term contracts undertaken by de la Rue. In 1879 de la Rue won the contract for 10 years for the 1 penny British stamp of about a billion / year. There was further growth into diaries, stationery, playing cards, before the death of founder, Thomas in 1866. Warren began to busy himself on the race course. 'Trayles' won the Ascot Gold cup, The Goodward Cup, the Alexandra Plate. Muller, Warren's top class chemist retired, and Warren's son, Thomas took more and more charge of the partnership.

Monopoly and complacency - the ivory tower

Complaints about lack of gumming was raised by colonies and later by British MP, Mr Mowbray but they were dismissed with contempt, but this gave rise later to questions about the stamp monopoly in Britain. Thomas was Governor of the Royal Chest Hospital and was honoured with a baronetcy. Author, Lorna, suggested that his father Warren with his huge scientific reputation should have been honoured rather than Thomas. Anyway when Thomas assumed control of the de la Rue partnership he turned this into a private company in 1898, with himself as chairman. Shortly afterwards he turned this into a public company. Soon, however, He was quarrelling with the Crown Agents over Ceylon and a little later the designs for Uganda were returned unacceptable - no customer orientation here, and the Crown Agents looked for other printers. The issue seems to be over the superior quality of copperplate printing in two colours, which other printers were doing. Thomas wished to retain the letterpress method. He did not have the innovative spirit to develop the technology of printing since the death of chemist Dr. Muller, nor the humanity to improve the conditions and pay of his workforce. In 1911 the Revenue mindful of the criticisms of the stamp monopoly decided to split the stamp contract into two, the higher denominations going to de la Rue, the lower ones to competitor Harrisons, but Sir Thomas was having none of this. It was to be all or nothing. But customers such as HMG do not like being treated with disdain so de la Rue lost the whole contract for British stamps, which they had printed for 30 years. Sir Thomas was so aggrieved at the loss of this contract that he died two months later.

Evelyn, Ivor and Stuart - 4th and last generation of family

The next generation of de la Rues consisted of three sons, Evelyn, Ivor and Stuart. Evelyn was scientific minded and wrote papers, but they did not achieve the public acclaim of his grandfather, Warren. However, he did want to get de la Rues to diversify and pioneered the fountain pen the Onoto, which was a huge success with a launch of £55,000 of advertising. It had a novel down plunger action and was beautifully crafted with gold nib. Sir Thomas had left the business evenly to the 3 brothers, but they did not get on well together, and 1911 was a crisis.

Some one third of the order book had been in the lost stamp contract and this was a time for leadership to slim the firm down to cope with a smaller business or to scour the world for new stamp contracts. But Sir Evelyn had other ideas. He got into partnership with an engineering boffin, Mr Taunton, and built a car factory in Liege in Belgium financing the whole project. Just as the first cars were rolling off the production line the first world war began and the £80,000 investment was lost and no new money had gone to revive the security printing. Both Evelyn and Ivor followed the call to the colours and the firm was left in the hands of Stuart, the youngest, just 32. Initially de la Rue prospered by printing the first £1 note and 10 shilling notes, but to their chagrin the long term bank note contract went to a small rival company, 'Sun Engraving' who had pioneered a new process called 'photogravure. ' The Company had begun the war with net assets of £90,000 but by 1918 despite having substantial war contracts, it was in debt for £90,000. Stuart had spent money on diversification into debt ridden enterprises - Philip Mead Crcket Bat, Cyclo Cars, Potterton Boilers and a plastics company, which eventually became Formica Limited. If only he had 'stuck to the knitting' instead of this unrelated expansion the finances might have been a lot healthier. When Ivor and Evelyn returned from war service in 1918 they were devastated at the changes in the company's fortunes. Ivor, had a nervous breakdown and never worked again for the company. Evelyn engaged in family pursuits and left Stuart in charge. The government approached the Company with a request that they print the Indian stamp order in India, but Stuart demurred and the last big stamp contract was lost. Stuart brought in a Mr. Gronow, as managing director, the head of the Waterlow's combine, one of the chief competitors of the de la Rue Company. What then emerged was that the de la Rue Company had been indulging in cartel pricing with Waterlows on bank note printing contracts. Stuart bowed out and Gronow went too, but the board called in Sydney Lambert to take over what was by then a leaderless company, No longer was any member of the de la Rue family involved in its destiny now in the 4th generation in 1923

Recovery with Lambert and Bernard Westall.

The Government of Siam requested a representative to go and quote for a banknote order using the copperplate printing which Waterlow's had brought to de la Rue, and young Westall landed a 5 year contract worth £125,000 and a new host of contacts in the Far East which once again filled the factory space of Bunhill Row.

An extravagance of Commission money,

They also employed a rather pushy salesmen, Avramov, who went to Bulgaria and landed a big order for bank notes with some commission paid in advance to the minister. Later the minister was tried for corruption and executed. Undeterred Avramow went to China and signed a contact for 4 billion stamps. At last in 1933 the de la Rue Company made a trading profit, the first time for 20 years.

China Market

The de la Rue Company and Dr Kung, Minister of Finance, struck a series of very good deals for banknotes ending with an order for 8 billion notes. The plant at Bunhill Row had to turn summasaults to achieve delivery without invoking penalty clauses. Dr Kung was the China representative to King George's coronation and the company did their best to make his stay in Britain a memorable one.

The Ball that killed the deal

Howard Pillow major shareholder in the British-American Bank note company in Canada let it be known that he wanted to sell out his interest and de la Rue was waning an alternative base from London to print banknotes so this was to be an agreed merger with much potential synergy. Westall flew to Canada with young merchant banker, Peter Kiek, to see the deal through. The first night Pillow gave a dinner party and his daughter Margaret, was present. A week later the deal was about to be signed when Kiek and Margaret went to the Governor General's ball. Next day Kiek and Margaret eloped and a furious Pillow rang Westall to say the deal was off.

*End

Portrait of Sir Evelyn de la Rue, author's grandfather, engrossed in cabinet making.

Sir Evelyn's Rolls Royce

6.5. Review of Biography of Runcie *'The Reluctant Archbishop'* by Humphrey Carpenter.

Runcie and Carpenter - who was the one sitting on the fence?

Archbishop Runcie was a larger than life figure so an excellent object of biographical study. Carpenter, his biographer, is the son of a past Bishop of Oxford, and able to capture all the theological nuances in the story, and like Trollop able to recognise the political moves and the course and impact of decisions of patronage. Carpenter had completed other biographies and acquired some reputation as a biographer. He spent 4 years having regular meetings with Runcie, going out on trips with him, and interviewing the main players on his staff, leading churchmen and politicians, many friends, his students, those who had supervised him. The tape recorder did Carpenter proud and left him a huge reservoir of first hand material. Much of this is anecdotal, and rather unsettling when reviewed in hindsight. Runcie did not appear to have anticipated what should be 'on the record' or 'off the record', or how he could exercise a right of veto over material subsequently seen as too sensitive or confidential. He kept coming across to the reader as 'such a nice, charming man'. Little did he realise how loose his tongue was and what Carpenter, his biographer, might do with what his wife Rosalind described as 'abundant indiscretions'. In the end Carpenter admitted that there were two biographies possible. One would attempt a dispassionate assessment of the man as an Archbishop, the other would be more of a hagiograph with lots of entertaining quotations, a story worthy of serialisation in the press. Runcie clearly expected the dispassionate version. Unfortunately it is the hagiograph version that is the book which was written for a wide readership. This is a book which once it is picked up cannot easily be put down. It is dramatic, racy, entertaining, but in the end very short in analysis. The reader is led through masses of conflicting assessments of Runcie and left to make the judgements unaided. Runcie is often accused of 'sitting on the fence' but was it not Carpenter who was also 'sitting on the fence'? Was he any better? He is the biographer who leaves a huge confusion of conflicting material and no framework from which to develop judgement about success or failure. The Erskine contribution in this critique is to attempt to convolute the journalistic version into a more dispassionate assessment of Runcie and provide a profile of what he will be remembered for in history.

Success or failure? - a framework for judgements

Erskine uses the Carpenter material and seeks out a framework which would be credible in the field of modern personnel management. The hypothesis tried out comes from Dr Lawrence Peter and is known as 'The Peter Principle'. This states that in general a manager rises in an organisation till he or she reaches a state of incompetence. Note that for a top person, such as a primate or archbishop, this might not be till a second term of office is contemplated. Thus for the readers here the relevant question is 'Would they have recommended a Crown Appointments Commission to extend Runcie's term beyond 1992 if the issues had not merely been related with his retiral age?' If the discipline of personnel management has any humanity at all then it is based on principles of achievement and merit. In middle management positions there is usually a job description to guide judgements? What job description was the person given and objectives and targets? How did he do against these? In the case of someone at the top of the organisation there is no job description as such but careful analysis of the biography material will yield clues of how the role of the position was perceived either by looking at manifesto style statements of the job incumbent or referring to the historical precedents about the various roles of the office. As Runcie was the 92nd Archbishop of Canterbury there are plenty of precedents about the roles of his final job, and they are rehearsed by him as he begins his term in Lambeth Palace. In his first sermon as Bishop of St. Albans he also lays out his manifesto of what he wants to do in the diocese of St. Albans. In the earlier parts of this biography it was particularly difficult to spot Runcie's manifesto style statements. He seemed rather immature and wavering, but by the time he has been appointed to a diocese his statements of role and manifesto have a concrete form from which the judgements of merit can and should be made and defended.

Progress through this paper

This critique now, in anticipation, lays out the interesting questions for the dispassionate biography of Runcie, which he thought was being written. Erskine then follows Carpenter chronologically through the journalistic version. Readers would be so very disappointed if they missed all that readable drama. At the beginning of the paper he raises the real questions which throw light on whether he was an effective Archbishop. By the end the reader should have some informed judgements and could recommend whether he could have been offered another term as Archbishop.

Critical questions

1. Was Runcie a committed ordinand?
2. How do you account for the rapid rise of Runcie to the position of Archbishop?
3. What roles did he target himself on as a bishop of St Albans? How did he do in these roles?
4. What roles did he identify in the position as Archbishop of Canterbury? How did he do in each such role?
5. What sort of legacy did he leave his successor, Dr Carey?
6. Do you really believe the assertion that the position of Archbishop of Canterbury is an impossible one?
7. Was the job bigger than the Archbishop or was the Archbishop bigger than the job? Which of these could or should be changed?

Professor Gillian Stamp

Carpenter's biography is littered with judgements about him. For instance Professor Gillian Stamp, "The job of diocesan bishop was too easy for him, even the archbishopric of Canterbury was too small for him."

Early Days in Crosby, Liverpool.

Robert Runcie was educated at the Merchant Taylor's School, a grammar school in Liverpool. His parents were lower middle class. His paternal grandfather was a taylor in Kilmarnock, and his Father grew up as an engineer, moving to Liverpool for a suitable opening. His Father was not an active Christian but young Robert was guided into the Christian faith by his elder sister Kathleen. He enjoyed his confirmation classes, mainly because of the romance they included when he met Betty Cook. However, he was quickly recruited by the rector into a course for servers and his commitment to the church strengthened. He was well liked in his school and captain of both football and cricket teams, and with some encouragement managed to get good enough grades in classics to pass into Oxford. Again Kathleen encouraged him to take up his place there. His father's view was "that it was not natural for a young man to take such an interest in religion and not be in sport on Sundays"!

Scots Guards

Runcie was rather slow to get accepted as a grammar school boy with slight Liverpool accent and learn all the regimental customs. At Pirbright no-one seemed to speak to him in the Regiment but he quickly learnt to talk proper and within a few months could soon pass as a charming guards officer. He liked the thrill of active service and won the MC after rescuing a guardsman from a burning tank when the turret had got stuck over the hatch, and then he went out on open ground in his tank to knock out the enemy tank which was holding up the advance of the whole armoured regiment. Rather modestly Runcie said that his commanding officer was good at writing citations. Runcie got to be very well liked in his regiment as being 'one of the boys', sometimes accompanying his brother officers to the London night clubs of the war era - 'The Bag o' Nails' or 'The Four Hundred Club'. "I drink, I make love, I smoke, I'm normal. My friends thought that I would have a career in drama or in the academic field, but for them a possibility that I would go into the church would make them roar with laughter."

Oxford

Runcie joined the Conservative Club also the newly formed Carlton Club. He served on the Committee while Margaret Roberts was President. "She was a hard working chemist. I always regarded her as rather tubby, with rosy cheeks. Not my sort of girl! I'm full of admiration for her, but it's like sitting next to electricity. She eventually sacked me from the Committee because she didn't like my association with the aristocratic Carlton Club."

"I read classics at Oxford, at Brasenose College, but as it was war time I lived in Christ Church. I much admired the beautiful ladies of Keeble College, girls from the Foreign Office, billeted in Oxford. At the end of my first tutorial with Derek Waters he said after two hours, 'And now let us have some sherry. ' A cut-glass decanter was brought out, and he went on talking and we emerged dizzy with sherry. This was my baptism with the Oxford tutorial system. The first part of the course, Moderations, related with the language and literature of the classics. The second part of the course, and for me interrupted by war service, was called 'Greats'. This was about philosophy and ancient history, and to everybody's surprise I got a first."

The decision to go for ordination

Principal Carey on Runcie at Westcott House, "I found when talking to Runcie that he had a far deeper spirituality than was common among the students. It was totally unostentatious. It was never explicitly paraded but I felt that he was a man of God. He was in the best sense a jolly person, a superb mimic and always full of fun."

The possibility of ordination had been with Runcie since the days of grammar school but eventually at Oxford he made the decision to go to Wescott Hall in Cambridge to study theology and it kind of 'happened' as a best option. Later he was asked if he could have become a Roman Catholic and he said "Yes". At that time even though he was a fun loving person he had some aspirations to be celibate.

Early career

Runcie was ordained from Westcott Hall and took up a curate's position in Lancashire under Rev Turnbull for two years. He was a priest in a working class area and fitting perfectly into his expectations of life, then to his surprise he got a call from the Principal of Westcott Hall inviting him to be a member of staff. He felt complimented by the invitation. His vicar, Turnbull, and the Bishop of Liverpool tried to dissuade him from becoming an academic so early in his career, but Runcie felt the call to return to Westcott. After 2 years he was invited to be Chaplain at Trinity Hall and a few years later to become Dean. In a Cambridge College the office of Dean is very important. He was at the hub of administration. Runcie had been popular at school; he was popular in the Scots Guards; he was the president of his junior Common Room at Brasenose College Oxford; now he was a popular dean at Trinity Hall.

Romance

While he was Dean he accepted a lady, Rosalind Turner as his secretary. She had recently had a romance which had not worked out, but anyway she was the daughter of the College Bursar, and the young sister of Jill, whom he had known and liked at Oxford. Rather off hand he asked her to a May Ball, and then sort of proposed to her. 'Would she like a ring'? Rosalind's story was that she fell for him as he was such a poor lost soul of a boy and she wanted to look after him! At Trinity Hall Runcie engaged in a lot of teaching, mainly classics, and some theology, but was not making progress at writing, and he thought that he would end up a 'college codger', with no strong academic reputation.

Cuddesdon Theological College

When he was approached to take on the Principalship at Cuddesdon he jumped at it - a way to climb the ladder without writing books! Cuddesdon needed a lot of reform from the very strict and oppressive regime of his predecessor who separated married students from their wives, and would not even permit them to eat together. Runcie had no previous experience as a parish priest but had to lecture on pastoral studies. He quickly gained experience as vicar of Cuddesdon, a joint job with the principalship. Among the students the warmth of his personality shone through. He was very popular. He was the clever academic with both a first in 'Greats' from Oxford and a first in 'Theology' from Westcott House, the charming guards officer with impressive war record, and aristocratic and political contacts. Runcie admired the questioning / thinking academics and invited David Jenkins, (later the Bishop of Durham) on to his staff. He seemed to approve of '*Honest to God*' by Robinson, (later a bishop) and Hugh Montefiore, later Bishop of Birmingham and author of the book which caused a storm by asserting that Christ was a homosexual. Montefiore to Carpenter, "My God, John Robinson's written a book which is going to cause mayhem - he's going to tell the world the sort of things *we* believe!" Runcie's friends and mentors were mainly from this 'liberal theology' persuasion. As they went through his hands he spotted the bright ones like a football 'scout' and he was sometimes able to promote their careers. The Archbishop's patronage secretary, was living in Cuddesdon village. He was Bill Saumarez-Smith, in a recently created job. Apparently the students of Cuddesdon sometimes used to follow Saumarez-Smith into Cuddesdon Parish Church with loud guffaws 'Derek, he's odds on favourite for Dean of Lincoln', just to take the mickey from poor Bill, who was described as master of discretion. Carpenter suggests that a close friendship developed between Runcie and Saumarez-Smith. Garry Bennett, academic of Trinity Hall Oxford, later accused Runcie of the charge of 'nepotism' in the famous '*Preface to Crockfords*'. A week after its publication Bennett committed suicide. Cuddesdon College had a history of promoting its principals to diocesan bishops, so Carpenter was to remark that soon Runcie's name was not only a matter for the guffaws of his students in their bating of Saumarez-Smith, but that the patronage secretary had really taken him on board. Runcie used his principalship as a means of widening his circle of church and academic contacts, always with the chance to offer them visiting lectureships, so he knew their abilities and their theology. With the relationships being so good he felt he could then brief a wide range of these acolytes to do ghosting for his addresses, sermons, lectures. Although he could not pay them for ghosting services, many would do it for the sheer thrill of having him adopt their text. In an organisation such as the Church of England, where patronage secretaries operate, significant power resides in just a few influential people who have their ear. The quid pro quo of ghosting may be the promise of a deanery, a bishopric, an archbishopric. The currency is thicker than blood!

Bishop of St. Albans - 3 objectives

In 1970 Runcie was appointed Bishop of St. Albans, after being considered for Dean of Guildford. St. Albans was ideal as being half way between Oxford and Cambridge, so Runcie could still hob nob with his academic friends. Three objectives were adopted by the new Bishop Runcie in his enthronement address:

- To make the church more aware of the place of questioning.

(This was the David Jenkins stuff, a 'manifesto' style declaration on his own theology).

- The second thing to make the clergy more professional in their role for social care.

(This also was a manifesto style declaration developed much later in Runcie's setting up the two Archbishop's Commissions, 'Faith in the City' and 'Faith in the Country').

- Thirdly, the church needed to face the problem of the world that there was such a gap between rich and poor.

(This also was a manifesto statement which later would show him in action in Canterbury as the Head of the Worldwide Anglican Church, which needed to be sustained in the 10 year cycle of Lambeth Conferences and showed his commitment to travel throughout the Provinces of Christendom). The bit about the gap between rich and poor inspired an agenda which was later to cause friction between Runcie and Thatcher.

Accident prone Runcie at St. Albans

Carpenter went to interview Runcie one day at St. Albans, and found him stuck in the attic. He was retrieving a suitcase for a trip to Australia, then fell and injured his ankle. A poem was written :

'Lament for the Archbishop's Heel'

Come, seers and poets, sweep the lyre,

And with united voice conspire

To tell a tale of dreadful woe!

Our good Archbishop is laid low,

An evil sprite with jealous frown

From ladder high has hurled him down,

And on the Magi's blessed feast,

Dear Robert could have been deceased.

Runcie's Leadership style with clergy In St. Albans Diocese

Runcie, "It was difficult for me to engage in strategic thinking, since I knew so little about how to organise such a framework." Eric James, Bishop's Chaplain, commented on Runcie's leadership style. 'He had a canny way of handling clergy who got into trouble - financially, sexually or some other way. Keep these people away from me so that you can handle it unofficially. You can consult me if you really need to , but not as the bishop, - just as Mr. Runcie". This meant that a lot of tricky cases were handled delicately and successfully. Eric James was encouraged to set up a course for part time clergy, the first of its kind in England.

Witheridge on Runcie's leadership at Lambeth

Carpenter, "What about the indecisiveness of Runcie, the apparent weakness or at least the unwillingness to make decisions quickly?" Witheridge, "His style of leadership had its own strengths, but that wasn't obvious to a nation that had Margaret Thatcher as Prime Minister. There was so much emphasis on 'strong leadership' and Runcie's style of listening to people, taking his time to make decisions, and leading from behind, was simply not in fashion. He clearly likes to have strong people around him. Richard Chartres, also Chaplain, encouraged me to behave like that."

Leadership - a business school model from Erskine 1991

It is so easy to have very woolly anecdotal discussions on leadership. One needs a little instrumentation to put it into perspective. Professor Henry Mintzberg suggests that a chief executive has 10 roles and if he is not competent in all of these then he needs team members around who can fill in the gaps. Roles: Figurehead, executive chairman of board, entrepreneur, monitor, disturbance handler, spokesmen, negotiator, liaisaion officer, disseminator of information, resource allocator.

Professor William Reddin asserts that effective leaders require the skills of 'situation sensitivity', so that they can weigh up the dynamics of situations, and the skill of style flexibility, so that they can articulate the appropriate style to fit the perceived situation.

Discussion

Thatcher's leading from the front style was appropriate in dealing with crisis situations, or the situations in which she wanted to change the whole paradigm of politics, but that style would not be very appropriate in a situation such as allocation of resources in which consultation was expected. Runcie's sitting on the fence position in the debates on women's ordination, were probably okay as he needed the consultation process to nudge the church on and avoid a damaging split. But he was embarrassed when Waite lunged for hostages. The consultation style was not effective. He needed to activate a monitoring skill and nudge Waite back on course. Although Runcie seems to excel in skills of situation sensitivity, he has great difficulties in flexing his leadership style around the different roles of an Archbishop. He could to considerable advantage have been coached by a strong minded business school expert in leadership. Chaplains Witheridge and Richard Chartres did not have the expertise to help much here.

Organisational weaknesses perceived

Professor Gillian Stamp, Head of the Organisational Capability Unit at Brunel University, knew Runcie when she was doing her doctoral thesis. She commented on the 'weaknesses of the Church of England's management structure. "The synod is a legislative body with no executive. This was the root cause of the Church Commissioner's disastrous investment policy. It was like leaving Whitehall civil servants to make policy decisions which ought to have been in the hands of ministers." She participated with Runcie in the setting up of Hitchin archdeaconry. She perceived Runcie as an expert on structures and strategies of organisations and of people's capabilities within them with a wide ranging judgement. They hop on from one thing to another once they see the limitations in one job, or form of study and they move on relentlessly. She believed that it was Runcie's intellectual restlessness accompanied by vulnerability to boredom that carried him up and up in the church. "The job of diocesan bishop was too easy for him, even the archbishopric of Canterbury was too small for him. "

Pigs and women

However, Runcie was vulnerable to pretty women. Jenny Boyd-Carpenter heard him say one day that he wanted a pig and in no time she had got him 60 black pigs and a rent-a-boar service for him, and with all the piggy husbandry which this required brought her into frequent contact. Jenny would wear low neckline dresses - sort of Nell Gwynne outfits. A few eyebrows were raised when Jenny accompanied Runcie on the confirmation visits. The Express published a cartoon of Runcie at the altar with a cope of pigs embroidered on it and gumboots protruding underneath, and all the choirboys holding their noses. Rosalind was really happy at St. Albans and her career in music and concerts started taking off. Later she was to claim that she had raised over £1 million for charities from her concert playing and promotion. Meanwhile, Rosalind had said that she would not play a role as bishop's wife travelling around the diocese with Runcie. She would entertain at home but kept her major role as mother for the children. She demanded a separate existence. Runcie accepted the position amicably. The marriage seemed to be a happy one.

Vacancy at York

In 1974 York was vacant as Dr Coggan was appointed to Canterbury. Runcie admitted that he was offered the post but Rosalind said "No. We went on holiday and I hid in the garden where we were staying, and drank gin!"

Canterbury vacant 1979

Runcie took a full 6 weeks to accept the prime minister's invitation to become Archbishop of Canterbury. "I feel that I'm so uncertain, it's wrong for me to do it. We went on holiday to Italy and Rosalind cried most of the time, but there was no bottle of gin this time. Rosalind did not want her private life to be taken away. And I did not think I was good enough spiritually. I can sparkle sometimes but there are huge areas of boredom, of inability to be enthused by ministering the faith to the country. I wasn't as interested in religion or the church as Coggan or Ramsay". Anyway Jenny Boyd-Carpenter drove him up to his former vicar in Crosbie, John Turnbull and he said "If God wants you to do something, he gives you the grace to do it".

Archbishop

Runcie found Lambeth like a tudor court. There was no job description for Archbishop. Runcie brought with him to Lambeth his very able chaplain, Richard Chartres. Chartres "With rather a hazy briefing from his staff Runcie's decision-making was put to severe test. His antennae were very, very sensitive but when so many contradictory signals began to be received by them things started to get clogged. He had a fantastically strong physical stamina, and he was happier if he didn't take much rest. He would come to less harm if he were constantly turning to the next task, otherwise anxieties would surface in an ungovernable way." Carpenter, "It struck me that, here at least the Chaplain seemed to have been giving the Archbishop his orders, rather than the other way about, or at least managing him skilfully like a statesman handling a tricky monarch." However as the 92nd incumbent of this office it had a distinct history and without much difficulty an observer would be able to define 4 key roles of an Archbishop. They were :

Archbishop roles

1. He is the diocesan Bishop of Canterbury, the pastor of his flock.
2. The Archbishop has responsibilities towards the national Church .... presides over General Synod, presides over the Church Commissioners. This is an administrative role.
3. He is chief spokesman for the Church of England, to offer an informed and searching commentary on events and controversies. He is a member of the House of Lords. He is the custodian of the Anglican faith.
4. He has an international role as head of the Anglican Communion with 65 million followers.

Well, what is all that worry about the missing job description?

If you look carefully Carpenter's data reveals how he managed each such role.

The pastoral role

In June 1980 it was announced that Richard Third, Bishop of Dover, a suffragan bishop in the see of Canterbury would take responsibility off Runcie's shoulders for all diocesan affairs. So this pastoral role was delegated. Later, Carpenter reported that Runcie was often in Canterbury doing diocesan things as he was such a perfectionist and somehow could not release himself from a part of the job which he really enjoyed, so Third did not inherit quite the autonomy he expected.

The administrative role

For Runcie his administrative role for the national church was something of a nightmare of responsibility. Runcie, "Gerald Ellison, Bishop of London, is a good man, definitely the Church Commissioners man. He was soon taking the chair instead of me as my deputy. Therefore, I did not have so much acquaintance with the day to day running of the Church of England." Did Runcie intervene in this sphere like he had done with Third at Canterbury? Oh no, there is much evidence that Runcie kept his distance from the Church Commissioners. For 10 years they did their own thing and then in 1992 Plender blew the whistle on the property losses in the *Financial Times.* Erskine subsequently followed up the work of the Church Commissioners in 1996 and reported that between 1982 and 1996 their assets had under performed as a pension fund by a gobstopping £5 billion. Runcie needed to have set up and retained some monitoring device to track what was going on. He needed a '*Management Information System'* This could have been as simple as a one page report tracking Commissioner Assets against the Financial Times 100 index. Any variance here would have alerted him to the true impact of the disastrous dash into speculative retail developments, seemingly unnoticed for an incredible 10 years! Runcie did have occasional discussions with the First Estates Commissioner, Sir Douglas Lovelock, on the topic of MetroCentre, the shopping complex at Gateshead, developed by the Church Commissioners. Lovelock persuaded Runcie that all the job creation it generated was 4 square within the policies laid out in the Archbishop's *'Faith in the City'* report. What Lovelock never told the Archbishop was that MetroCentre absorbed investment of £272 millions of Commissioner funds. Ironically in 1995 the 80% interest in MetroCentre was sold for a mere £80 million, a huge loss for a pension fund to absorb. Unfortunately, Runcie, had much difficulty in distinguishing between delegation of role and abdication of role. He seemed to have been easily taken in when communicating about finance or business, for which first class honours in Greats and Theology, was not a particularly relevant training.

The International Role

This was a role which could have absorbed Runcie almost full time, and he had a huge enthusiasm for it. Soon after he entered Lambeth he was visited by Hector Laing, an old chum from the Scots Guards, chairman of United Biscuits and joint Treasurer of the Conservative Party. And he was prepared to put up some real money - refurbishing for Lambeth Palace, and place money in what is now a Lambeth Fund for Runcie's personal staff, including Terry Waite, as 'Archbishop's Assistant for Anglican Communion Affairs'. There is a job description for this post in the Lambeth files, "The job will include a Research element addressed to evolving a general strategy for the Archbishop's visits to the various provinces of the Anglican Communion and providing adequate briefing to ensure that he goes not just as a tourist but with the clear understanding of the opportunities to be grasped ... also a 'trouble shooter' a low profile emissary for the Archbishop to send to places where he is asked to intervene ... It would be difficult to think of anyone better equipped for this complex task than Terry Waite." Carpenter reports many successes in the Runcie / Waite partnership. The well informed Archbishop is really loved as he globe trots around the Anglican Communion, determined to lay the foundations of a mega successful Lambeth Conference in 1988, and the opportunities for the Papal visit planned for 1982. But Terry Waite wants to do much more than play the 'warm up' man for the overseas pastorals. He gets absorbed with hostages and his love for an active negotiating role. Runcie seems unable to box Waite into the expected 'low profile' role of his job description, and Runcie is hugely embarrassed when Terry himself becomes a hostage. Carpenter plays tribute to Waite's courage and being prepared to risk his life to spring hostages, but reports that Runcie is nervous about all the 'blood money' and 'arms money' that became the currency of the deals. Runcie, "Waite was initially a good friend and a good companion, and we worked well together. But he always enjoyed centre stage; he was what Oliver North once called 'a grandstander' - but forgivably so. Of course it was totally absorbing to him, but if was going to be an international negotiator he oughtn't to be on my staff". For 5 years Runcie's press secretary had to concentrate on the Terry Waite story. In some ways Runcie, like President Carter, also became an unwilling prisoner of his office, while the hostage crisis ran its course and became a black hole for absorbing his time and energy. Carpenter, however, rationalised on the Runcie enthusiasm for globe trotting. "It got Runcie away from Lambeth, when the relationship with Rosalind was going through a bad patch".

The role as custodian of the faith

Garry Bennett, Trinity Hall academic, in the *Preface to Crockfords* was uncompromising in his comments on Runcie's role in faith. "He was not trained as a theologian, and though he makes extensive use of academics and speechwriters, his own position is unclear." Yet this was a period when reaffirmation of the faith was sorely needed. There were many themes of change flowing through church life, revised attitudes to women's ordination, to divorce and remarriage, to homosexual unions, to the possibility of admitting homosexual priests, to the Resurrection story. The flock needed their faith reinforced, but found Runcie backing the doubters. Notice in the Runcie manifesto statement as Bishop of St. Albans he stuck his mast to the questioning Church, the Robinson, Montefiore, Jenkins, fraternity. To allow this hangover from 'Greats' to continue was a devastating error of judgement. Many Christians found the attack on the Resurrection Story of deep offence. How could he possibly have stood back and given the platform to the doubters? Incredible for an archbishop to be so careless. Erskine took a peep at the 1990 accounts of the Church of England Commissioners. His eye strayed to a section devoted to the 'Redundant Churches Committee'. In between 1969 and 1990 1,292 churches in England had closed. But with the doubters in the bishoprics isn't it amazing that 2,000 churches had not closed?

Runcie's Views on Royalty

Runcie in the Royal wedding sermon, "Here is the stuff of which fairy tales are made". Carpenter to Runcie "What do you think of the difficulties of the Prince of Wales"? Runcie, "It depends whether the Prince wins his way with the British people over the next 5 to 10 years. Also it would quite help if he loved the Church of England a bit more. And when he came to Lambeth for his pre-marriage talk he said in a kind of nostalgic way, 'I came and served here sometimes'. But it was something that had passed away. And I think that he was deeply into the Laurens van de Post spirituality. I don't think that he took the Church of England very seriously. I remember my chaplain Richard Chartres - a very observant man - saying to me when he and Diana came to see me for the first time 'He's seriously depressed. You can tell that by his voice'. The person I admire is the Queen. She is the only person who has the ability to arise above it. I've always felt that she wanted to encourage the Archbishop of Canterbury and to listen to what he had to say - to ask him his opinion about things. Now, I never managed to strike that sort of relationship with the Prince of Wales".

Placing Tutu as Archbishop of Capetown

Runcie "I remember Waite ringing me up in 1981 during the World Council of Churches and saying that he had met a South African delegate who thought we should give more profile for Desmond Tutu. And I asked him about the diocese of Johannesburg, where a pupil of mine was then the bishop. And I said, 'I think he could possibly come home now. If we could engineer a vacancy for him in England could you, do you think, get Tutu elected Bishop of Johannesburg?" Waite, "Yes". Runcie, "And if you manage that do you think that when Philip Russell, the Archbishop of Capetown, retires, you could get Desmond elected there". Waite, "Yes". Runcie, "I managed to persuade the Crown Appointments Commission to get Portsmouth to accept my man, Timothy Bavin. This gave the ANC Tutu who was in a position to communicate that the party wasn't a bunch of communists. This had a big effect on world affairs".

The Pope visits Canterbury May 28th 1982

The Kentish gazette reports "The Pope arrived in Canterbury by helicopter. He drove into the city. A great round of applause echoed through the Cathedral as he entered. The service was a Celebration of Faith and began with the choirs of Canterbury and Rochester singing anthems. Pope and Archbishop walked in procession down the Nave to the Altar. The two men knelt in silence, then said the Lord's prayer, and exchanged the kiss of peace. Runcie, 'This is a service of celebration, but the present moment is so full of pain for so many in the world. Our minds turn to the conflict and tragic loss of life in the South Atlantic, and we also remember the sufferings of Your Holiness' fellow countrymen in Poland. In 597 Pope Gregory sent Augustine to bring the word to the English race. I rejoice that the successors of Gregory and Augustine stand here today in the church which was built in their partnership in the Gospel.' Archbishop and Pope moved to St. Augustine's chair where they kissed the 6th century gosples, the gifts of Pope Gregory to Augustine. The Pope preached a 45 minute sermon, 'My dear brothers and sisters of the Anglican Communion, whom I love and long for, how happy I am to be able to speak to you in this great cathedral. May the dialogue we have already begun lead us to the day of full restoration of unity in love and faith'. Afterwards Primate and Pope prayed side by side just near the spot where Becket was murdered. During the service they both put their signatures to a Common Declaration to set up a commission to examine the outstanding doctrinal differences which still separate us." Erskine comment: "This meeting certainly gave a boost to the ecumenical movement and established much more normal communications between Anglicans and Catholics, but the differences in attitudes about sex and ordination, abortion, and divorce were if anything increased in the 1980s and 1990s. But when a new Pope is elected progress might be possible from this improvement in communications.

Runcie sitting on the fence April 1981.

Runcie on women's ordination. "There are arguments which I respect both for and against, but I think the best arguments for the ordination of women are these - if priesthood is to represent God to mankind and mankind to God in days when an exclusive male leadership is no longer the case in most walks of life, it's hard to justify the fact that men alone can represent God to mankind and mankind to God. I therefore now think that the best arguments are in favour of opening the priesthood to women. But there *are* arguments on both sides and I have opposed the ordination of women simply because I think unity among Christians is more important than ordination of women as a particular topic - a topic that can arouse strong feelings both ways."

Sermon in St. Paul's 26th July 1982, Service of Thanksgiving

"Thanks are due for the courage and endurance of those who fought in the South Atlantic and praise be given for the lack of triumphalism of the victors. At the hard fought battle of Goose Green the reaction was not the conqueror's triumph, but 'thank God it's stopped. It is right to be proud of such men.' It is impossible to be a Christian and not to long for peace. War should belong to the tragic past, to history. It should find no place in humanity's agenda for the future. In our prayers we shall quite rightly remember those who are bereaved in our own country and the relations of the young Argentinian soldiers who were killed."

Denis Thatcher on the House of Commons terrace after the service, "The boss was angry enough this morning, now she is spiting blood".

Runcie's Visit to Malborough College and impression of James, his son

James Runcie, "I was 16 when my Father was asked down to Marlborough to preach. That was excruciatingly embarrassing, because I thought he was going to cock it up. In fact he was brilliant. From then on I realised how exceptional a speaker he was, and how exceptional a thinker."

The Runcie / Thatcher relationship

When Runcie was at Oxford reading 'Greats' he clashed with Margaret Roberts. "Not my sort of girl. Very plump and serious, and like sitting next to a coil of electricity." It is amazing that she appointed him archbishop, but very soon they fell out over the Falklands Victory Service; Whitelaw, Home Secretary, (Runcie's ex Squadron Commander in the Scots Guards), told him that Thatcher referred to him as 'king wet' and later his commission's report 'Faith in the City' was rubbished by her as a Marxist Manifesto. I have read 'Faith in the City', and it was very critical of the poverty of inner city areas and the lack of compassion or political will to cope with the sense of helplessness of the people. The report had two pages of recommendations to the Government. Thatcher was not amused at receiving instructions from the archbishop, whom she had appointed!

Use of ghost writers

To Garry Bennett from Runcie, wanting material for his Presidential address to the Synod, 'I don't know whether you would like to have a shot at something to help me, or to talk sometime by telephone or face to face .... You are the only person to date who in my present naked state has produced a brief which I could actually use.'.

Appointments

'According to Bennett's diary, George Austin, Archdeacon of York, produced an interesting computer read-out which showed how virtually every episcopal or decanal appointment was Bob Runcie's nepotism. The list demonstrated that liberal churchman had been preferred to Anglo-Catholics and evangelicals'.

The anonymous preface to Crockford's

The first time the Church Commissioners assumed direct responsibility for printing this reference book they asked Bennett, a theology don of New College Oxford, ghost writer to Runcie, and often promised a preferment of a deanery by Runcie, but never getting the appointment, to write the preface. It caused a storm and within a week of publication Bennett committed suicide by gassing himself in his car. His preface began with a eulogy of Runcie, ended with a savage attack, amazing for this to be in an official Church Commissioner publication.

The eulogy -

"Since 1980 Robert Runcie has established himself as a notable holder of the Primacy. He has intelligence, personal warmth and a formidable capacity for hard work. He listens well and has built up a range of personal contacts among clergy and laity far wider than any of his predecessors. His speeches and addresses are thoughtful, witty and persuasive.

The attack

"He often took the line of least resistance on policies. He was not trained as a theologian, and though he makes extensive use of academics and speechwriters, his own position is unclear. He puts off all questions until someone else makes a decision. He is described by Mr Field M.P. as an archbishop who is usually nailing his colours to the fence."

The attack found other targets -" The appointment of David Jenkins, as Bishop of Durham. a man of such imprecision of mind and expression, under the guise of being a theologian was a minor Anglican disaster." (He was the Cuddesdon College academic promoted by Runcie, who questioned the miracles and the resurrection of Christ. Three days after his enthronement in York Minster a thunderbolt struck the roof). "The General Synod was virtually powerless and consistently ineffective; most of the debates were for show".

And the coup de gras "Let's hope that the Church of England can be rescued from its present suburban captivity and become once again a

Church for the English people."

Runcie on marriage and divorce

"Every marriage has its incompatibilities. Every couple has its ups and downs. But what people must understand is that very often by getting over the hump and working through the problem, you can produce a richer relationship. Some of the deepest experiences of life come not so much from neat harmonies but from something askew that is worked through together. You come out the other side feeling that you've learnt something about yourself, about each other and the nature of your marriage."

The legacy of the position inherited by Dr. Carey

Erskine. Dr. Carey was generally regarded as an Evangelical. This means that he defends a faith which is a strict interpretation of scripture. He would not have much truck with modernists such as David Jenkins. The first crisis which blew up was Plender's whistle blowing report in the *Financial Times* on the property deals of the Church of England Commissioners. Carey immediately set up the investigative machinery to find out what was going on and what to do about it. Sir Michael Colman, an experienced business man replaced Sir Douglas Lovelock, a Whitehall mandarin, as First Estates Commissioner and in addition a Finance Manager was appointed to the Assets Committee, and professional pension fund managers were appointed. Bishop Turnbull was commissioned to provide a blueprint for radical re-organisation of the national church *'Working for one Body'.* This recommended that the Church Commissioners should be reduced from 95 to 15. That a new Archbishop's Council should be created to enable them to rediscover their role of leadership. This Council would make the main decisions on spending. Management of the Church assets would largely be 'outsourced' and given over to professional fund managers working under contract. A controversial implication of this radical reorganisation is that the link between Church and State as manifested by the Church Commissioners is much weakened. Turnbull is possibly the first step to a progress towards disestablishment - a way of avoiding a supreme governor who espouses a Laurence Van de Post spirituality. Amazingly, in August 1996 reports were circulated in the press of the 'Balmoral' meetings on the future of the monarchy, and disestablishment of the Church of England was on the agenda.

Definition of the 'impossible job of Archbishop'.

Rev John Witheridge, Runcie's Chaplain, now Headmaster of Charterhouse, argued that the position of Archbishop of Canterbury was in its present form unworkable. "As it stands the job that Runcie will bequeath is an impossible one. It has been so for at least 100 years .... Randall Davidson said that it was an 'impossible job for one man'; and Cosmo Lang complained that his work-load was 'incredible, indefensible, and inevitable'. William Temple did 'the work of a Prime Minister with the staff of a Head Master', and Geoffrey Fisher believed 'that the first requisite of an Archbishop is to be as strong as a horse'."

Erskine "The Archbishop's job can be defined in roles which reflect the history of the position and the contemporary pressures and priorities. The present incumbent must then prioritise his time and decide which bits are the 'core' parts of the office requiring direct attention, and which must be delegated to others. He needs the management nous to determine how to delegate without abdicating. He needs to monitor all delegated roles. He can then breathe. He doesn't need the energy of a horse all the time! The restrictions which seemed to imprison Runcie were dramatically cut away by his successor.

Reader

Now you are gently invited back to the beginning of this report, to get off the fence, and make judgements about Runcie. Could he be recommended for another term? Don't forget to apply, among other things, the principles of good practice personnel management!

Two Erskine brothers disagree about the role of merit assessment.

Major Philip Erskine, Scots Guards, "In 1996 they introduced merit assessment at Stellenbosh University, activated by the students, and the staff were livid. I remember as a boy all those masters who were such characters at school, and I am sure they would never have survived 'merit assessment'. Later in life I saw Archbishop Tutu in action. You know he appointed a bishop here with a record of convictions for child abuse. He would never have survived a merit assessment from his own diocese! And now you look at our government here and its crime record, and the police will not confront the gangsters in the townships, and they just cannot deliver. I cannot think of any prime minister or archbishop who would ever really survive 'merit assessment'. If we really had and applied merit assessment we would never have a government, or a university or even Coca Cola. You forget that at the top appointments are politically motivated. The man or woman appointed is usually one with the qualities nearest the agenda and aspirations of the appointing power group. And of course if circumstances change during the 'reign of the top person, you will almost certainly get dissatisfaction. And you, brother Robert, want your readers to merit assess Robert Runcie. It's all for the birds".

References

Carpenter, Humphrey, *'Portrait of Runcie,'The Reluctant Archbishop,*

Erskine, R.K., *Business Management',* Prentice-Hall 1991

Erskine, R.K. '1982 - 1996 Case of the Church of England Commissioners ', Case Clearing House, Cranfield 1996.

Erskine, R.K. '*Strategic Positioning of Robots,*' Case Clearing House, Cranfield 1996.

Plender, John, '*Unholy Saga of the Church's missing millions,* Financial Times 11th July 1992.

Reddin, W., *'Managerial Effectiveness',* McGraw-Hill, 1970

Turnbull, Michael, Bishop of Durham, *Working as one Body. The Report of the Archbishop's Commission on the Organisation of the Church of England,* Church House Publising 1995.

*End

6.6. Book review of *Escalation in Decision-Making* by Helga Drummond, Oxford University Press 1996.

21/2/97

The overview

This book gives an analysis of the Taurus Stock Exchange system for paperless settlement, which failed after absorbing £500 million of funding after a development time of 3 years. Helga seeks an explanation of the behaviour behind this loss making phenonemum. For an overview of the contents of this book she suggests that the reader moves firstly to her conclusions in chapter 14. This offers a triangulation of three academic paradigms as lenses to explain what happened. She defines escalation as a point in decision-making when those with power persist in continuing with a course of action long after when the reasonable person would have abandoned the project as being unviable. She finds that Peter Rawlins, Stock Exchange Chief Executive, did not really support this project on his appointment and failed on two further occasion to abandon it through his lack of power and conviction to get an abort decision carried. This research recognises that actual decisions are the result of power struggles and not necessarily based on grounds of rationality or economics. This final chapter summarises the different approaches to escalation, and points to further research to helping the recognition of escalation behaviour and ways of confronting it before the waste is allowed to become a crisis. Helga's approach will appeal to social scientists and also to risk managers as she uses this case to examine the behaviour of a chief executive engaging in a high risk situation.

Chronology

This gives a 3 page summary of events in the Taurus case beginning with 1970 and the recommendation of the Heasman Committee to streamline the settlement system. Then are given the main events from 1986 till abandonment in 1993. After the stock market crash in October there were unsettled share bargains worth a total of £13.4 billion.

Chapter 1 - What causes escalation?

This chapter reviews the behaviour of executives when they make decisions in a risky environment, and draws some attention to the executive, who having risen to the top thinks he or she is infallible and just masks out negative feedback. When the executive persists in this course of action it is labelled escalation. Social-psychological theory suggests that persistence is driven by ego forces. Decision dilemma theorists suggest that decision-makers are simply helpless and they can do nothing till market forces exert themselves.

Chapter 2 - Researching Taurus

The researcher used press reports as basis for making up interview lists with the key players. Her key question was why did they persist with escalation? She gave them in advance the questions to be asked and then taped their replies. She looked for a pattern and used 3 basic perceptual lenses for interpretation and analysis. Interesting points emerged. Vista software imported was not popular among some stakeholders. There was much conflict in the Siscot project management group reflecting the conflict of interests of Stock Exchange and City players. Progress never seemed to be fast enough.

Chapter 3 - Time, Gentlemen, Please!

This is a useful background chapter to help understand the culture of the City before and after de-regulation. The Stock Exchange had got rid of the trading floor and replaced it with a computerised market making system, so the market makers thought themselves able to computerise settlements with equal competence as the Stock Exchange. Also the balance of power in the City had changed following de-regulation in 1986. The Stock Exchange had much less clout with market makers.

Chapter 4 - The scandal that never was.

After de-regulation there was the stock market crash of October 1987, and at the peak there were one million unsettled bargains worth £13.4 billion. It was amazing that this level of chaos did not bring down the credit structure of the City, but it didn't. It was perceived that Taurus would become the pathway to rolling settlement in a shorter time and thus reduce risk in unsettled bargains.

Chapter 5 - The Mad Hatter's tea party

This chapter reveals the discussions and progress of two key committees supervising Taurus. Firstly, Siscot, which consisted of members representing the stakeholders, i.e. the Stock Exchange and brokers representing private clients and the institutions. The members of Siscot were expected to fight the interests of the industry sector they represented. "We started walking through water, then it became mud, then it became honey, then it became glue, and in the end it was quick-drying concrete". Siscot's primary role was to get the providers of the system to come up with a specification, which they could approve. No less than 16 designs were considered. People disappeared into working sub-groups to come up with compromises, but these were never agreed with any clarity for the satisfaction a year later of project director Bill Wills. Meantime consultants, Touche Ross, stated that Taurus could only be justified on grounds of prestige; the commercial case was dodgy. They disputed that Taurus was essential as a mechanism to reduce settlement time and therefore risk of default. London had never had a history of default, so Taurus was pursuing a non-problem and at huge cost. Meanwhile a 'Group of 30' influential bankers, with role of defining international settlement standards decreed that there should be rolling settlements on T + 3, i.e. within 3 days. Philip Hooker, representing City firm Hoare Govett, joined the debate, rubbished the report of the 'Group of 30', and declared that Taurus was a white elephant. This was in 1989, before the big money was invested and wasted. Why was the plug not pulled at that stage? There was no agreed business system to pass for development to the technical people. (Any money spent would have been like funding a building project with land that had not got planning permission). Several members of Siscot were coll about Taurus as they saw this as a settlement system in competition with themselves and there was a lot of money from settlement which would be lost. The final design of Siscot was to weld together what was known as Taurus 3 with Taurus 7 & 8 and run two systems in parallel. This design was a complicated nightmare and a hopeless brief to send to any of the provider community.

Chapter 6 - an opportunity lost.

Peter Rawlins, Chief Executive, was head hunted into the Stock Exchange by the Bank of England. He was asked to implement a programme of drastic reform but to keep out of Taurus! After 12 years of arguing a compromise had been developed and no-one was interested in any further delay. Rawlins was not convinced. He couldn't seem to find who owned the project, yet 30 committees in the Stock Exchange and the City had some involvement. Despite the doubts expressed by consultants, Touche Ross, John Watson, partner in Coopers and Lybrand was appointed project director. He had an impeccable track record as the project manager of Talisman, the current settlement system. As part of Watson's new job description was a clause that there should be no interference from the Chief Executive. The project was funded. In light of Watson's position Rawlins did not have enough other IT competent people around him who could make the case to stop it, and his own brief had been that Taurus was OKAY, let it continue. The opportunity to abort had arrived and was not taken.

Chapter 7 - The origins of escalation.

In this chapter Helga threads the data so far collected through her analysis. The most interesting set of observations were those of the power relationships. When Rawlins, chief executive arrived on the scene Siscot had after a year of great argument adopted a compromise design, Taurus 3 + 7 + 8, and did not wish to open up further argument despite the negative feedback which was around. Also, Watson, had been appointed project director on condition of 'no interference'. He played the role of the all powerful provider and had the budget to steamroller the project through. The group of 30 bankers wanted to make London the financial capital of the world and they saw electronic settlement as the instrument to get there. For Rawlins to abort was like a fly trying to stop a juggernaut. The project had become institutionalised. And the providers naturally wanted to continue as this work for them was a gravy train. Although Rawlins had an instinct to abort, he had neither the time, nor energy, or priority, or expertise to abort. Helga explains the dynamics that make escalation a reality.

Chapter 8 - Building Taurus.

This soon became a nightmare. There were considerable gaps in the high level business specification yet there was a huge pressure to deliver a working system. The options were to program the system from scratch or to buy a proprietary package, and adapt it. Vista software from USA was reviewed and taken on board for trials. The technical team under Watson admitted later that they regretted this decision. The package adopted needed root and branch modifications. The package was not very well documented, so it was a major effort to understand where changes needed to be made, and the only Vista manager who really knew the system suffered a heart attack. Other Vista people did not have a grasp of the dynamics of the whole system and the vital points of interaction between the modules. Meanwhile the specification for Taurus was constantly changing and

Vista staff, were re-programming again and again. Meanwhile the DTI announced that they would refuse to grant regulations unless the Stock Exchange agreed to insure the private investor against settlement losses; the final coup de gras from HMG was that Taurus had to be a voluntary system and would have to be sold to the public. Nearly 100 pages of legal drafts were prepared to give effect to the de-materialisation of the paperwork.

Chapter 9 - Chickens come home.

Coopers and Lybrand were constantly urging City firms to get ready for Taurus though by now many were skeptical. In May 1992 Watson was saying that the specification was virtually complete; and the project 95% complete; the programmers were faintly amused at what he meant by virtual! Anyway completion dates were constantly being revised. The provider group kept reporting to the Taurus monitoring group that everything was okay. Peter Rawlins just kept his distance despite lack of real progress. He put yet another Cooper's and Lybrand man in to check if everything was okay and he recommended a delivery date 13 months later still, but with the proviso that it was still possible to implement Taurus. When Rawlins appeared before the newly formed Board of the Stock Exchange he raised the question of whether Taurus was the right sort of project to be involved in, but they would not accept such a radical agenda, and approved funding for another year. (The providers heaved a sigh of relief. The gravy train was flowing for yet another year for them.)

Chapter 10 - A second opportunity lost.

Helga analyses the data leading up to the funding decision despite so much negative feedback of project progress. She finds a huge force of institutionalisation which is articulated to keep the project going; and the providers lap up the challenge of doing something difficult. Provider / client communication had become ritualised. Rawlins defended Taurus in public. Noone seemed to notice that expected benefits were shrinking rapidly, while costs were escalating. This was no longer a value for money project by the wildest imagination, yet there was no natural forum where these issues could be objectively debated. The opportunity to abort came and went. Helga summarises: The root of the escalation was the overarching influence of the 'great and the good'; The immediate causes were - a complex project, decision-makers working at the boundaries of knowledge, inadequate control and communication mechanisms, an authoritarian culture; Escalation was the observance of due diligence - 'This is what some committee said we ought to do'.

Chapter 11 - The final months.

Rawlins was concerned about Taurus project costs, so re-negotiated the provider contracts unilaterally, and sent the Touche Ross advisers packing. They cannot staunch media criticism of Taurus. Stock Exchange Board members kept a stiff upper lip over Taurus, and 'lunched their way out of criticism'. Hooker attended a breakfast briefing. 'Nowadays people are not spending several years building an ideal system, they are instead determining their strategic direction and making a series of small, pertinent, low budget moves in that direction ... The trouble with Taurus is that it is a Seventies idea, with an Eighties budget, which has become dislocated from the tough, competitive trading conditions of the Nineties'. IBM's communications server for the security interfaces failed. They were working just too close to the edge of technology. Confidence eroded in the testing methods proposed for the much re-programmed Vista Software. The providers felt let down by Rawlins' lack of real support and his reference to the project as his albatross. Rawlins finally put in two more IT gurus, a consultant from Anderson, and another senior Coopers and Lybrand consultant, to see if Taurus was okay. Finally he went to the monitoring group and announced 'I have scrapped it'.

Chapter 12 - Revelation

In October 1992 Anderson, reported on whether they would be able to operate Taurus after completion. In 8 pages this consultant laid out a devastating summary: 'There is no operating system. There is no centre. It isn't designed, let alone built. If you want us to operate it, then we have a list of 15 things, which we have reservations about.' This became the point at which Rawlins decided to abort the project, but he took another two months preparing Stock Exchange directors for this decision. Stuart Senior of Coopers and Lybrand was called in and soon there was enough provider or independent corroboration for Rawlins to carry the abort decision and resign.

Chapter 13 - Withdrawal.

This chapter is an analysis of the decision to withdraw from Taurus using the escalation frameworks. The discussion relates with the breaking down of myths and substitution of other myths and issues of accountability. The board were really miffed at the cancellation decision. Rawlins turned on them and blamed them for the pressure to continue an ambitious, but non-essential project. The board now had no option but to go along with Rawlins, for continuation would require another tranche of funding, and the technical people were still wanting another two years of development time and further one year of systems test time, and would make no guarantee that the system delivered was anywhere near value for money. Helga had a fascination with the fact that withdrawal took so long, nearly 3 months. Rawlins had to manage the power politics, and ensure that abortion was achieved against much opposition and strongly entrenched interests.

Judgements

This book is a superb case study, readable, well structured, a fascinating blow by blow account of the IT project which absorbed £500 million for nothing. Helga used lots of public domain material, but this was backed up by extensive interviews with the key players and also committee members and programmers, who told much more than what the public pronouncements declared. Helga is primarily a social scientist and used to probing issues of motivation, power, and organisational dynamics. She has a good track record developing the theory of escalation, and there are many references to that work in this book.

A profile for escalation - use in other cases?

Helga has nudged forward the academic understanding of manifestations of escalation, and this is a framework which could be used to explain seemingly irrational behaviour in many of the disaster case studies. She makes the point that successful executives become corrupted by their success and stop hearing what their colleagues are saying. A common observation disaster analysts make is that the disaster making decision was often made by a chief executive persisting on an ego trip and failing to listen to colleagues. This was the prime cause of the disastrous merger of Ferranti. This company had net assets of £1.5 billion and decided to merge with a US defence company, ISC in 1987. Sir Derek Allun-Jones was the CEO of Ferranti, and he could not 'hear' the distinct warnings of senior colleagues that the merger was with a dud. This ended with the bankruptcy of Ferranti. But there is a bizarre implication to all this. As fat cat executives get huge self delivered pay rises they become more and more prone to escalation and disaster. High pay high risk. Modest pay, and the board acts as a problem solving team with its feet on the ground. Perhaps there is a negative correlation between company performance and chief executive compensation. That will make you think! Helga's book on escalation decision-making has given us an uncomfortable nudge in a new direction.

The criticism

Helga aspired to take the reader beyond understanding escalation to offer a strategy to prevent waste. But this final bit is not really convincing. What advice does escalation theory offer victim operators like Rawlins? The Bank of England has picked up the torch of Taurus in the making of CREST. But there is a probability that CREST will fall the same way as Taurus, and Helga does not really give the CREST team a focus of bullet points to avoid another shambles.

An alternative academic approach to the Taurus disaster.

There is a relevant approach to apply in the management of large IT projects such as Taurus, which is much simpler in application than the social science approach of escalation theory, and easy to articulate. The alternative approach is to declare adherence to three industry good practice standards which if applied could prevent Taurus style disaster manifestations. It is well known from the case study literature that there is frequent friction at the client / provider interface. With the use of three good practice frameworks the friction can be prevented and IT Projects can follow an almost certain route of gathering added value. The key to this golden route is to contain 'provider' power, and substitute it with client power. Three good practice frameworks follow.

1. Strategic Application Search.

Messrs Michael Porter and Michael Earl [1] offer a useful framework for getting sound Information Technology Methodology. The secret is to be creative both within the business and the technological environment and work with teams of line managers combined with IT resource people. This requires awareness of what IT can contribute, combined with a vision of what competitive forces are crucial in the business situation. The starting point is to seek out the concepts of Michael Porter's model of Competitive Forces and then his model of Strategic Application Search

Stages of SAS

1. Concepts briefing. Brief review of the Technology of I T
2. Market Analysis, Threats and Opportunities.
3. Strategic evaluation and selection.
4. IT Opportunity Scan.
5. Application Selection.

Examine possibilities on Porter's Value Chain

- There are cost drivers and added value activities.
- Consider purchasing, manufacturing, dispatch, sales and marketing, customer services.

6. Implementation

Assign 3 teams consisting of both IT resource people and client managers and staff to look at the following possibilities:

- Deploy I T to improve automation
- Alter the linkages in the business system to get quicker responses and better decisions.
- Look for information lying around which could have value added by IT.

2. Basic stages of design for IT systems, follows after SAS

Erskine [2]

1. Feasibility study:

done jointly by client and resource provider.

(a) systems proposal by provider after consultation and investigation.

(c) economic evaluation, clients predict benefit, providers predict cost. NPV and rates of return computed.

2. Proposal validation.

Need to pass green lights, (a) The project is technically viable, (b) Has sufficient added value, (c) The client has made an assessment of the pain of change and resourced its implementation, (d) accepted the security implications.

The project champion uses this stage to secure senior management authorisation, prioritisation of the project and then development through later stages.

3. Detailed systems specification.

Provider develops this phase.

4. Specification validation.

Client manager and operating staff do this with their own appointed business analysts.

5. Program specification.

Provider systems analysts do this.

6. Program validation.

Provider programmers accept specifications.

7 Program writing and testing. Jointly done by programmers, systems analysts and client analysts.

8. Data collection. Teamwork

9. Systems testing. Teamwork

10.Implementation: Teamwork

(a) management and clerical training (Note later Zuboff Principles apply at this phase).

(b) issue of implementation manual,

(c) pilot runs,

(d) 'go live' decision. A quality control point for senior management.

11. System maintenance and post-system audit. Teamwork.

From the above activities it will be noted that the activity of validation is given equal prominence to that of proposal and investigation. When budgets are set the resource provider has resources so that he can 'push' the design forwards. Also the client needs funds so that he can 'pull' the design through. In practice there is a subtle balance in the budgets. If the resource providers have too much resources they may steamroller the design and compromise the validation points above. If the client has all the resources, he may buy an incompatible set of robots. The project champion has to play the role of referee, and in particular reconcile conflict at the feasibility stage between different client stakeholders. If there is no clarity and support for the business vision of the IT project then computing is a waste of time and effort and should not be authorised. The golden rule of operating this way may be summed up 'Always work with validated specifications'. This protects the project from changes in staff during development and offers the possibility of aborting the project if new unforeseen specifications are imposed. The abort process is the re-crank of the feasibility stage, and particular examination of residual value for money in new circumstances.

A project starting point may also be an assessment of a proprietary package. In which case the design phases will generally be much reduced, but the validation processes are still necessary, otherwise the wrong package may be bought! Beware skipping the feasibility study phase. A point of major interest is that UK Government are by far the biggest waster of resources identified in this archive, estimated by Collins[5] at £.5 billion a year for the previous 10 years! Some of this waste occurs because of bad 'outsourcing' decisions for development or management of IT systems and glitches which occur when legacy systems are brought up to date. The major waste occurs because Her Majesty's Government, (like many other bureaucracies), gives large budgets to providers who 'push' IT design without client validation, and this is rejected at the implementation phase.

3. Zuboff's Framework.

In a prime source Zuboff[3] explains how technology affects the motivation of people doing their jobs. She develops a framework to predict what the job outcome might be and then offers simple case studies to illustrate these principles. Resistance to robots has a variety of causes - people prefer to see and touch source material; they may resist a 'tube', (this is another word for robot); they don't like; the 'tube' to observe and measure their productivity; they dislike the 'tube' breaking up a social grouping; they may feel stress in learning new unfamiliar skills required by the tube; managers often in positioning robots forget to make them 'user friendly' enough to all the stakeholders, employees and customers. She suggests that managers should welcome the manifestation of people resistance as it generally signals a problem about the quality of the working environment and this needs attention! Possible outcomes of introducing robots to the workplace are :

the job might be eliminated altogether; it might be dehumanised; the job might be enhanced; it might be made more challenging; it might be made less challenging; it might create a different social environment of doing work with more teamwork or less teamwork; it might require new skills, new styles, new economics of scale.

The requirement is that managers learn how to position robots strategically to get positive effects. If they do not anticipate the human reaction at the workplace to the robot, then sabotage may ruin a system that has cost £ millions to set up. Alternatively a 'clumsily' positioned robot can cost £ millions of lost added value.

A few key dates follow which illustrate the way Taurus was developed with an abuse of provider power.

Key Dates

May 1986 Stock Exchange embarks on Taurus

December 1987 Group of 30, influential bankers, (the great and the good) decree a settlement period for dealings of T + 3.

November 1988 Siscot Committee was formed by and for clients of Taurus to supervise Taurus and approve specifications. Members represented their constituency interest. Touche Ross, consultants advised in the monitoring role till Rawlins removed them as a cost cutting measure in 1991. Many corporate intricacies such as transfers, rights issues and benefits, and the legal implications of dematerialisation were still unresolved when Siscot stood down.

August 1989 John Watson, seconded from Coopers & Lybrand, appointed Taurus project director. (No interference clause in his contract)

November 1989 Peter Rawlins appointed chief executive of the Stock Exchange. Told not to interfere with Taurus.

March 1990 Taurus promised for October 1991, Vista software adopted. Decision later regretted by Watson.

January 1991 Taurus promised revised date, May 1992, delay blamed on unforseen regulatory implications.

1991 Date uncertain, Richard Wilson, partner in Coopers and & Lybrand, moves in for 2 weeks at Rawlins' request. Advises him that Taurus is okay.

October 1991 Taurus promised revised again to May 1993, because of software writing problems. Total funding now £90 million.

June 1992 Stock Exchange fund a further £25 million of Taurus, developments costs underestimated.

October 1992 Anderson Consulting reported to Rawlins that Taurus could not be implemented as a long term viable system.

January 1993 Stuart Senior of Coopers and Lybrand corroborated Anderson's opinion.

March 11th 1993 Rawlins announced abandonment of Taurus and resigned

Failure to adopt good practice in Taurus

Good practice observations

The good practice school would aver that Taurus was a 'no hoper' because the team never conducted a proper feasibility study; they introduced a technical solution before there was any clarity on what the stakeholders might be prepared to validate, and half way through the project Government intervened with a demand for extra requirements, which had not been anticipated and was difficult to graft on to the design as currently specified. There are many examples in the literature where top management has expected to change the culture of an organisation by imposing an IT system, but failed abysmally at the point of implementation when disgruntled stakeholders, unfamiliar with what is being imposed, sabotage the system with little difficulty. Taurus was a very difficult IT prospect, as the stakeholders were so diverse - the Stock Exchange, the Traders, Companies with Share registers. Moreover, this was also a time of evolution for the Stock Exchange itself for its business mission and role after 'big bang' and the de-regulation of the 1980s. This was a very high risk environment for IT development. When Rawlins arrived and found that Taurus was up and running and funded all he needed to do was to ask to see the documentation of the feasibility study and the documents of proposal validation. We know from Helga's account that Taurus never got through systems validation and that Siscot membership, the body supervising the project, did not have enough IT competence to walk through design at the operating level with their colleagues at home base. Watson just seemed to assume validation by client stakeholders of working design was not a part of good practice IT development. How wrong could he be? It would have caused delays, but without a depth of client validation any system being built is a structure built on sand, not the basis for sending to programme development. It would have been so tempting to tear up the 'no interference' clauses in Watson, the provider's, contract. What arrogance for a provider to think he could operate without accountability to the line executive, Rawlins. The data suggests that once a majority on Siscot were happy as they adopted Taurus 3 +7 & 8, they virtually disbanded, yet no-one had seen the final specifications, and there had never been the expectation that members would walk through the design at the operating level to validate it. The provider had a blank cheque to progress. Meanwhile disaffected members of Siscot could walk away unconcerned. They didn't need the Stock Exchange in the post 'Big Bang' era of de-regulation, thank you very much. This was a white elephant which was being paid for by someone else. With IT good practice frameworks in place Rawlins can test out his intuition that this is not a project for the Stock Exchange to get involved in. Very soon Rawlins would get directly at the data which will get support at a meeting with the Stock Exchange Council, without them thinking 'Rawlins has thrown a wobbly'. Rawlins does not need a series of external consultants to advise him. He just needs to keep his calm and demand to see the evidence of project validation - no evidence, no more funding, the project is aborted full stop. As other crises occur in the project and Helga relates with yet a further opportunity to abort, all Rawlins has to ask for is a re-crank of the feasibility study reports, and it is so obvious that the case can be made to carry an abort decision before the waste accumulates to scandalous proportions. In May 1992 Watson was saying that the specification was virtually complete; and the project 95% complete; and it has not even passed the feasibility stage. His no interference clause is a complete block for line management knowing what is really going on. But providers like Watson, must operate within the framework of the good practice models and then they are forced to put forward objective reports on progress, which relate specifically to the 11 stages of design for the overall system and then its component modules. As it is Rawlins cannot get objective information from the provider executives. He keeps having to bring in more consultant experts to advise him and they love the gravy train too and tend to empathise with the providers. These are the optimistic men who say for ever that everything is possible, whereas they should be asked whether it is worthwhile.

Completion date infinity

From Chapter 8 we hear that the specification for Taurus was constantly changing and Vista staff, were re-programming again and again. The golden rule of professional IT project development is to work with validated specifications . A coach and horses were riding through this basic rule on Taurus. The programmers were reacting to instructions from 4 different groups! No specification, no validation, no progress; the logic was inevitable. Of course, the people working at this lower level never had access to any of the supervising committees, so decisions higher up were always taken in a state of uncertainty, and could it be said unreality? Boss promises 1 year of testing. The punters downstairs directly working on the project predict infinity!

Zuboff rules compromised

The objective of de-materialisation, (i.e. abolition of the stock certificate), was highly contentions. Many operators used share certificates as collateral for loans. Under de-materialisation the Taurus people would have instead to provide a document giving the holder entitlement. The writings of Zuboff relate how sensitive people are when their direct file is taken away and it is replaced with the tube. Under good practice computer systems require design, validation and finally positioning in a user friendly way to the clients. Taurus was breaking all these fundamental rules.

The copper bottomed armoury to protect chief executives from hijack.

Rawlins armed with the three good practice frameworks can have used them to recover delegated power from the providers. Never again should any chief executive allow providers to hijack him for 3 miserable years and cost him his job! Helga's social science models of escalation theory could usefully be integrated with the IT good practice frameworks, then this would be an considerable contribution to good management practice.

References

1. Porter, Michael and Earl, Michael, The Search for Competitive Advantage, *in video from TV Choice* of 1989.
2. Erskine, Robert, *Business Management*, Prentice Hall. 1991
3. Zuboff, Shoshana, *New worlds of computer-mediated work*, Harvard Business Review, Sept / Oct 1982 p 142 - 152.

*end.

Postscript

I first met Helga Drummond at the Whitehall Think-Tank (see item 7.1) above. Since then she has earned a professiorial chair for her work on Taurus. We have kept in touch for our mutual interest in 'disentrepreneurial behaviour'.

Chapter 7 - Academic adventures and causes.

These newsletters cover a research phase beginning in 1994 and still active. They begin with experiences in Whitehall 'Think-tanks', which arouse much irritation in the author over the manifestation of massive waste in the UK economy, initially in failures of computer projects, through non-compliance with the rules of 'best practice'. They include a copy of a letter to Prime Minister, Tony Blair. The intervention is a challenge to save in Britain £3 billion a year in waste arising from useless computer projects and poor control of large contracts in the Public Sector. Erskine calls cheekily for the importation of an Italian statute on regulation, designed to beat the Mafia, and 'Erskine best practice rules' to be the instrument to eliminate complacency and waste in the civil service of HMG. The letter is a passionate plea for reform, which was sent indirectly through local MP Tam Dalyell to a Whitehall Minister, Helen Liddell. This generated a considerable pile of correspondence in June - August 1997.

This section ends with the copy of a paper to the British Academy of Management outlining a new field of study - 'Disentrepreneurship'. The author suggests from research from many large mature organisations which glitch, that this behaviour and manifestation is mainly preventable.

7.1. A Day in a Whitehall 'Think-tank' October 1994

This week I am flat out preparing for the Thursday meeting in London sponsored by the Programme for Information and Communication Technologies (PICT), where they have a day's forum on Computer Disasters. On Wednesday evening As I get to Glasgow Airport who should come and sit next to me in the departure hall, but our university chancellor, Lord (David) Nickson. He has been a family friend for 30 years and started his career renting 'Lettre Cottage', Susan's old home, and was introduced to the university by me in 1991, when he came to make a speech at the launch of '*Business Management*'. He received the only life peerage in Scotland in the 1994 New Year's Honours for public service to industry, banking, and the state in addition to being first chancellor of Glasgow Caledonian University.

"Where are you going"? I ask him. "I am off for a meeting of the civil service pay group in company with the Lord Chief Justice. We have to recommend how much the redundant civil servants from the Treasury are to get. And Robert what are you going to London for"?

"My mission is to report on computer disasters and their prevention together with a number of Government and White House advisers."

"Oh that sounds interesting. I am about to 'outsource' the facilities of the Clydesdale Bank." (David is chairman).

I reach for my briefcase and pick up two articles. "Never, never, never as a bank 'outsource', or you will lose control of your own destiny. I have a file of over 100 outsourcing disasters. It will be the end of Clydesdale and the peerage days. You will become the 'case study' disaster' of 1995!"

Anyway, David grabs my papers ... the flight is called, and that's that.

The day the 'Yes Minister' characters visit their chums in the think tank.

One always has expectations. Do the experts know how to handle and prevent disasters? Will they teach me many new lessons and offer new insights? Will we be concentrating on clarifying what best practice is to prevent disasters, or will we be trying to understand better how to communicate already known solutions to reluctant listeners? Will I be able to find a way of developing a research proposal for a chunk of PICT money? Will I be able to offer a course on disasters and their prevention to the university sector? Will I be on the short list to write the prescribed textbook for such a course?

And of course there is always a social agenda. What is it like being in with a group of Whitehall and White House advisers? Are the characters in 'Yes Minister' such as Sir Humphrey, the ever winning senior civil servant, and Hacker the ever clueless minister just funny or real? Would it not be profitable to open up Pandora's Box and discover the characters in the world of academia, and the researchers from the think tank, who strive to make Sir Humphrey the formidable and ever winning character. According to our agenda in the evening we move to a reception in the Principal's Residence of Imperial College in Queen's Gate and some journalists will join us and also Sir Kenneth Warren, MP, Chairman of ITCOM, the Parliamentary Computing Committee which is so concerned about computer disasters. My goodness, we have all the personalities who could so easily come alive in a script for 'Yes Minister' and with the choreography of the Imperial College dining room, with a huge chandelier and full life sized portrait of Albert Prince Consort. The theme is obviously the 'Yes Minister' characters cavorting around with the members of the 'think tank'. Indeed at 5.30 pm we leave the Policy Research Institute near Euston, Real think tank, in Professor Frank Land's Rolls Royce for Imperial College. If I had ever wanted 'Jim to fixit for me' it would have been a ride through central London in a Rolls Royce. (Well, so much for setting the scene in a mild flight of fancy and reality).

First Half of the day in the think tank.

The professors are assessed!

We begin with coffee. I find Helen Foster, the PICT Administrator and give her a bundle of 36 envelopes all made up for each participant and a label on each package. She agrees to go into the conference suite and put a package on each place. Hurray, my papers are circulated to everyone. Yes, they have got the equivalent of an Erskine newsletter, an Erskine critique on disasters, and they are junkmailed with the following contents:

a personal covering letter from me, saying how interested I was to have read their own position paper; a one paragraph summary of my interpretation of what they were contributing, and a one paragraph comment from me giving a constructive appreciation of their paper and sometimes referring to one or more of my own articles in an enclosed archive which supported or disputed the position taken; finally a request that they too would give me the courtesy of comments on my position paper or the archive.

You may smile at this little exercise, which is basically what I do every week to my own students when they hand in their course assignments in the university. The only difference is that the prestigious think tank professors are getting the same treatment from me! There is nothing like a little one-up-manship to start a few hares running. The chairman and vice chairman each get 4 sheets extra. These contain my summaries of interpretation and comments for all the position papers. A few were participants but had omitted to offer position papers. So on letters to them I just said I was disappointed not to have a paper to comment on, but they still got the Erskine archive and an opportunity to comment back.

First Session

We are shepherded in to the conference suite. It is a large room and the tables are laid out in a huge square, 10 seats each side. The two forum chairmen sit at a diamond point in the square for maximum vantage point and control. I am seated immediately opposite the chairman and next to Professor Frank Land of the LSE. He was the only one I knew personally before. In 1972 I had been on a working party chaired by him to produce a specification for the first undergraduate degree in 'Information Systems'. He is a dear old man and delighted to receive my package with a comment on our 1972 working party. Participants take ages to settle down. They are thumbing their way through the Erskine junk mail package and reading my comments, and it is fascinating to watch their reactions!! And at this stage they don't know who I am. The participant names on the tables are too small to be read from a distance. But anonymity didn't last long.

Our first task is to go round the room introducing ourselves and our interests. My platform is as a 'generalist comfortably crossing the domains of strategic management, computing, risk management, behavioural science and practical work as a successful project manager, and with a recent archive of 750 disasters and an article prepared for the Harvard Business Review.' Amazingly, I am the only generalist in the show. Most of the professors had one specialism only; a few had two. Engineers, computer scientists, mathematicians, telecommunications specialists, sociologists, were thick on the ground. Some were consultants, sometimes they were directors / managers of their business; 6 were specialist advisers to government. Today's main chairman, David Firnberg, is a past President of the British Computer Society, director of the National Computing Centre, adviser to the World Bank. There was a spread of talent in depth, but generally not in width.

Our first work assignment was to agree a definition of computer disaster, and then identify at least 3 themes, for debate for the next three sessions. Not quite as easy as you might think. Was Concord a success or failure? Clearly an engineering success, but a commercial failure. London Ambulance, clearly a failure as it didn't work. Was it a disaster? There were no people directly killed, but being 'a mission-critical' failure it had all the attributes of a disaster. The Gulf War Incident of the Vincenne which shot down the Iraqui airbus, clearly a disaster as 300 people perished and it was an international incident. Taurus, the London Stock Exchange paperless system, abandoned after £400 million spending, a failure but no-one was killed so hardly a disaster. Frankly, I found this discussion rather sterile. For me a disaster was just an extreme form of failure, but we should give our attention to all failures, ie.

when stakeholder expectations were dashed. This would keep in the net the accumulation of waste which is my key interest. And when waste in the UK public sector runs at the rate of a £1 billion / year on failed and abandoned computer projects someone needs to sit up. Others wanted to have a much more restricted definition, otherwise there would be no focus to the day's contributions. Fortunately, the broad boys won that round. The chairman then summed up and put some ideas on the flip chart to set the pathway for the rest of the day.

Causes of disasters, decision-making process in disaster cases, procurement, project initiation, project development, project implementation, project maintenance and abandonment, what to learn? who has to learn? new research issues and projects, deliverables.

Session two - Causes of disaster, decision-making processes

One realised that there were an awful lot of issues to discuss and everyone wanted to contribute. The 1 1/4 hours / session were gone in an instant. But it was oh, so difficult to catch the chairman's eye, when I was an unknown, and most of the other participants were chums of David Firnberg. For every session I managed at least one contribution, sometimes two, but without follow-ups often some unsound thinking went unchecked. Frank Land, on my immediate right, was a great help. He was well known to David Firnberg, and sometimes I would scribble a note to him and he would put up his hand and then generously offer me the spot, so with some conspiracy I got slightly more than my fair share of the debate, but at times I felt so like Kruschev, when at the United Nations he got so frustrated and angry with MacMillan's speech he took off his shoe and banged the table! I will assure you that I managed to maintain good behaviour, but it was a bit of a problem.

Now, some issues which infuriated me. Discussion developed on how computer projects should be initiated. An early contribution from me asserted that there should always be a broad ranging feasibility study to which both the providers and owners would provide financial and other information from which the best solution could be outlined and a return on investment calculation made. The argument was that with this commitment all the owners would want to buy the project and there would be no question of the computer people imposing an unworkable solution. But oh dear, our MOD adviser said that the MOD now wanted to discontinue feasibility studies as in 20 years none had come up with any other conclusion but go-ahead! There was always someone who would profit from the project.

That morning in the Daily Express a story ran of the losses in MOD procurement projects which had overrun in £ billions and caused savage cuts in the armed forces, which were unnecessary, had this waste not taken place. The reason of course was that the MOD never controlled their procurement projects tightly enough. Only once a year would a stock take be made and if you were a £ billion overspent then it was too late to stop, and the irregularity was indulged. Good practice, suggests of course, that you check your budget once a month, while there is still a bottom to kick, but with a year's delay the bottom has moved out of range and there is no corrective mechanism! At next coffee break I nudged the MOD adviser with the comment that they should go to Enid Blyton to learn the first lesson of budgetary control, and he immediately became defensive, with the words, "No-one, but no-one can change Treasury Rules and Practices, not even God". Naturally, I was filled with pessimism, as this point about Treasury rules kept coming back unchallenged to the forum several times in the day.

Session 3 - Implementation of projects

Much attention turned to the vital decision to go-live without a disaster. In the London Ambulance fiasco 999 calls were being answered as late as 10 hours after the initial call. The operating standard is 15 minutes. In one case the crew turned up to a house in Sheperd's Bush to find that they had been preceded by four hours by the Co-op funeral service. My goodness, the undertaker's manual system had beaten the LAS computerised system! Anyway from this point the forum explored more widely the issue of how a 'safety culture' can be recognised and developed. In the case of London Ambulance no-one had taken account of the risk of breakdown as the implementation happened. In this session I had a good chance to inform the forum of the safety culture issues from the King's Cross Disaster, Piper Alpha, Chernobyl, Zeebrugge ferry disaster. Most other contributors found it difficult to impose a safety culture via outside inspection etc until a disaster had occurred.

Gaff of the century!

In the final session of the day Brian Oakley, a former Secretary of the Science and Engineering Research Council, turned to a Church of England priest / computer boffin, Rev Michael Cavanagh, and said they should pray for more disasters so that organisations would learn quicker. That must be the 'gaff of the century'! I had worked so hard to convince the forum that a safety culture can be appreciated by an effective independent check, so that, disasters are usually preventable; Oakley throws in the towel. His comment was not meant facetiously. He and many others didn't see a way through. My shoe was so nearly off once again to wack the table. I don't know how I restrained myself!

I made 16 pages of handwritten notes during the day. I have just brought a few highlights to your attention.

Evening banquet at Imperial College

Professor Frank Land and Professor John Buxton, (a Buxton of South Essex who is related to the Norfolk Buxtons), gave me a lift in Frank's georgeous Rolls Royce to our banqueting hall. We were joined by a bevy of journalists and the MP, Sir Kenneth Warren. He really had no time for the think tank fraternity or for any of the professionals in the computer industry. He delivered 6 of the best to all present for having chronic problems of lack of standards and waste for 20 years and not being able to get any form of best practice defined or implemented. No wonder we have so many disasters, and it was all our fault. He certainly was not praying for more! I don't know what he would have done if he had been present when Oakley made his gaff!

Kettles and pots

I would love also to have challenged Sir Kenneth. This summer I have read many reports of the House of Commons Public Accounts

Committee and there are passages of interviews between the Chairman of a Regional Health Authority and the PAC, and it is agreed with no argument that £100 million has been wasted and that the money was spent beyond the statutory powers of the Authority, that this was illegal, and that a prosecution should be initiated of the management of the Authority, and then nothing happens. In one case an erring regional authority chairman got the sack with a £300,000 golden handshake and then got the chair in another Authority. It is unbelievable. Isn't Sir Kenneth a kettle calling the pot black?

We have a very pleasant dinner. Stephen Flowers, author of a book on computer failures is on my right and we avidly compare notes. He is made keen to get a sight of my 750 archive of disasters. On my left is Michael Cavanagh. He tells me about his work in Manchester at the National Computing Centre. I tell him that I used to teach one of the NCC courses at Glasgow. Yes, he says, it is still running and profitable. Has it changed much? No, very little change. I tell him I didn't like some features as the project control standards were very weak. Yes, he does agree with that point too, but the course is still profitable. It never seemed to have occurred to Michael that if the National Computing Centre admits that its standards are weak then Sir Kenneth Warren did have a point to make! Anyway, the brandy was too good to talk any more shop and we compared Glasgow and Manchester till The Queen and the after dinner speech was made by Professor Hoare, first regius Professor of Computer Science at Oxford University, a Fellow of the Royal Society. If ever there was an eccentric professor then that must be Professor Hoare. During the day a constant theme among many forum speakers was the need for a better understanding by the computer man of other disciplines, particularly human relations and management, so I thought he might reinforce that theme, but not one bit of it. We got a real bellyful of rigourous science and mathematics. People and organisations who have disasters were not even on the map! Earlier in the day he had said in forum that managers would never understand computing and should always look to the expert. In coffee break I said to him that was most unwise as the computer man often took his chance and management lost control. Professor Hoare was indifferent.

I could not help feeling that many of these prestigious professors were victims of. Tunnel vision. I would never give them £ millions to spend on computer disasters, which requires a very wide range of disciplines to beat the problems.

Academic journals where research is reported have very low circulations. No wonder the computing industry never seems to learn. I think the only way of progress is via the mass international journals, like the Harvard Business Review, with its readership of a million. Books are no better. Just a few thousand copies sold will not make the impact, but the tv, that is the mass communication vehicle for the 1990s.

I am convinced that a 'Yes Minister' episode is the obvious way of bringing to the general public the message that disasters are preventable. With the heros and villains of PICT forum 20th November 1994 there are the bare bones of a super script. I shall have to track down the BBC producer and get a script written. I think that I could do it in two weeks!

7.2. More adventures in a Whitehall 'Think-tank' May 1995.

This week's think-tank was the PICT international conference running as the grand finale after 10 years of funding from the Economic and Social Research Council for the study of large computer and telecommunication projects. It ran for two days, Thursday and Friday, 11th, 12th May. The site was the Queen Elizabeth II Conference Hall, positioned between the Methodist Hall and Westminster Abbey, just off Parliament Square. I travelled by sleeper overnight, and then by tube to Westminster. I was most taken with the Churchill statue, a dominant feature of Parliament Square, and got to the Conference Hall by 8.00 am arriving just the same time as the director, Professor William Dutton of South California. We swopped greetings, and then I made myself comfortable in the coffee room, deciding which particular sessions to attend. There were 4 slots each day with 5 parallel sessions. These took the form of a keynote speech, followed by a panel discussion, ending up with questions from the floor, or alternatively 4 shorter papers followed by a panel discussion. All contributions were taped, and I suppose there will be another report on the conference outcomes. There were about 340 participants present. The list included university representation from all over the world, mainly EC, and those in communications and media interests, consultants, civil servants from Britain and the EC Commission, members of research councils, Members of Parliament and Ministers, a think-tank with a huge capacity. Conference papers were available if you put your name on a sheet, or lobbied the speaker.

Paddy Ashdown and the kids

The first session I attended ran on the theme of Computer aids for Education, and the keynote was Paddy Ashdown. He spoke very forcefully and energetically and enthusiastically about what he wanted to do for education. You may remember he wanted to put on a penny on income tax to improve education. He rather light heartedly said that he wanted to be Prime Minister for just half a day and then hand over at 1.00 pm to Michael Portillo! Then he waxed with some charisma over his three hours as premier. He said that Knowledge equated with Power, and Ignorance with Isolation. Computers must transform the United Kingdom into a well informed society; this would alter the nature and structure of society, particularly education. Schools should be on the new 'Superhighway' network. This would equip people to handle information, and at the same time revolutionise the education process. A sea change would be coming to society from education. There were lots of strategies and he favoured a high cost / high return option. This would benefit both gifted children and those with learning difficulties. There was much need for flexible learning. Top priority was for nursery education, then primary, finally secondary. The youngsters would have computers galore. This rather reminded me of the Johnny Andrews cartoon of the baby, who had already become a computer buff at 6 weeks! Paddy then set his sights on Hoy in the Orkneys and his enthusiasm for setting up telework stations, (Alison wanted to do this in Coll so that with a telephone and a fax and a computer she could have run a business remotely and put together penpals from all over the world!). Then Paddy wanted to adopt a project from Liverpool whereby computers are used in a school during the day and the school is used for commercial training at night. The universities of Britain would market their courses worldwide through computing and earn a bomb of foreign currency. Paddy spoke of his recent conversation with Vice President Gore about 'cyberspeak to heaven' as though computing would be an answer to all problems of government! After this very upbeat assessment of computing Paddy quit the platform before questions. There was urgent Parliamentary business across the road. I think he wanted to vote a no confidence in Virgina Bottomly over the London hospital closures.

When Taiwan gets the bit between its teeth!

Anyway most of the other panel members were supportive of Paddy's line. They pointed out the reality of no computer, no degree for the student studying at university, and no computer literacy, no job in the work place. A leading executive of British Telecom reported that he had given all his under teenage children powerful computers and prided over the fact that they were more computer literate than him! Unless education could provide enough instant gratification then children would want to learn at home. Another speaker was a bit concerned about the UK universities selling their wares worldwide. Weren't we already a victim of the Holywood threat with 24,000 cd roms which deliver US culture; they capture material on our art galleries, and sell our technology back to us. My goodness, Taiwan might impose their management courses on the UK from very low cost university lecturers, and we would be down the tubes for foreign currency. The 'information superhighway' has two lanes! The debate was open for questions.

No, Paddy not the 3 year olds, but the 43 year olds first!

At the sixth attempt I caught the chairman's eye, got the microphone, and rehearsed a few of my civil service disaster stories, ending up with a plea that they let off the under 18 year olds from over exposure to computers and put the money into an intensive program for senior managers and civil servants to make them more computer literate and more aware of management best practice. The session is nearly ended and in the coffee break I am mobbed by other researchers into disasters who are all a little sceptical of Paddy's brave new world. We swop cards and I give them a copy of my next week's conference paper. I then get taken aside by the official PICT conference photographer for a picture of a contributor. I am looking around the coffee room and wow; there is Cousin Quinton Rappapport, just a month as Public Relations Adviser for British Telecom. So friends and relations are never far away! No, Quinton says his children have given computers a big thumbs down. They much prefer playing football, and he agrees with me that it is the 40 + age group who should get first priority in a distribution of 'computers for all'.

*End

7.3. Conference report on 50th Anniversary of Keynes' death, Kings College, Cambridge, October 1996.

Forum at King's College Cambridge, 18/10/ 1996

This was a gathering of all those of King's College who had read economics as undergraduates, or done post graduate study of economics in the college, plus the leading economists of the world, who had been associated with the economic theories of Keynes.

Forum style and format

The forum took the form of a meeting at 4.00 pm in the Keynes lecture theatre of King's College. This was a two tiered room dominaterd by a huge bronze bust of Keynes. The forum started with an address by Professor Frank Hahn, 17 years Professor of Economics at Cambridge, now Professor of Economics at Harvard, currently writing a book 'Towards a sane approach to macro economics'. This lasted 40 minutes and was followed by questions for 20 minutes. After a short break we were re-seated and Lord Annan, ex provost of King's, gave an address about Keynes and the Bloomsbury group of intellectuals, who were known as the Apostles. This address was also followed by questions and the session wound up at 6.30 pm. We then went to the Senior Common Room of King's for a reception, and a visit to an exhibition of the Keynes papers in the top floor of the College Library. I checked the availability of the Erskine textbook 'Business Management' 1991, as part of their collection of the publications of Kingsmen, and it was there. Finally, we sat down in the Great Hall of King's for a commemoration banquet. This is a most impressive hall, capable of seating 300 easily. On either side are 25 stunning portraits, of academics, divines, statesmen. . The centre piece is a full length portrait of Robert Walpole, first prime minister of England. In the corner is a mid 19th century portrait of an Archbishop. I could not help smiling, an archbishop, just put in a corner, but of course, when there is an embarrassment of riches that can happen. The cuisine was excellent. Smoked salmon filled with smoked trout mousse and creamy horseraddish sauce, followed by well cooked fillet of venison, crouton of pate, hot Cumberland sauce, braised red cabbage, two wines. The lady at the porter's lodge told me that in vacation the college is turned over to conferences, and the cuisine has to appeal to the internationals, so the standard of excellence just becomes the norm. One of the newly appointed custodians of King's told me that 300,000 tourists visited the College / annum. After this very appetising meal Provost Bateson rose and introduced the Commemoration speaker.

Professor Sir Hans Singer - a eulogy for Keynes

Hans came up to Cambridge as a post graduate student in 1930. That must put him in the 90 plus age group! When he came to King's his thesis was supervised by Keynes. It was on housing development to reduce unemployment and the site was a greenfield one, Milton-Keynes, (called after you know who). Hans gave us vivid descriptions of how small groups of about 5 or 6 would go down on the Backs and discuss the drafts which were emerging from Keynes as he was developing the 'General Theory'. They would pool their ideas and criticisms and pass them on to an inner group of dons of economics, who again would give a critical assessment of comments and then pass them on to Keynes. Keynes introduced Hans to Sir William Beveridge, who later wrote the Beveridge Report in 1945. This was a foundation document for the welfare state and laid out a strategy for combating the three evils of ignorance, health and housing. How these students loved this process of debate and consultation. They felt that they were part of building the most important book in the world in the field of macro economics. In the archives there were over 1,000 letters of correspondence between Keynes and his supporters and critics over this book alone. When at Caledonian we become so besotted about the brilliance of teaching / learning strategies developed apart from research, I cringe. When the teaching incorporates minds who are working at the very frontiers of knowledge, the learning experience is that much more rewarding! Without the critical weekly seminars with Keynes and his pupils the quality of thought in the 'General Theory' would never have reached world recognition. With this succulent meal and the gee up speech by nonagenarian Sir Hans I felt I had had an abundance of feel-good factors in commemorating Keynes. He really was an academic hero. Hans then remarked that though Keynes theories went out of favour in the 1970s and 1980s he was now back in his own as debate developed on the European single currency.

A little hob nobbing with the VIPs

My two tablemates were Dr. Simon Keynes, great nephew of Maynard Keynes, currently a fellow of Trinity College, with a fellowship in Anglo Saxon History. He told me that he lectured 4 hours / week to a university course, and did another 4 hours of 1 to 1 tutorial supervision in Trinity College, but this load gave him plenty of time to research and publish. His strategy was to get a publisher to give commitment to a whole series of books, and with the numbers virtually guaranteed in sales to libraries, set up costs were already covered and that left virtually no risk to publishers. His books were generally sold for £30 - £40 but his latest was on the market for £1,000. This was in facsimile style of ancient manuscripts, and he was very proud of it, but thought that only libraries would be able to afford it. On my other side was Mr.Tom Rivers, Chairman of Associated Press, formerly with a lifelong career with Reuters in the Far East. He came up to sit his entry examination to King's in uniform in 1944. Keynes had spotted him sitting in uniform and left word with the invigilator that he would be pleased to entertain him for dinner afterwards. Coming out of the examination hall he was amazed to find this invitation pressed into his hands for hospitality with Lord and Lady Keynes. They were both charming hosts to him and he was the only guest. Lydia was a star of the ballet, stunning and such an amusing talker. It was through her influence that Keynes developed his interest in the arts and drama and the founding of the Cambridge Arts Theatre. Needless to say our Commemoration evening was a jolly one of stimulating conversation.

A Noble Prize winner - some politicians

On the top table was an amazing collection of the world class economists, including Professor Stone, a Nobel prize winner for economics of just 2 weeks standing. There were also two politicians, David Howell, ex minister of Transport, "Robert, when are you going to publish your report on the Church Commissioners"? Also, Tam Dayell MP for Linlithgow. Yours truly, "I am now a constituent of yours". Tam, "Where were you in digs in Cambridge"? Y.T. "9 Newnham Terrace, same as David Howell". Tam, "So you were under the tender loving care of Mrs Marshall"? Y.T. "Yes".

Lord Annan

I got to speak to Noel Annan too. Y.T. "Do you remember in your provostship the hospitality you gave to Dean Acheson, US Secretary of State, when he came to deliver lectures in Cambridge on the post war Marshall Plan in 1957? You asked me to get a group of undergraduates together in my room in Bodenham Court? Noel, "Yes indeed, I do. He was a very stimulating guest to have. I remember he had a passion for martini. He consumed it in gallons! I was glad to find other hosts for him during his stay Of course, after the debacle of the peace in 1919, the free world was determined to leave a re-constructed, democratic Europe after the second world. The Marshall Plan orchestrated by Dean Acheson, was the instrument".

Professor Robin Marris.

Y.T to Robin Marris, "Do you remember the traumas you had in supervising me in first year economics in 1956"? "Yes indeed, you did find economics a bit of a struggle then. What are you doing now"? Y.T. "I teach 'strategic management' at Glasgow Caledonian University." "My goodness, I have always wondered what went into a strategy course. What do you teach them"? Y.T. "I will send you a copy of my book 'Business Management', 1991 and some syllabuses. Economics is but one of the building blocks of the discipline. The others are management accounting, organisation behaviour, information technology, risk management. Particular models of strategic management have also developed independently of economics. I will gladly send you material. The top British writer in this field is Johnson and Scholes. They have a sale of over 100,000 per year in the Business Schools of Britain."

Professor P.K. Basu

This gentleman was very much a man after my heart. He was about 2 years ahead of me at King's and while he was up he courted and married a graduate of Newnham College. The two of them then got into teaching management studies, and he founded the Gysei International College in UK. It currently has a branch in Japan and they run very successful courses for the MBA there. Y.T. "We are always glamorising Japanese management methods and styles here. How have you managed to get the Japanese interested in Western Management Education?" No real answer but we swapped cards. There might be some mileage in following up this contact.

Judges Management Centre

Basu told me that fees for the MBA programme run at the new Judges Management Centre in Cambridge were £90,000 / year, and their books were well subscribed.

Train reading South 18/10/1996

In order to get the most out of the commemoration addresses for Keynes I took for refresher reading my copy of the book 'Life of Keynes', Roy Harrod, 1951. During the journey I made a few notes on my palm top computer. The notes offered a simple profile from which the addresses could be understood. I was intrigued by Harrod's comment that the inter-war years were characterised by political crises, which had their root causes in crises of economics. If Keynes had had his way in 1919 at the Peace Conference, we might have had a stable Europe, and a United States, who were involved instead of isolationist.

Undergraduate

Keynes came from Eton as an Undergraduate to King's, read mathematics, then started a second degree on economics, but went for the Civil Service Examination, came out second. He was disappointed in results for economics paper. Thought he knew much more than his examiners! However the Oxford school of economics then never put a Cambridge economist on the reading list so an examiner from the other place could end up blinkered!

Under worked at India Office

Gets posted to India Office, is very under worked. Does excellent paper on currency reform for the rupee. Became member of influential Indian Currency Commission under Austin Chamberlain in 1913. Persuaded it to adopt pure gold standard for the rupee. He then began an ambitious thesis on 'Probability' and published this in 1921. Rave reviewed by Bertrand Russell.

To the Treasury - 1st World War

Keynes moved to the Treasury and became a major player in arranging the basis of war time finance and borrowing, reported directly to the Chancellor of the Exchequer, was credited with the greatest civil contribution to winning the war. He was present at Versailes for the Peace Treaty and very critical of the clauses. He wrote a book 'The Economic Consequences of the Peace' and predicted what the clauses on reparations would do to the Weimar Republic. Quoted Lenin 'If you want to destroy a country you start by debauching its currency'. The hyper inflation which followed in Germany created the circumstances for revolution. In hindsight the clauses concerning re-armament should have been stringently applied; those relating with reparations related more with a capacity to pay. Keynes stinging riposte against the establishment figures of the Allies made him unpopular in Britain, and for the time being he was out of 'The Treasury' and back as a don in Cambridge.

Inter-war years

Keynes moved back to Cambridge and had an active period of lecturing on new economics tripos. He developed the work of Alfred Marshall and Pigou, both distinguished economists of King's. He divided his time between London and Cambridge. When in London he associated with the 'Bloomsbury group', a clique of intellectuals who strove for truth and candour in their relationships. They appreciated the arts. They had a reputation for some promiscuity in sex. Keynes had developed a relationship with this group from about 1910. They were generally anti establishment in their outlook. Members were as follows: Adrian and Virgina Wolf, Vanessa and Clive Bell, Lytton Strachey, Duncan Grant, (A portrait of Keynes by DG hangs in the Senior Common Room of King's), G. E. Moore, Roger Fry, E.M. Forster, John Shepherd, David Garnet, and from Oxford, Stephen Tomlin, Philip Ritchie and Edward Sackville-West. In the inter war years Keynes published prodigiously through his books and journals. He was much in demand at conferences all over the world. The full extent of these publications were on display in the King's Library upstairs, and evident in the Provost's notice that the College had received £27,000 for the repair and re-housing of the Keynes papers. and was currently appealing for a further £107,000 for papers of Kahn, Kaldor, Joan Robinson and Nobel Laureate Stone.

Keynes Publications

The Economic Consequences of the Peace September 1919, written at Charleston.

A Treatise on Probability 1921

A Tract on Monetary Reform 1923

Does Unemployment need a drastic remedy? 1924

The Economic Consequences of Mr. Churchill.

General Theory of Employment Interest and Money 1936

How to Pay for the War 1940

Notes on the symposium 18/10/1996

This was opened by Provost, Professor Bateman, with fund raising request for the archives of Keynes and his disciples (see above).

Key note speaker, Frank Hahn

Frank Hahn, is a distinguished economist currently authoring in America 'A sane macro economics'. He was 17 years professor of Economics at Cambridge. This was a critical appreciation of the economic theories of Keynes. To digest the points made you needed some familiarity with his General Theory. My understanding was a bit modest, two hours in the train that day from the Harrod chapter in his 'Life of Keynes', and built on a few days of study from undergraduate days in the 1950s. Hahn's main points were that although Keynes was by upbringing a mathematician he rejected the rigour of mathematics in his economics, a pity. (Strange to me. If economics is about behaviour in the real world, then it should go beyond the confines of mathematics). Hahn then admitted that it was quite hard to find substantial criticism of Keynes. The nub of his work was the search for a theory of equilibrium in unemployment. This is what the 'classical' school of Marshall had been unable to deliver. Keynes had wanted to find the instruments to guide an economy between the twin evils of inflation and deflation. He was upset by the manifestation of involuntary unemployment, i.e. the situation that pertains when simply the reduction in wages has no impact in reducing unemployment. Currently there is 5% unemployment in US, 9% in most of Europe.

Keynes' vision was for a liberal decentralised economy with low unemployment.

Discussion of the Hahn address

Professor Robin Marris averred that flexibility in the labour market, one of Keynes pet themes, did not matter, because there was imperfection in the goods market. Hahn, "No, no".

Howell "Common currency is a no hoper. It will produce huge recession in 1930 style gold standard."

Tam Dayell, "What are you gong to do when Germany and France are already in a common currency? We will be forced to join.

Hahn, "When Germany and France have a common currency, where is the danger? "

Dayell, "We will have a micky mouse currency".

Hahn, "No micky mouse does not have a currency. (laughter). Keynes did not want a competitive devaluation at Bretton Woods."

Yours truly did not intervene in this debate, but I was very tempted to make the observation that in this part of the century the major forces creating unemployment are the structural forces of technology, particularly information technology, which almost overnight make some skills obsolete, and promotes vacancies elsewhere. The crucial strategy for reducing unemployment then becomes the nation's ability to attract foreign investment to enterprise zones with appropriate start up rewards, or the imaginative provision of re-equipment capital to keep old style industry up to date.

Address by Lord Annan, ex Provost of King's - 'The Bloomsbury connection.'

Noel Annan, aged (80), began with some verses from Virginia Wolf. She was one of the Bloomsbury Group of intellectuals of London. They were mainly writers who formed an elite clique with the purpose of cross fertilising one another from critiques of their works. They were inspired entirely by their pursuit of truth and candour. They developed their own private language. Members were called apostles. Keynes admired their intellectual prowess and in turn they admired him for the clear logical analysis which he offered in papers and in criticism. Bloomsbury was a mutual admiration society and its values professed that ethics was about the pursuit of goodness of human affairs. When Keynes came to King's as a fellow, he thought the College was pretty inefficient, but that you needed to run a college with a number of abuses! The address continued with a wide sweep though Keynes' contributions to art, economics, and good living.

Keynes exhibition

This was an exhibition of great fascination. The books, the pamphlets, the critique letters of contemporary economists, the essays of students, their pleas for clarity in points made and not understood, a wealth of original manuscript with pencilled comments, wild pictures of Lydia and her ballet movements, this gave one a feel for the humanity of Keynes, his interests in the arts as well as academic discipline, his voluminous correspondence. He was busy all his life. The focal document of this exhibition was the angry letter he wrote in resignation to the prime minister from his place in the British delegation at the Peace Conference.

Keynes' Memo to Prime Minister, Lloyd George

(original is in the exhibition archive on display 18/10/1996)

Peace Delegation Paris

19/6/1919

Dear Prime Minister,

I am writing to you with my immediate resignation from the Treasury. I feel that there is nothing I can do here any more. These last few weeks have been terrible. The terms for reparations in the Treaty are an abomination of unrealism. Germany will not be able to pay that much, will go bankrupt, and become an easy target for revolution. This is indeed a black day for the future of Europe. As

I see it is now too late to negotiate any amendments to the Treaty I wish to leave your service forthwith. Ward will quickly pick up the remaining items in my portfolio.

Yours Sincerely, John Maynard Keynes.

Commemoration meeting in perspective

For a short time I felt I was plunged back 40 years into the hothouse and stimulation of continuous academic debate of King's. The pursuit of learning, the persuit of excellence. That must be the core activity of a university. The dons are open. They develop their theories with a critical mass of colleagues of their own discipline; they expose drafts to colleagues for candid criticisms; they share the thrill of research with their students; they are not too big to learn from their students; they carry their ideas and publications outside the academic world to nudge governments and business. I could not help musing over Hans Singer and his housing dissertation supervised by Keynes, leading to the new town, Milton-Keynes, and the contributions he made to 'General Theory'. Today once more economists such as Robin Marris was re-stoking old arguments about flexible unemployment. Thank goodness the Cambridge spirit of the search for truth still burns so brightly.

*End

CAMBRIDGE UNION SOCIETY

LENT TERM, 1959

THIRD DEBATE

TUESDAY, 3rd FEBRUARY, 1959
at 8.15 p.m.

"This House approves Her Majesty's Government's handling of affairs in Cyprus"

Proposed by Mr. R. K. ERSKINE, King's College.

Opposed by Mr. B. M. LAPPING, Pembroke College.

Mr. A. B. ADARKAR, Gonville and Caius College, will speak third.

Mr. LAKSHMAN KADIRGAMAR, Balliol College, Oxford, President, Oxford Union Society, will speak fourth.

Captain JULIAN AMERY, M.P., Balliol College, Oxford, Parliamentary Under-Secretary of State, Colonial Office, will speak fifth.

Mr. FENNER BROCKWAY, M.P., will speak sixth.

Tellers:

FOR THE AYES	FOR THE NOES
Mr. P. N. FOWLER, Trinity Hall.	Mr. A. C. RENFREW, St. John's College.

King's College.
29th January, 1959.

JULIAN GRENFELL,
President.

Order paper for Cambridge Union debate - An early political contribution by Robert Erskine

King's College Chapel

7.4. Letter to Prime Minister advocating saving of £3 billion / annum

16/5/97

Rt Hon Tony Blair, PC., MP.,

Prime Minister,

10 Downing Street,

London W1

Dear Mr Blair,

Top Priority for attention - do you wish to adopt a strategy for saving £3 billion / year in Britain which is not tagged to the Windfall Tax?

Savings of this magnitude become possible as the direct result of 31 'leading edge' operators meeting for 'Software Quality Engineering '97 in Udine, Italy, 5th - 7th May 1997.

Introduction

It is not often that one is inspired to write directly to the prime minister with advice, so you will want to know who I am? After graduating from King's College Cambridge, I had 13 years industrial experience on large information technology projects, followed by 24 years of teaching and research in a Scottish University. Latterly, I specialised on the manifestations of waste and failure of IT systems and became an 'expert' with a strong portfolio of publications, ending up with presenting a paper at an international forum in Italy in May 1997.

These are the bullet points of this international conference.

1. Erskine opens with a paper : Erskine, R., United Kingdom 'A methodology for getting added value into computer mediated jobs'. P135 in Conference proceedings.

In this paper 3 'best practice' frameworks were offered as waste prevention strategies in 15 case studies. The main cause of poor performance of the computer industry was laid at the apparent inability of organisations to manage the client / provider relationship both during the design process and in the final strategic positioning of the IT system. The main sources for this paper came from interpretations of a 750 item archive set up in Glasgow Caledonian University in 1995 of UK computer glitches. Erskine quoted Collins of Computer Weekly, 'The wasted Billions' 19/5/1994 p16, summarising the waste in UK Government IT projects as having run at £.5 billion a year for the 10 years of 1985 - 1994. Erskine included in his paper two Government Glitches, the West Midlands Regional Health Authority, the Foreign and Commonwealth Office. He also developed the circumstances in which the Stock Exchange absorbed £400 million from the failed Taurus system, the system which was supposed to bring electronic settlement to London. He reviewed the failed computerised system of the 'London Ambulance Service' at the third attempt to computerise absorbing a total of £7 million public money. He commented on the underperformance by £5 billion of the Church of England Commissioners in their stewardship over funds between 1984 - 1996.

Erskine's pleading

Erskine ended with an impassioned plea to the world providers of Information Technology to work to 'best practice' and take on board his suggestions about improving the client / provider relationship. He explained his involvement in a

Government 'thinktank' under the 'Programme of Information and Communication Technology' forum in October 1995 when MOD people were not aware of such practice as feasibility studies!

2. Ambriola, V., et al, 'Monitoring the Software Process: a solution from the customer point of view', p 169 in Conference Proceedings.

Monitoring of public administration contracts.

According to the Italian law, monitoring is a kind of quality control that must be performed during the enactment of contracts related to information systems of the Italian Public Administration. In this paper the authors describe and analyse the aspects of monitoring as a tool to guarantee the quality of software production, and as a consequence to assure customer satisfaction. The paper presents the administrative context where monitoring is applied, its purposes, the application areas, and the relationships with other kinds of quality control. In particular, the authors emphasise the novelty of monitoring and its characteristic of customer initiative. This is a brilliant paper illustrating how an independent Statutory Authority obliges the Public Administration to present their contracts in a structured fashion so that monitoring is done throughout the project life cycle. This Italian solution is so very innovative. This paper is essential reading for all those interested in improving the client / provider relationship.

Overall Comments on SQE'97, participant point of view from Britain.

SQE'97 was a very rewarding conference. Leading edge operators were reporting progress in many fields and sharing their successes and concerns. There was no complacency anywhere. Most interesting of all to the British were the reports of the Italian contingent of professors of Public Administration and Informatics. ("Italy is run by academics. The mayors of the major cities are nearly all academics. They realise that governments must be monitored to reduce waste. The professors of informatics worked with the professors of public administration and articulated a change in the law so that all large public contracts are now monitored by an independent Authority. Informatics is the instrument to generate the pressure to squeeze the review process and prevent large scale waste.") The conference participants responded to Erskine's call to set up a world database on the internet to report on IT glitches and the prevention strategies. The Italian Professors of Public Administration and Informatics were positive to the suggestion that they come to Britain and offer their Informatics based solution to the new government of Mr Blair. This is an opportunity which cannot be lost!

Rationale of waste reduction

The Italian monitoring mechanism was primarily targeted at Information Technology projects. In Britain the estimated waste here in government departments and QUANGOS is £.5 billion. In Britain there is also very large waste in Public Sector building contracts, possibly as much as £2.5 billion, and these contracts should also be monitored also, which would require an extension of the Italian legislation. but could and should cover all large projects in the public sector.

In Britain monitoring is done within departments and my strong assertion is that the monitoring is incestuous and ineffective. For instance, the Ministry of Defence never starts projects with a 'value for money feasibility study'. (Observation from PICT forum under Professor Dutton). They only appear to take budget variances every 18 months, by which time the variance is invariably in excess of £ .5 billion, the money is long since spent, the horse bolted two miles away from the stable! Although monitoring Italian style with an independent Authority might seem expensive, the very discipline of having to develop a contract with specifications open to scrutiny by the informatics experts forces a much clearer specification in the first place, which is a huge influence on cost reduction. The literature is full of business projects which overran dramatically because the original specification was so weak. For instance, the assets committee of the Church of England Commissioners authorised £.5 billion of commercial property development, and promptly spent £1 billion!

Cost of regulation?

There would be the obvious cost of putting legislation into place, but operational costs could be very low. At the moment ministries have some internal project monitoring process, (incestuous and generally ineffective), but that part of the work could be compulsorily 'outsourced' to a statutory monitoring authority, (no change in cash flow). This monitoring authority could be public or private sector based and would build on the skills already in the private sector for project monitoring. The AUTHORITY would also be staffed by business leaders and those with expertise in informatics to ensure that the monitoring process grew along with current 'best practice' and was independent of any single government department. The Italians want to progress from 'monitoring' to 'quality assurance' for contracts in the public sector. In their language 'quality assurance' is aimed at giving value for money at the initiation of the contract, i.e. a tough feasibility study to kill off the many 'no hoper' projects, rather than having to abort more expensively later on. In the private sector in Britain much of this project monitoring skill is already available, for instance, the GEC company has recently landed a contract worth £ billions for the 'Batch 2 Trafalgar' and they have in place an advanced internal project monitoring system. An effective AUTHORITY to do this job would could be franchised to the private sector and thus generate minimum cost to government. In any event we could rely on our Italian partners for giving us a more detailed cost / benefit analysis.

Appointment at number 10

Can you find a place in your diary for the academics of Glasgow and Pisa in Italy? We will come running on the nod from you to Downing Street. We believe that you should set up an AUTHORITY for monitoring all large contracts from the public sector and use the instrumentation of informatics to flush out the potential waste. This could also be the instrument to enable CCT work to be monitored from local authorities, and the CCT mechanism to deliver real savings.

This is the one way to help you honour your promises to the British electorate. Our estimate of the potential net savings to the Revenue is £3 billion a year.

What about it Tony?

Supplementary Material

1. Erskine's paper, 'A methodology to get added value into computer mediated jobs. Delivered at SQE'97. Covers manifestations of waste in UK Public Authorities. Offers 'best practice' prevention strategy.
2. Ambriola's paper from conference proceedings at SQE'97. 'Monitoring the software process: A solution from the customer point of view'. Offers the Italian regulatory mechanism.
3. Book review of Drummond, Helga ' Escalation on Decision-Making' Oxford University Press, 1996 (about the Taurus collapse, review unpublished yet. Gives blow by blow account and prevention strategy for Taurus losses of £400 million).
4. Erskine '1982 - 1996 Church of England Commissioners' case study registered in The European Case Clearing House, Cranfield University. Gives rationale and blow by blow account of £5 billion under performance by the Church Commissioners.
5 Erskine, Robert., 'Preventing Computer Disasters: Lessons from Contemporary Cases', Conference paper at 'Risk in Organisational Settings', ESRC funded May 1996. Gives overview of patterns of disaster from 27 cases.
6. cv Robert Erskine.
7. Dutton, William., MacKenzie, Donald., Shapiro, Stuart., Peltu, Malcolm, 1995 *'Computer Power and Human Limits: learning from IT and Telecommunications Disasters'.* Policy Research Paper no 31, (Outcome of PICT programme on Information and Communication Technologies, ESRC). (Write-up of forum attended by Erskine).

Yours Sincerely, Robert Erskine

Postscript

Before communicating directly with Tony Blair I considered the intervention would have more chance of being effective if it were preceded with political support. How busy is a Prime Minister in his first month of office with the world at his in-tray fighting to get into the ministerial red boxes? I communicated in the first instance with local MP, Mr. Tam Dalyell, who agreed to pass on the proposal and its supporting papers to Helen Liddell, the Minister responsible for Regulation in HMG. She in turn passed it on to Junior Minister, Mr Geoffrey Robinson, who replied in a short note of June 26th 1997. This returned documents which were heavily marked with a highlighting pen. He had passed these on to officials and they had noted the contents. In his view it was too early to establish a conference. I was soon to reveal that this cause would soon be platform fodder for the academics of the world. I sent the following reply.

Date 17/7/97

The Right Hon Geoffrey Robinson MP

Treasury Chambers, Parliament Street,

London, SW1P 3AG

(Copy Mr Tam Dalyell MP)

Dear Mr Robinson,

Re Correspondence Liddell / Dalyell - proposal for saving £3 billion waste / annum in Britain by regulation

Thank you very much for responding to my constituency Member of Parliament, Mr. Dalyell, relating with my file of papers developing the case for a very substantial saving of money in the public sector. I was most encouraged to see that the file had been carefully read and many salient points marked in coloured pencil.

However, I was a little disappointed that I had not had a chance to make the case face to face with a Labour politician. I do appreciate that members, particularly Ministers, are incredibly busy, and the natural instinct is to pass correspondence to officials.

Need to make Political case for regulation first

It must be noted that the core of the thrust of my proposals is aimed at a considerable reform of the Whitehall regime itself, thus officials will find plenty of pleasure in rubbishing something perceived as a threat to current practice themselves. I was a participant in October 1994 at a one day forum / thinktank presided over by Professor Dutton, director of the PICT programme. Proceedings were published in the following book:

Dutton, William., MacKenzie, Donald., Shapiro, Stuart., Peltu, Malcolm 1995 'Computer Power and Human limits: Learning from IT and Telecommunications Disasters.' Policy Research Paper no 31, Outcome of PICT Forum (Programme on Information and Communication Technologies, ESRC)

During the discussions the Ministry of Defence was being tweaked for not adopting the 'best practice' process of value for money feasibility studies before authorising large Information Technology projects, and doing variance analysis just every 18 months on other major contracts. A civil servant from MOD said, "No one can change Treasury practices. Not even God can change the Treasury". Later that day another civil servant urged the cleric present "to pray for more disasters, so we would have a better understanding of their causes".

In a democracy political power should be articulated by politicians.

For me both contributions were infuriating. Firstly, Treasury rules, like all other rules in a democracy, must be responsive to the articulation of political power. Secondly, we have had in this decade our bellyful of disasters and to be wanting to pray for more is blasphemous and absurd. Absurd, particularly, because most of the really significant disasters were preventable - Taurus, London Ambulance Service, Alpha Piper, Kings Cross Fire, Zeebrugge, Church of England Commissioners (they underperformed by a staggering £5 billion in their asset management and half their funds were gifted by Parliament in 1947 when Queen Anne's Bounty was passed into the control of the Church Commissioners. The documents of stewardship, the annual accounts audited by the National Audit Office, connived at a terrible cover-up as the money was haemorhaging at the rate of £500 million / year!) -

The tv "Yes minister" series has far too strong a flavour of reality. Politicians must be very weary that their power is not usurped by 'Whitehall'. I thus wish to generate the support for reform with the instrument of independent regulation of public sector contracts first among politicians. The officials can be involved later once the principle of regulation has been won.

Lobbying and advocacy for regulation

As a member of the public naturally I will lobby this initiative till real progress has been made.

In September I shall be on the platform at two academic conferences

- Bounemouth University 4th - 5th, and 8th - 10th for the British Academy of Management annual conference at the London Business School. In both places I am presenting papers once more promoting among academic colleagues the merits of regulation. Naturally, I would hope that with the oxygen of publicity and advocacy this cause will develop some momentum. It remains to be seen whether the momentum becomes unstoppable! As previously, I renew the offer to meet with politicians to make further the case for regulation of public contracts, and would if necessary break the vacation. I shall be on vacation till 27th August

Yours Sincerely, Robert Erskine.

The abstract of a further paper under consideration for presenting in Saudi Arabia in March 1998 is enclosed. I wonder whether Britain will be the last Government in the world to adopt regulation of public sector computer contracts?

Title "The case for regulation of public sector Information Technology Contracts"

Abstract

Recent experience in the United Kingdom is that the Public Sector has a very poor record of getting value for money in its Information Technology projects. Collins estimated £0.5 billion annual waste for the years 1984 - 1994. Typical cases are: the London Ambulance service glitch after 3 days working having absorbed £7 million funding and two previous abandonments; the Taurus system of the London Stock Exchange for paperless settlement after absorbing £400 million funding was abandoned. Drummond In 1994 an archive of 750 items was set up relating with information technology glitches reported in the press. Analysis of this archive suggested some simple causes of failure, Erskine, highlighted major problems in the client / provider relationships, which should yield to the adoption of already known 'best practice' design and development solutions. Much of the problem seemed to be cultural in nature. Bureaucracies have a tendency to fund providers with substantial sums and tight deadlines, so that provider / client validation at the operating level is by passed and the 'imposed solution' from the provider's ivory tower is rejected on implementation. Ambriola introduced a novel solution in an Italian statute which obliges the Public Sector in Italy to register their information technology projects with an independent AUTHORITY for the process of regulation using the techniques of variance analysis and informatics. The disciplines of regulation enforce clients to think through thoroughly the business merits of their projects before committing them to information technology contracts. The monitoring process is seen as an effective vehicle for raising the level of quality assurance in the management of IT projects. Erskine currently is lobbying Her Majesty's Government to adopt Italian style regulation in Britain, and to embed in proposed legislation some key features of 'best practice'. This paper gives a summary of the academic content and political process aimed at raising significantly the effectiveness of large scale information technology projects through a constructive and practical system of independent regulation.

Governments of the world, there is something in this for you.

Further progress on this cause will doubtless be a feature of newsletters after September 1997.

7.5. 'Disentrepreneurship', a paper for the British Academy of Management, 1997

Abstract

Much of contemporary thought in the field of 'Strategic Management' has concentrated on the processes and behaviours of entrepreneurship starting with the family business, and ending with a pathway to 'excellence' in the environment of a competitive market. A pressing and outstanding problem is that 'excellent' companies have a dreadful propensity to shed their 'excellence' and the 1980s and 1990s have witnessed a distressing number of organisations which have glitched while in maturity. Research reported in this paper reviews manifestations of disentrepreneurial behaviour in three key areas:

1. *Information Technology glitches dominated by a failure to adopt 'best practice' design and project management principles.*
2. *Financial glitches manifested in severe losses following changes in strategic direction and generally accompanied by a headstrong unstoppable chief executive and weak accountability.*
3. *Physical glitches manifested in substantial loss of life and dominated by the failure to respond to weaknesses in the safety culture of the organisation;*

The methodology of the research reported here is the examination of a wide base of case material on glitching organisations to induce from these common causes and then offer some prevention strategies. In the interests of space just a synopsis of a few of the leading case studies are discussed in this paper. This paper is ambitious. It strives to open up a new field of study, the study of the dynamics and behaviours of 'disentrepreneurship'. Whereas the study of entrepreneurship examines incremental growth of capital in a competitive environment, disentrepreneurship is a study of protection of the sum total of capital invested in organisations. There is huge leverage in the attempt to master and respond to the principles of disentrepreneurship. The outcome is a new paradigm of strategic management, one which embraces the study of entrepremeurship alongside a study of disentrepreneurship. This paper as a bonus profiles an act of intervention to HMG to save £3 billion / annum in the public sector alone in Britain.

Disentrepreneurial behaviours in Information Technology Projects

The cases examined in this section are 'Taurus The London Stock Exchange project'; 'the London Ambulance Service Failure'; 'West Midlands Regional Health Authority buyout failure', 'Expensive robots at Edinburgh Waverly Station Car park'.

Glasgow Caledonian University set up in 1994 an archive of 750 items relating with computer glitches. The UK Government emerged as by far the biggest waster of resources identified in this archive, estimated by Collins (1) at £.5 billion a year for the previous 10 years! Some of this waste occurred because of bad 'outsourcing' decisions for development or management of IT systems. The major waste occurred because Her Majesty's Government, (like many other bureaucracies), gave large budgets to providers who 'pushed' IT design without client validation, and were then rejected at the implementation phase.

A few simple principles of 'best practice' are used in the analysis :

1. Strategic Application Search. This develops a sound dialogue between client and provider at the policy making stage when I T projects are contemplated for strategic advantage. (Porter & Earl) (2).
2. 11 stages of design. This framework offers a step by step approach for proposal and validation of projects through the stages of design to enhance client / provider relationships. (Erskine (3)
3. Zuboff principles. These offer guidelines for preventing rejection of I T mediated jobs at the time of implementation. (Zuboff) (4). They concentrate on making the instruments of I T super user friendly.
4. Principles of 'outsourcing'. (Mary Lacity) (5) and Dutta (6).

As each case is developed a short summary is given of the underlying principles of 'best practice' which were broken.

Taurus

The Stock Exchange was a mature organisation, which somehow could not come to terms with getting added value from the goodies of Information Technology. In essence it was a failure to manage the client / provider relationship. Top management, unsure of how to manage the IT part of the business, passed control to an IT Facilitator, and expectations were dashed. The Stock Exchange, abandoned the paperless trading system, Taurus, after £500 million funding had been absorbed. Drummond (7).

The good practice school would aver that Taurus was a 'no hoper' because the team never conducted a proper feasibility study; they introduced a technical solution before there was any clarity on what the stakeholders might be prepared to validate. Taurus was a very difficult IT prospect, as the stakeholders were so diverse When Rawlins, Chief Executive, arrived and found that Taurus was up and running and funded all he needed to do was to ask to see the documentation of the feasibility study and the documents of proposal validation. It is that Taurus never got through systems validation and that Siscot membership, the body supervising the project, did not have enough IT competence to walk through design at the operating level with their colleagues at home base. Watson, chief IT provider, just seemed to assume validation by client stakeholders of working design was not a part of good practice IT development. How wrong could he be? It would have caused delays, but without a depth of client validation any system being built is a structure built on sand, not the basis for sending to programme development. It would have been so tempting to tear up the 'no interference' clauses in Watson, the provider's, contract. What arrogance for a provider to think he could operate without accountability to the line executive, Rawlins. With IT good practice frameworks in place Rawlins could test out his intuition that this was not a project for the Stock Exchange to get involved in. Very soon Rawlins would get directly at the data which would get support at a meeting with the Stock Exchange Council, without them thinking 'Rawlins had thrown a wobbly'. Rawlins did not need a series of external consultants to advise him. He just needed to keep his calm and demand to see the evidence of project validation - no evidence, no more funding, the project should be aborted full stop. As other crises occurred in the project and there were further opportunities to abort, all Rawlins had to ask for was a re-crank of the feasibility study reports, and it was so obvious that the case could be made to carry an abort decision before the waste accumulated to scandalous proportions. In May 1992 provider, Watson, was saying that the specification was virtually complete; and the project 95% complete; and it had not even passed the feasibility stage. His no interference clause was a complete block for line management knowing what was really going on. But providers like Watson, must operate within the framework of the good practice models and then they are forced to put forward objective reports on progress, which relate specifically to the 11 stages of design for the overall system and then its component modules. As it was Rawlins could not get objective information from the provider executives. He kept having to bring in more consultant experts to advise him and they loved the gravy train too and tended to empathise with the other providers. These were the optimistic men who said for ever that everything was possible, whereas they should have been asking whether it was worthwhile. Just three pages of 'good practice rules applied' would have saved Chief Executive, Peter Rawlins, from 3 uncomfortable years at the Stock Exchange and resignation. But there are around countless organisations which break the most elementary rules of good practice, and immediately their value for money IT £ de-values to 30p and high risk, and in the case of the Stock Exchange, to nothing!

London Ambulance Service Failure

This must be the classic of all computer failures, much discussed in the literature with an official report. Bottomly (8). This was a system which had absorbed £7 million in development and this third version was the only one which got as far as implementation for 3 days and then an ignominious abandonment. Sadly, London Ambulance Service never seemed to be able to learn from its previous failures. The good practice 11 stages of design Erskine (3) were ignored with devastating effect! There was no proper feasibility study completed as an initiating process. The system go-live date was written in stone some 9 months previously as the director was committed to improved 999 response times by that date, so this masked off any attempt to apply risk management or quality control principles as the project progressed. Project control methods were recommended but not adopted. There was no role separation between owners of the project and providers, so validation of the design by those who were to adopt it was never done; this meant that neither ambulance crews nor controllers were familiar and comfortable with the system when it went live. A risk management presence would have 'heard' that there were still 80 bugs in the working system, 30 of which were serious functional errors, and pointed out the high risk of breakdown. The back-up computer had been planned but not yet commissioned. So there were no lines of defence in event of hardware failure. There was no proper mechanism for monitoring progress. The London Ambulance IT manager was appointed without previous experience of IT. He had a background of ambulance management and was destined to lose the IT job after implementation. He should have been a project champion but had neither the skills nor the terms of reference to fulfil this role. When he decided to involve a software house to facilitate the design the lowest tender was selected for a software organisation which had never previously introduced a mission critical system and were soon out of their depth. The system testing was done late and was never comprehensive. The implementation plan was badly flawed with one large final step in which the 3 divisions of the LAS had to operate as one mega Pan London system without trials in that format, in a new poorly equipped operations room. In the manual system of London crews were dispatched by a controller via a radio message, which was required to be acknowledged. Voice contact made a bond between crews and controllers. All the Zuboff (4) rules were ignored in the new system. Ambulance crews resented direct instruction from the computer. Controllers were never fully trained in their new posts. The new system was perceived as not being user friendly. The ambulance crews were irritated to be distracted from the intense medical duties involved with emergencies, and were prepared to sabotage the system. The system always sent the nearest available ambulance to the scene, so crews over a shift might work further and further away from home base. The controllers felt a loss of control without direct voice contact with the crews.

Note that Avon, the West Country Authority, had successfully introduced robots in the City of Bristol to assist the dispatch of ambulances with striking improvements to response times to 999 calls. But in Avon the robot indicated to the 'controller' whether the address was valid. The robot showed the 'controller' where there were ambulances available. The 'controller' with voice communicated via radio to the ambulance crews. Crews and controllers were directly involved in the design and deployment of the robots. They were not unfamiliar or lacking in user friendliness. A very modest investment in robots achieved significant business results. When Zuboff (4) principles were adopted added value would flow in spate.

West Midlands Regional Health Authority Case Study of a Disastrous UK Management Buyout.

This is manifested most clearly in the much publicised failure at West Midland Health Regional Authority as investigated by the Public Accounts Committee 57th report in 1993. Some extracts are given of a disastrous outsourcing episode done with a management buyout at WMRHA, (9). As computer systems are not homogeneous products like potatoes migration from one outsourcer to another will be fraught, so fraught a failed outsourcer will have to be rescued on any terms dictated by the subsequent receivership! No balance in commercial power whatever!

"The use of the National Health Service funds by the West Midlands Regional Health Authority has been characterised by serious shortcomings in the management, control and accountability of the Authority's Regionally Managed Service Organisation. These shortcomings have led to the waste of at least £10 million. This was at the expense of health care for sick people in the West Midlands. We note that the Accounting Officer for the

Management Executive said that he would describe what had happened as 'a shambles'"

The Regional Authority wanted to privatise its Management Services Division (MSD) without incurring liability for redundancy payments. There were no bidders when MSD was put up for sale, so the Authority decided to offer MSD the opportunity to have a management buyout. The terms were very favourable in salaries and staff working conditions and turnover guarantees and a scheduled payment of the purchase price to the new company, QaBS, which still managed to go bankrupt after 3 years. As MSD ran critical systems for the Authority, such as pay-roll and medicine inventory, it could not be allowed to fail. A 'white knight', AT&T, was sought and a rescue package put together by the Authority, on even more generous terms such as a larger turnover guarantee and 3 months' prepayment of fees. It is amazing that WHRHA were so oblivious of the principles of risk management and NPV calculations in authorising this buyout. They allowed the computer provider to become all powerful. There was no project champion around to get a better deal.

Much of the waste in the Glasgow Caledonian archive on Computer Disasters in the Public Sector seemed to be attributed to failure in the 'outsourcing' decision. A recent paper, Dutta (6) , affirms that IT management is something which cannot be outsourced. The WMRHA case reaffirms that position.

Expensive robots at Edinburgh Waverly Station Car park'.

This case illustrates the need for strategic positioning of technology. This was an organisation, which funded substantial IT projects, but glitched at the point of implementation, because the IT agents were not positioned strategically and adverse human reaction caused rejection by the customer. At Waverly Station in Edinburgh there is a carpark controlled by robots. When you arrive the robot issues you with a ticket. When you leave you take your ticket to another robot which on payment stamps the ticket, so that the robot at exit will let you out - all very simple. The problem is that the robot at exit will not accept plastic money. The user may be nonplussed at 7.00 am in the morning off the sleeper train from London with demand for £28 in £1 coins or a note reader, which is often out of order. This is perceived by users as very unfriendly, and for 18 months now the carpark had very poor utilisation. Railtrack had been losing approximately £1.5 million / year.

They could restore user friendliness by providing a plastic card reader for less than £1,000. This must be the classic case of unnecessary losses owing to a failure to position the robots in a way perceived as acceptable to customers. This must have been the most expensive robot in Edinburgh! A few simple Zuboff (4) principles were ignored at huge cost. Erskine (10)

Beyond a prevention strategy - regulation for enforcement

'Best practice' is relatively easy to identify but quite hard to enforce. Ambriola (11) from the University of Pisa in Italy threw new light on this problem in May 1997 in his paper 'Monitoring the Software Process: a solution from the customer point of view'. This paper offered the monitoring of public administration contracts. According to the Italian law, monitoring is a kind of quality control that must be performed during the enactment of contracts related to information systems of the Italian Public Administration. In this paper the authors described and analysed the aspects of monitoring as a tool to guarantee the quality of software production, and as a consequence to assure customer satisfaction. The paper presented the administrative context where monitoring was applied, its purposes, the application areas, and the relationships with other kinds of quality control. In particular, the authors emphasised the novelty of monitoring and its characteristic of customer initiative. This was a brilliant paper illustrating how an independent Statutory Authority obliged the Public Administration to present their contracts in a structured fashion so that monitoring was done throughout the project life cycle. This Italian solution was so very innovative. This paper is essential reading for all those interested in improving the client / provider relationship. Erskine is currently doing an intervention (June 1997) to HMG through the Minister for Regulation, Helen Liddell. This is aimed at transferring and customising the Italian concepts of regulation. Erskine would advise the embedding of 'best practice' into such a system of regulation in the United Kingdom. Beamed at the IT contracts these measures could save £.5 billion a year of waste reported on above by Collins (1). It is ironic to contemplate that measures designed to thwart the mafia could become so productive in Britain. Effective accountability and stewardship is a huge problem in Britain with a recent mushrooming of public QUANGOS and government departments which only play lip service to professional budgetary control, variance analysis and project management. Monitoring by an independent authority would change all that. Regulation and monitoring should be extended to apply to all major public sector contracts, IT and others; the savings from effective monitoring could exceed £3 billions / annum, some prize to work for.

Financial Glitches - Disentrepreneurial behaviour in mature organisations

The cases considered here are the Church of England Commissioners, Ferranti Limited, University of Oz. The theoretical concepts underlying these cases are all simple. The disentrepreneurial behaviour is easy to recognise. Common causes are abuse of executive power and the inability of the organisation to survive with its present culture. The major triggering event is usually a change in strategic direction generally accompanied by a headstrong unstoppable chief executive and weak accountability. The chief executive becomes unstoppable when he believes that he does not need to listen any more to professional colleagues, and they operate within a 'Munich' spirit of groupthink unable any longer to take rational business decisions and assess risks. Prevention strategies will be considered at the end of each case. The disentrepreneurial behaviour recognised is difficult to treat as it can be dangerous and uncertain to challenge legitimate power.

1982 - 1996 Church of England Commissioners, Erskine (12)

Managing assets is like managing a business, and the Church of England has a turnover of £600 million a year. Assets are held at the level of parish, diocese, and nationally. 95 Church Commissioners oversee the national assets, which in 1982 amounted to £1.7 billion; much of this was in agricultural land inherited from the 16th century; there was a portfolio of offices and housing; there was a portfolio of equities and gilt edged stock. The Commissioners are accountable to the General Synod and to Parliament.

Appointment of Sir Douglas and his briefing

The First Estates Commissioner, Sir Douglas Lovelock, was appointed by the Crown in 1982 as the chairman of the staff at Millbank in London, to manage the assets. Sir Douglas is a distinguished civil servant, ex chairman of HM Customs, and ex Private Secretary to 2 cabinet ministers, but he was not an 'expert' in property. He was picked by the Cabinet Secretary, Sir Robert Armstrong, after a chance meeting at a Yacht club with Sir Ronald Harris, the former First Estates Commissioner, after being identified as a Christian knight. On appointment he was sent without competitive interview to Lambeth Palace for tea with Archbishop Runcie, who told him that he would soon find his way around the Commissioners' offices in Millbank, and appreciate what worked or didn't work.

Retail property development

Sir Douglas in 1982 immediately faced pressure to increase income by 7% to pay for increases in stipend, pension provision, and housing for retired clergy which had been voted by the General Synod. He reviewed the various portfolios and decided that returns were poor on agriculture, that farm ownership gave rise to fox hunting protests and environmental protests, so he decided to reduce this drastically. Retail development appeared very attractive with good growth prospects. So Sir Douglas thought in 1982 that he could steer the Commissioners back through the golden days of property boom of the 1960s and 1970s when the magnates made big money and sometimes the booty was shared with a grateful church. The investment policy thus went through a very radical change, initially very successful. 37 property development companies were spawned in Britain and USA and borrowings of the Commissioners at its peak in 1990 reached £517 million from banks at between 9 - 10% to fuel this development. The development companies were limited companies which paid tax, but covenanted income back to the Commissioners, who reclaimed the tax. Despite the inherent tax advantages of using a mechanism like this, there were still losses. Lovelock was not a magnate. The Church of England Property Commissioners did not have 'magnate' expertise. In a new and unfamiliar business they became very vulnerable to disentrepreneurial behaviour. The losses were awful.

Metro Centre Gateshead and Ashford Park

The flagship development was Metro Centre in Gateshead encouraged by Mr. Howard, of the Commissioners' Assets Committee, a director of Marks and Spencer. This was done in partnership with Sir John Hall. The Commissioners budgeted £130 million and then upped this during development to £272 million. (Field 1995) (13). Sir Douglas Lovelock, the First Estates Commissioner, found "Sir John impossible to deal with and forced him to exercise his option to withdraw from the partnership." Subsequently 90% of the Church of England interest in Metro Centre was sold in 1995 for £80 million. (Montefiore 1996) (14). Sir Douglas revealed in an interview on 23rd May 1996 that Metro Centre was the most successful commercial development in Europe! (Erskine) (15). As an investment it had cost COE £184 million in losses. Sir Douglas, encouraged in the entry to retail development via Metro Centre, then master minded his own vision to build a mini town at Ashford in Kent near the Channel Tunnel. When a developer made a proposition to Sir Douglas he was quick to progress this project and put together £60 million of COE funding to buy the land. Subsequently, planning permission was refused and the land value was reduced to between £1 and £10 million in the accounts. Sir Douglas reflected "You win some you lose some. If you never take a risk you never make money. Many proud firms went bankrupt in the recession. At least the Church Commissioners survived".

Lack of Internal Control of projects through the Commercial Property Department

Investigators Coopers and Lybrand (1993), (16), made some observations in their report at Page 44 para 918 Project cost overruns. "There were no formal guidelines setting out the circumstances in which expenditure should be referred to the Assets Committee and in consequence major additional expenditure was on at least two occasions (Ashford and Hemel Hempstead) authorised without such referral." Appendix 4 of the Lambeth Committee report showed a summary of commercial retail projects approved and the eventual cost. They were approved at £592 million and the eventual cost was £1,003 million.

Lambeth Committee reports

John Plender of the Financial Times wrote an article very critical of the Church Commissioners in July 1992 'The Unholy Saga of The Church's Missing Millions', (17). He revealed that the capital assets had haemorrhaged £800 million between 1989 and 1991. Newly appointed Archbishop Carey, unaware of the extent of these losses till Plender reported, immediately set up the Lambeth Committee to investigate the losses and set in motion a recovery plan. The Lambeth Committee were most concerned at the concentration of power in the hands of the First Estates Commissioner, Sir Douglas Lovelock,who chaired the Assets Committee and the Board of Finance and was a key member of 14 other committees. They were concerned about dividend stripping, (buying securities before the dividend had been paid and then selling them afterwards, to convert capital assets to income).

Field Committee, Turnbull Committee

The House of Commons Social Security Committee under Field MP (13) conducted a 'pensions investigation' in 1995 and interviewed the key players. They found that the Church of England did not employ an actuary to advise the pension fund committee, that auditor recommendations had been rejected. The archbishops commissioned Bishop Turnbull to propose a re-organisation of the National Church. They found the existing set-up a "dismembered jellyfish". They proposed the virtual dismantling of the Church Commissioners reducing numbers from 95 to 15 and shifting power to a new Archbishop's National

Council to manifest a new structure 'Working for One Body' (Turnbull) (18) for the church. The intention is for "The archbishops to recover their role of leadership and be responsible for the major expenditure decisions". Implementation measures are now progressing through the Synod in 1997.

National Audit office difficulties

The Church of England was not itself a plc, but a charity with 'exempt status' This meant that accounts did not have to be lodged with the Charity Commissioners. Accounts were audited by the National Audit Office, which had limited powers. They advised the Commissioners to consolidate accounts with the subsidiaries in 1982, but this was rejected by Sir Douglas every year till a new First Estates Commissioner was appointed. Without consolidation the NAO admitted that "the accounts were misleading to the layman, and in any event concealed value for money in the deals undertaken". (Erskine) (19). The NAO succeeded in stopping the Commissioners doing 'shell company trading'. This had been another mechanism to convert capital assets to income through making advances to a subsidiary company and then using it as a sub-contractor for Commissioner work. (Primary research).

Under performance - £5 billion

Most pension fund managers attempt to get their funds to grow at least in line with a leading indicator i.e. the FT 100 index. The investment policy assumed is one of assets growth, and the assumption is that income only is distributed to beneficiaries. Church of England net assets in 1982 were £1.7 billion and by 1996 they had reached £2.25 billion. This represented an annual growth rate of 2% in that period. But the FT index grew at 11% during that period. Putting an 11% growth rate onto the 1982 assets they should have grown from £1.7 billion to £7.57 billion by 1996. This reveals an 'under performance' gap of £5.32 billion in a realistic stewardship of the Commissioners for the period 1982 - 1996 the accounts as audited by the National Audit Office, (another Government department), did not alert the Archbishops to the huge haemorrhage of assets that was taking place over 10 years. They needed a layman's simple one page report tracking the assets against pension funds and the leading FT index. Armed with such a focussed summary it is most unlikely that under performance on this scale could have occurred. There is a crying need to develop the positioning of robots, or Management Information Systems, particularly to track the performance on core activities.

Summary of disentrepreneurial behaviour from this case and prevention strategies.

1. The appointment of Sir Douglas Lovelock as 'First Estates Commissioner' was done without competitive interview. The present system of Crown patronage needs revision.
2. Lovelock's briefing was minimal and he had no realistic framework of accountability. Turnbull has offered a radically new structure with power shifted from the Commissioners to an Archbishops' Council, but progress will still be elusive till the Church of England develops the skills of strategic management.
3. Lovelock inherited a rent collecting portfolio of assets, and moved into the new world of the magnate doing property deals without realising the need for risk management and

magnate skills relevant for the new business strategy. Top management need to absorb and apply MBA skills.

4. Lovelock was permitted to become dominant and unstoppable within the committee structures of the Synod and Commissioners. There need to be more efficient checks and balances built into organisation structure to control the executive and ensure that policies are properly debated in the organisation.

5. He was able to conceal the extent of losses for 8 years through weak auditing by the National Audit Office. Auditing must be of a value for money orientation. Independent regulation 'Italian Style' (see above) would be so much more effective than NAO auditing. Also the Commissioners need performance reporting related with what other pension fund managers are doing.

6. Internal controls within the Commissioners were very weak for property management - £.5 billion authorised, £1 billion spent. You just need management who are competent in the skills of project management and monitoring. These are skills available in abundance in the private sector.

Ferranti

The major disentrepreneurial behaviour illustrated in this case study was a company merger which went badly wrong. Ferranti had net assets of £1.5 billion and decided to merge with a US defence company, ISC in 1987. The vetting of the merger partner was done with support of a large consulting firm of accountants, Peat Marwick, yet after acquisition Ferranti realised to their horror two years later that the company was £300 million in debt and had no established product lines. This debt forced part of Ferranti to be sold immediately and the remainder of Ferranti went into receivership in 1994. Ferranti recovered £40 million in damages from its accountancy consultant. James Guerin, CEO of IFC went to jail for fraud. Sir Derek Allun-Jones was the CEO of Ferranti.

The merger between Ferranti and International Signal and Control (ISC) was announced in Sept 1987. The company had net assets of £1.5 billion. The merged company would expect to have greater financial muscle to take on bigger projects included in the space industry. "We certainly hope to get further up the food chain in space projects", said Guerin, the chairman of ISC. (Scotsman 22/9/87), (20). Ferranti discovered financial irregularity in its subsidiary ISC Technologies Ltd in 1989, and left the Ferranti Group with a debt of £300 million.

Business rationale for the merger

There was a number of reasons listed by the management at Ferranti for the proposed merger. One of the objectives for the merger was the "opportunity of growth and development." (Scotsman 16/9/89) (21). Ferranti was a small fish in the big ocean of defence contracts. Before the announcement of the merger with ISC, Ferranti was under pressure from the stock market with rumours that giant electronic companies (defence contractors) like GEC and Thomson of France was interested in Ferranti (a takeover bid was likely). In a way this merger was a survival strategy - to remain independent. Although the cold war was still in its high point in 1987, the defence spending was in decline since the second half of the 1980s. SDI or Star War project of the US, (it was the biggest defence project in the world to date), was in full swing. In order to penetrate the US defence market the merger with ISC (a UK listed company with proxy establishment in the US, and currently a US defence supplier), which already had a business relationship, present the company with an opportunity to bid for US defence contract without the trouble to either establish a proxy or set up a shareholding trust to satisfy the US Defence Department for Ferranti being a foreign company. Moreover, ISC takes Ferranti into the world of "turnkey" defence contracts - making entire defence systems rather than components. Sir Derek said "There will be very little duplication of processes and no direct overlap. The two companies are very complementary so there will be no rationalisation and no closures." (Scotsman 22/9/87), (20). Ferranti makes missile guidance seekers, while ISC makes missile propulsion systems a contract which Ferranti had earlier wanted to gain from Royal Ordnance. Ferranti dropped its bid for RO this Spring (1987) because it did not want to buy unrelated parts of RO. Other complementary aspects of the two companies' product lines include Ferranti speciality in airborne radar, tying in with ISC's ground and ship surveillance radars, and Ferranti's development of safety and arming devices for munitions of the tactical airborne type which ISC already makes. (FT 22/9/87), (22). The group would have a better geographical spread, bringing together Ferranti's strong position with the MOD with ISC's large US business. (Investors Chronical 25/9/87), (23). One is strong in the US, the other in the UK, one is well placed in Southern Europe, the other in the North and ISC has substantial sales in the Third World while Ferranti had not. (Financial weekly 24/9/87), (24).

Judgements made in situation of uncertainty.

Sir Derek Alun-Jones, chairman of Ferranti, appeared to have relied on his personal confidence that James Guerin, head of ISC, was a decent chap. The purchase of ISC in Nov 1987 was a leap in the dark for Ferranti who paid £415 million for a company whose products were secret, sold to buyers whose identity could not be revealed, and to countries which could not be spoken about. The Ferranti board saw Guerin as an international deal maker who could inject world wide streetwise sales potential into a traditional British group whose virtue was that it was good at making clever high technology equipment for the British armed forces, but incapable of selling into overseas markets. (Scotsman 16/9/89) (21). The conspiracy between management at ISC i.e. false accounting could not be easily detected due to the complex nature of the industry and the secretive environment of the company. Although there were warnings on ISC's accounts, the information given was general and vague in nature. Flemmings, the financial adviser to ISC were forced to admit in research document circulated to big institutional share buyers that "the anonymity of international customers and its heavy reliance on two of them is naturally a source of concern for investors". (Guardian 18/9/89), (25). This particular warning may arouse interest in Ferranti, but it is difficult to see that Ferranti's management should suspect that there was a management conspiracy in ISC, given their long standing business relationship. With careful consideration, and environmental analysis the management from

Ferranti might have been able to discover the inflation in the order book, as well as the under-estimation of the cost of contracts which involve secretive third world customers. But also the non existence of some of the contracts. The accountancy firm KPMG then the accountant "auditing" ISC's books forced the company to accept a substantial write down in the value of the overseas contracts. (Scotsman 16/9/89), (21). However, this by no means indicates a general conspiracy - false accounting in ISC, rather than a simple and innocent over optimistic view of the profitability of their contracts. Since the merger, Ferranti's accounts have been given an unqualified audit report, stating that they give a "true and fair view" of its financial position. And both Peat Marwick and Grant Thornton issued similar reports on ISC and Ferranti for at least the 5 years leading up to the merger deal. Three issues are highlighted by the affair:

1. If the suspicious contracts relates to before the merger, why did Peat Marwick not discover them before the deal was done?
2. Why did neither Peat Marwick and Grant Thornton spot them while advising the merger?
3. And why has neither firm uncovered the irregularities in the two years since the deal was completed? (Scotsman 16/9/89), (21).

One may put the responsibility on the shoulders of the auditors. Touche Ross technical partner Ken Wild said "The auditor is really only looking for material mis-statements in the accounts. If there is a significant fraud he will often find it. But if there is management collusion then it can be virtually impossible". (Accountancy Age 28/9/89), (26).

Summary of disentrepreneurial behaviour and its treatment.

Ferranti were making a very high risk decision in merging with ISC with unknown order books, unknown customers, and eventually concealed debt, as an international merger. Many voices within Ferranti warned the CEO, but he and his board did not appear able to 'hear' such warnings. They relied too much on 'friendly' but weak auditors, who had dual interests. Ferranti would have been well advised to do a more modest step by step growth, and culturally checked by free debate in the boardroom, and with much more affirmative information about products and contracts. The CEO, appeared to be autocratic and would not permit full discussion of risk with the Ferranti Board. Those who were involved in the merger programme became victims of CEO's inspired 'groupthink'. Sir Derek Allun-Jones, CEO of Ferranti, was too easily taken in by James Guerin, CEO of IFC. The company needed more depth in its MBA level talent and the capacity to use them.

University of Oz - case study of financial glitch in UK Public sector.

This university was a post 2nd world war founded institution and the case covers the circumstances in which its first 3 principals left in ungracious circumstances . Dr Pipkin built an institution which received CNAA validation for its degrees, but he fell out of favour after CNAA criticised the academic maturity of Oz through the autocratic leadership style of Pipkin. He was also criticised for two cases of sex discrimination and unfair dismissal then disloyalty to his employer, the Regional Council, for having discussions with HMG to become centrally funded. His deputy, Dr Popkin, well in with the local director of education, moved in to Pipkin's office, seized the HMG papers, and passed them to the director of education. This led to a short sharp session between Pipkin and his employer and with three misdemeanours on the table Pipkin was doomed. Dr Popkin assumed acting Principal role immediately and was soon confirmed as Principal. He had a dislike of consultation on matters of technology and soon started ignoring the advice of his Information Technology Committee. He got involved directly with major suppliers of equipment. Dr Mopkin was then appointed as his deputy. Within a month Mopkin had conducted an unauthorised interview with the local press and Dr Popkin took much exception to this and threatened Mopkin in public with disciplinary procedures. Mopkin surreptitiously got possession of Popkin's suppliers' files and passed them to the chairman of the Governors, where irregularities were uncovered. Popkin was out. Mopkin was appointed Acting Principal. Mopkin then enjoyed a 10 year reign and saw the institution achieve university status in the early 1990s. However, power went to his head and he soon thought that he was walking on water. He recommended the appointments of a majority of the university court. He put all ex officio members of the senate on 3 year contracts with bonus schemes. If they ever put a toe out of place they risked losing bonus. If they put a foot out of place they lost the job. The Munich spirit of appeasement wafted through court and senate, but the staff rebelled with a vote of no confidence when he attempted to delayer the university by removing faculties and departments during the vacation period. After 9 months and further votes of no confidence the auditors moved in to investigate financial irregularity. Eventually he was confronted with the abuse of £1 million to a wholly owned subsidiary company set up as a consultancy company. Mopkin left suddenly when the Court received the auditor's preliminary report. Subsequently spreadsheets revealed a wide range of unnecessary expenditure and bad academic judgements which totalled over £8 million. He was a very expensive Principal.

Summary of disentrepreneurial behaviour and prevention strategy

This was a third glitch of stewardship of the Principals of Oz. Clearly there was not an effective check on Principal's power and the organisation did not seem to be able to learn from its own mistakes. In some ways the behaviours of Lovelock and Mopkin were very similar. Accountability failed badly with substantial losses in both cases. In Britain we have centuries of valued experience within Westminster for curbing the powers of a strong executive in Parliament. But in the QUANGOS and universities it appears that accountability machinery is easily abused. Stronger structures need putting in place to recognise and cure this rampant form of disentrepreneurial behaviour. There needs to be a recast of the instruments of university governance. Ways forward are much more democratic structures of management or a 'jury' system with audit powers to curb the executive. We need better to steer the techniques of informatics so that core activity is rigourously monitored and less reliance is placed on accounts in stewardship documents which can be corrupted with creative accounting. Many QUANGOS are at risk from abuse of their chief executive officers, who are capable so easily for articulating the Mopkin style abuses of power.

Disentrepreneurship - Physical glitches manifested in substantial loss of life and dominated by the failure to respond to weaknesses in the safety culture of the organisation.

There are many organisations which glitch unnecessarily because they cannot take on board the principles of risk management. In many enterprises there is conflict in spending money on safety, and surviving in a competitive environment. But company culture and chief executives have a tendency to ignore risks which could be managed relatively cheaply. In the Piper Alpha disaster there were several warning signs that the rig was dangerous, but they were not heard by a non-risk conscious management. The King's Cross Fire disaster, and the Zeebruggee ferry disaster are both manifestations of lack of an ability to audit their own safety cultures and proactively manage the threats of physical disaster.

Alpha Piper

The crucial issue here was the failure of management to 'hear' the reports of safety inspectors and respond to them with a professional risk management culture. Six months before the explosion the DTI inspectors highlighted the high risk of having oil and gas pipes running so closely together beneath the accommodation module, and pointing out that a fire ship would not likely be effective in event of the fire spreading from the oil to the gas pipe. No action was taken on this report even though it did identify a serious risk and get communicated to senior management. The right communication channel was in place, but top management were indifferent. The actual explosion occurred when a pump under maintenance failed through poor communication between workers of different shifts, and the gas leaking caused an explosion which ignited the main oil pipe. A 'mayday' call was made to all adjacent rigs. The expectation was that they would immediately stop pumping to Alpha Piper and participate in rescue, but that action was not taken. The fire in the oil pipe consumed the oil in the reservoir of Alpha Piper and then continued with the boost flow from the other rigs. (Some fire prevention that one!) With such a strong flow of fuel the temperature of the fire continued to increase till the adjacent gas pipe fractured. When the second explosion occurred the rest of the rig was almost completely demolished. The evacuation programme was also completely flawed. It assumed that workers could assemble in the accommodation module and be helicoptered to safety. But there was no way a helicopter could land after the first explosion in the oil pipe. The only survivors were those who dived into the sea from the platform. A risk management response would have ensured:

1. The documentation of jobs would alert those handing over work that they were aware of the status of the job, in the event of it not being

complete. The pump should not have failed.

2. The oil and gas pipes would have been separated and re-routed away from the accommodation platform.

3. Evacuation exercises with other rigs would have been conducted. In any dangerous process it is necessary to have lines of defence to combat the threat. (Lesson from 3 Mile Island).

4. Reports from DTI inspectors would be rigourously analysed for risk identification and response at the highest operating level of the company.

5. All employees would have freedom to report concerns about safety without fear of reprisal. Perhaps it would be necessary to guarantee anonymity to the employee, but it would be essential that all such reports go to the platform manager and also a senior manager ashore for investigation and action. Perhaps a copy too to the DTI inspectors.

It is impossible not to make the observation that any official with a minimum training in risk management techniques and skills, who visited the rig in the days before the disaster would have noticed the absence of a safety culture. Management seemed not to be able to hear of any interference with the production schedule, even for safety reasons, but when the gamble turned sour the penalty was £ millions of production loss. Ironically the overhead cost of incorporating a risk management presence would have saved £ millions. Piper Alpha Disaster, (1990). (27) .

King's Cross Fire

London Underground was the classic case of an organisation blind to learning from its own fire fighting experiences, even though they were often re-inforced with internal enquiries and recommendations, which amazingly gathered dust, and made marginal impact on the culture. In the 10 years preceding the King's Cross fire, in which 38 perished, the enquiry report found that there had been 60 previous incidents of 'smoulderings' in the underground, but oh dear, none of these had been taken seriously and acted upon as there had been no loss of life. Top management seemed oblivious of the need to know and the need to act. Significantly, they had refused to opt for independent certification of the underground by the London Fire Service basing their opt out on a technical interpretation of the statute making an underground station a 'structure' not a building, and therefore outwith the act. The fire was caused by a smoker dropping a match on to the escalator. As there was 30 years' of grease accumulated without any cleaning, the fire in the debris soon gathered momentum. But the inspector on duty panicked and walked past the water fog equipment on the escalator, which could so easily have been turned on. There were many other failures of personnel and operating management as the fire got going, and great difficulties of evacuation. The booking office clerk after reporting the fire continued to sell tickets till just a few minutes before the flashover, which completely engulfed the booking hall with fire. There was a closed circuit television system on the underground platforms for view by a controller, but it didn't work, and on the night of the fire the controller was in an 'outback' office as his own office was under maintenance, so he did not participate in the first 1.5 hours of the emergency! There were no telephones in operation on the platforms so communication with the surface failed. Communication with the trains in the network also failed. They continued to drop passengers at Kings Cross after the fire had been declared. In the absence of a working London Underground line management structure it was left to the police to take control. Some of the vital escape routes from the station were barred by locked gates, and the keys were not available. Fennell, Desmond, (1988). (28).

In the aftermath of the disaster significant investment was made to make the escalators safe; the wooden panelling was removed; safety officers were given direct access to the board, and safety was the mandatory number one item on monthly board meetings of London Underground, to be looked at before the statements of profit! A safety culture had been born out of this disaster. But how many other transport companies had taken this lesson on board? In 1908 a fire in the Paris metro was serious and caused loss of life, yet out of sight out of mind, nearly a century ago; London Underground would never have a serious fire! But without a safety culture anything can happen! The layman would have thought that 60 recent incidents of smoulderings would have alerted management to the possibilities of a very serious fire. Indeed a risk manager would have no difficulty in recognising this.

The single most significant lesson to be learned seemed to be the need for London Underground to welcome certification by the London Fire Service. An independent and expert body is much more likely to recognise cultural weaknesses in fire fighting and safety than a complacent London Underground.

Perhaps the insurance industry has a positive role to play here. They might with advantage offer cover conditional on certification, or offer discounts to premiums whenever certification is completed.

Chernobyl.

In the Soviet Union the public view was that the Soviet nuclear industry was safe. The reactor at Chernobyl was commissioned 4 months early. There was much jubilation among the sponsors and contractors of this project and several awards were granted to participants in recognition of this feat. They were made 'heros of the Soviet Union'. Unfortunately, there were major flaws in the life cycle of this project. The original design was weak. The power station was not even built to specification. When materials arrived on site if they were defective they could not be sent back to the ministry. The builders had to make do with the materials which had been sent. The designers and operators did not have time to communicate sufficiently with one another to leave the operators comfortable in understanding the dynamics of the power station, particularly under unusual conditions. A major gap in the risk assessment of the commissioning procedure was the handling of a possible thunderstorm, which might cause a powercut. Eventually, this horrible and unwelcome risk got recognised and a special programme was constructed to simulate the condition. Unfortunately, the operators were given insufficient training in running this simulation. They lost control of the 'bubble'. The panic button was pressed. The expectation of the operators was that by lowering the control rods into the reactor there would be a drop in temperature, but no, the designers knew that this action would initially cause an increase in heat. The reactor exploded sending a very dense and toxic cloud of radioactive material into the atmosphere. Soviet Nuclear power was still 'safe'!

Three days later a May Day parade was held in nearby Kiev. A million people were exposed to very dangerous radiation as the party bosses would not admit that Soviet nuclear plants were not safe. Grave errors of safety and quality control simply repeated themselves. This cultural assumption about the safety of Soviet nuclear power had a devastating effect on the need for openness and action in protection of the population. The operators were so poorly trained no wonder they 'lost the bubble'. Where were the lines of defence in depth, which had been recognised at Three Mile Island or evidence that principles of risk management had been applied or that any effective audit of the safety culture had been done? Reid, (1993). (29).

Zeebrugge disaster.

The ferry business was particularly competitive in the years immediately before the opening of the Channel Tunnel. Management saw the very fast turn around of ferries as crucial for surviving in the competitive battle; captains of Townsend Thoresen's fleet were even encouraged to sail 20 minutes early out of Zeebruggee if they had a full payload. The ship's staff showed concern for safety devices to ensure that there was a direct line of sight between the bridge and the bow doors. Captains perceived that ro/ro ferries were very vulnerable if sea came into an open car deck. Many memos were sent from the captains, and finally through the master captain requesting this safety measure to be adopted by the shore based operating management, but the company regarded this as unnecessary expenditure. 'Don't we already pay a bosun whose job it is to report that the doors are closed? One day he may be asleep in his cabin'! Formal Investigation into MV Herald of Free Enterprise, (1987). So it was, and nearly 400 people perished in the capsize of the Herald of Free Enterprise. Townsend Thoresen as a company name disappeared. The company re-emerged with new company colours as P & O. They distanced themselves as much as possible from TT. Normally when things are dangerous there are several lines of defence. Positive reporting would have forced the captain not to sail without an affirmative report that doors were closed. But the fast turnaround culture meant that negative reporting had been adopted. Only report when something is wrong. But open doors cannot speak! There was much friction too between ship and shore over the number of passengers carried. The staff of several ships in the TT fleet felt that they were often pressurised to carry more than the legal limit of passengers and vehicles. The shore based staff refused to accept the ship based 'head count' figures. Management could not seem to 'hear' news of illegal activity, or to calculate the net present value (npv) of a line of sight system as against the costs of an upturned ferry and loss of 400 lives and a company name. The application of even the most basic risk management principles in arguments about capital expenditure on grounds of safety would have prevented this disaster. As so many of the captains in the fleet were also disenchanted with the way they were treated by shore based management in the management of safety the availability of whistleblowing for them to a government department would have forced some hearing on a deaf shore based management. Within a few months regulations were in place to have boarding cards so that excessive numbers were not carried. On the bridges of the ships devices were erected to enable the master to confirm the closing of doors at the time of sailing. As there had been previous incidents in ro/ro ferries going to sea with bow doors open the industry was very remiss in not learning from its own lessons. The Zeebruggee enquiry, (30), was also critical of poor role clarification between captain and officers, and the abuse of power by management in the pursuit of profit without safety. Any independent audit of the safety culture of TT would have been able to recognise the considerable gaps.

Conclusion - A new paradigm of strategic management thought.

This paper reviews briefly the current paradigms of strategic management and then develops the subject of disentrepreneurship within three themes which are essential for glitch prevention. The paper is heavily dependent on case study data and the recognition of a pattern of manifestations of disentrepreneurial behaviour, its prevention and treatment. The outcome is an enriched and practical approach to strategic management thought leaving many possibilities for further development.

References.

1. Collins, Tony, 19/5/1994 'The wasted billions' *Computer Weekly* p 16 (from Caledonian University disaster archive).
2. Porter, Michael and Earl, Michael, The Search for Competitive Advantage, *in video from TV Choice* of 1989.
3. Erskine, Robert, *Business Management,* Prentice Hall. 1991
4. Zuboff, Shoshana, New worlds of computer-mediated work, *Harvard Business Review,* Sept / Oct 1982 p 142 - 152.
5. Lacity, Mary, 'The Information Systems Outsourcing Bandwaggon', fall 1993, *Sloan Management Review.*
6. Dutta Soumitra, 'Linking IT and Business Strategy: The role and responsibility of Senior Management,' *European Management Journal* Vol 14 no 3, June 1996.
7. Drummond, Helga, *Escalation in Decision-Making,* Oxford University Press, 1997, (Analysis of Taurus).
8. Report of the Inquiry into the London Ambulance Service, February 1993, ISBN 0 905133 70 6, commissioned on instructions of Virgina Bottomly, by South West Thames Regional Health Authority, 40 Eastbourne Terrace, London W2 3QR.
9. West Midlands Regional Health Authority: Regionally Managed Services Organisation, House of Commons Committee of Public Accounts 57th Report, October 1993, HMSO.
10. Erskine, Robert, 'Strategic positioning of Robots', *Cranfield University, European Case Clearing House,* 1996
11. Ambriola, V., et al, "Monitoring the software process: A solution from the customer point of view.", *Conference proceeding published 'Software Quality Engineering '97', editors Tasso, C. et al CMP* 1997
12. Erskine, Robert, 'Church of England Commissioners 1982 - 1996', *Cranfield University, Case Clearing House,* 1996.

13. Field, Frank MP, (Chairman, Social Security Committee, House of Commons), 'The operation of pension funds: the Church Commissioners and the Church of England', HMSO 1995

14. Montefiory, Hugh, 'Commissioners: a large turning circle', *Church Times* 26th April 1996

15. Erskine / Lovelock interview notes May 1996.

16. Coopers and Lybrand, 'Report to Archbishop of Canterbury', pp 15 - 16. 1993.

17 Plender, John, 'Unholy Saga of the Church's missing millions', *Financial Times* 11th July 1992.

18. Turnbull, Michael, Bishop of Durham, '*Working as one Body. The Report of the Archbishops' Commission on the Organisation of the Church of England*', Church House Publishing 1995.

19. Erskine / NAO interview notes May 1996

20. Scotsman 22/9/1987 'Ferranti'

21. Scotsman 16/9/1989 'Ferranti'

22. Financial Times 22/9/1987, 'Ferranti'.

23. Investor's Chronicle, 25/9/1987 'Ferranti'

24. Financial Weekly, 24/3/1987, 'Ferranti'

25. Guardian, 18/9/1989, 'Ferranti'

26. Accountancy Age, 28/9/1989, 'Ferranti'.

27. '*The Public Enquiry into the Piper Alpha disaster*', HMSO 2v Cm no 1310.

28. Fennell, Desmond, '*Investigation in the Kings Cross underground Fire*', 1988 HMSO.

29 Reid, P.P., '*Ablaze,*' Secker and Warburg, 1993

30. The Merchant Shipping Act 1894, MV Herald of Free Enterprise, formal investigation, HMSO 1987.

Appendix - Robert Erskine, Curriculum Vitae August 1997

Present Position

Lecturer, Department of Management, Glasgow Caledonian University.

Qualifications

MA (Hons) Law and Economics 2nd class 1964 from Kings College, Cambridge University.

Member British Computer Society, 1972.

FE Teacher Training Certificate from Jordanhill College of Education 1975.

Mlitt by Research from University of Glasgow 1985.

Experience

Army Commission 1954 - 1956

Imperial Tobacco Company, 1959 - 1965

Honeywell Limited 1965 - 1973

Bell College of Technology 1973 - 1974, Lecturer in Management.

Glasgow College of Technology 1974 till current date, now as Glasgow Caledonian University. Lecturer in Corporate Management.

Course development

I was a member of the development board for the MBA programme at first validation 1988.

I was a founder member of the development board of BA Risk Management which was validated in 1982.

Publications

Textbook With Prentice Hall, "Business Management", 23 chapters with foreword by Bill Reddin of Canada, January 1991. The textbook develops six main themes ending on 'Excellence' and is widely used in GCU has made some 4,000 sales to date, is highly recommended by the 'Long Range Planning Society', has had some 10 reviews, mostly favourable.

Other publications

"Under a Work Study Microscope". (A comparison of the techniques of work study and systems analysis). Computer Weekly May 1967.

"Explosion Technique". Computer Weekly. (An early paper on manipulation of an engineering database, leading to MRP techniques). July 1967

"Exception Programming", IFIP International Congress, refereed paper 1968.

Mlitt Dissertation, "Effective Management", 1985

"Quality Assurance in Mission Critical Systems", a refereed paper presented at Scottish Quality Assurance Conference in Edinburgh, July 1994. Published in Software Quality Management II Vol. 1. 'Managing Quality Systems, editors M. Ross et al, published by CMP 1994

"Preventing Computer Disasters: Lessons from Contemporary Cases", A Conference paper delivered to ESRC Risk and Human Behaviour Programme, May 1995 White House, London. This paper attracted an author award of £300 from ESRC.

"1982 - 1996 Church of England Commissioners", Case study for Cranfield Case Clearing House, 1996.

"Strategic Positioning of Robots", Case study for Cranfield Case Clearing House, 1996.

"A Methodology to get added value into computer mediated jobs", A published conference paper for SQE'97 University of Udine, Italy. Book reference: Tasso, Adey, Pighin, 'Software Quality Engineering' CMP, 1997

"Glitch prevention in Effective Organisations." for International Research Symposium on Effective Organisations 4 - 5 September 1997 at Bournemouth University

Paper for British Academy of Management 7th - 9th September 1997 "Paradigms of Strategic Management, embracing manifestations of glitch prevention' leading to the study of 'disentrepreneurship'".

*End

Iona Andrews, daughter, and Tommy, grandson on Christening Day at Maxwell Court.

Robert and Susan's descendants and in-laws, July 1997. Back row Iona, Johnny, Hamish, Sandy. Front row, Tommy, Morna, Timothy, Carl, Jonathan on Nicola's lap, Carina, Robert Junior.

Generals Eisenhower and Erskine in the field

Field Marshall Montgomery and the 8th army veterans

Back row

Henry LLewlyn, Oliver Poole, David Belcham, Sidney Kirkman, Brian Horrocks, Geoffrey Keating, Sandy Galloway, Gerald Templer, Johnnie Henderson, Bill Williams, Charles Richardson

Front row

Oliver Lease, Bobby Erskine, Monty, Henry Broadhurst, Freddie de Guingand, Slap White, Brian Robertson.

BUCKINGHAM PALACE

4th May, 1995.

Dear Mr Erskine

Thank you for your letter to Sir Robert Fellowes about The Queen's visit to South Africa. Her Majesty was most interested to read this account of her visit which undoubtedly was a great success and very much enjoyed by The Queen and The Duke of Edinburgh. She was very glad to have the opportunity of seeing Philip Erskine again in Cape Town and to meet your cousin Anthony at the end of the tour in Durban. It was indeed a splendid and memorable week for all of us lucky enough to be involved in the tour.

Yours sincerely

Robin Janvrin

(ROBIN JANVRIN)

Robert Erskine, Esq.

Her Majesty's response to the Erskine newsletter about her State visit to South Africa in 1995

4000/1375

PAYMASTER GENERAL

Treasury Chambers, Parliament Street,
London, SW1P 3AG

Robert Erskine Esq
Cornaig Lodge
Isle of Coll
Argyll
PA78 6SY

26 AUG 1997

Dear Mr Erskine,

Thank you for your further correspondence of 17 July.

I note the points you raise but, at present, I am afraid I have no time in my diary for a meeting. I will however continue to read your correspondence with interest.

With best wishes.

Yours sincerely
Geoffrey Robinson

GEOFFREY ROBINSON MP

The door of HM's Treasury is opened ajar to accept the Robert Erskine requests for 2 spots in the Queen's speech for the millenium year - one to reform the universities - a second to bring regulation to the public sector contracts and save £3 billion / year in UK. Geoffery Robinson , MP., responds

Index